DEADLY DILEMMAS: DETERRENCE IN U.S. NUCLEAR STRATEGY

James H. Lebovic

DEADLY
DILEMMAS
DETERRENCE IN U.S. NUCLEAR STRATEGY

 Columbia University Press   New York

Library of Congress Cataloging-in-Publication Data

Lebovic, James H.
Deadly dilemmas : deterrence in U.S. nuclear strategy
   James H. Lebovic.
p.   cm.
Includes bibliographical references.
ISBN 0-231-06844-1
1. United States—Military policy.
2. Deterrence (Strategy)
3. Nuclear warfare.
I. Title.
UA23.L44   1990
355'.033573—dc20   89-25266
                              CIP

To my Parents
Joseph and Grace
for their devotion
and in the hope that we can learn from
what they have known in war

CONTENTS

PREFACE

This book was completed in the first days of the Bush administration. As with any book on the subject, it could be overtaken by events soon after it appears in print, particularly with a Presidential transition. The Reagan years were marked by alternating periods of stasis and hyperactivity: Policy seemed to drift aimlessly when it could even be called policy, or else it was consumed in the frenzy of bureaucratic competition. Yet the Reagan period will also be known for its dramatic initiatives in strategic defense and proposals for arms reduction.

Even if President Bush engages in major initiatives and policy departures, the contentions of this book will likely still apply. This book alludes to broad forces that are not fully appreciated by policymakers and, even if they were, could not easily be controlled by any one leader or administration. This book also shows the policy debate to be at least recurrent when not persistent: The debate runs in irregular cycles when not driven and framed by an organizational and technological context that changes ever so slowly.

These observations are grounds for both pessimism and optimism: They provide little comfort to those who hope for radical change, but they will relieve those who fear departures from a *status quo* that has inhibited nuclear weapons use. Nevertheless, given the stakes at risk and the costs of existing policy, the basic conservatism of the strategic policy process must not be cause for complacency. The United States is now at a critical juncture: Weapons research has made revolutionary technologies possible and appears to offer new solutions to old strategic dilemmas

—solutions in the form of strategic defense technologies, anti-satellite weaponry, and ever-more accurate and responsive missiles. Against this backdrop, the United States and the Soviet Union have again turned to arms control. It would be tragic if history comes to judge these as times of lost opportunity.

ACKNOWLEDGMENTS

This book has been influenced by many people, not all of whom can be mentioned here. I am particularly indebted to Jeffrey Richelson and Edward Rhodes for their informed comments and for providing what is a very precious commodity in this business—sincere, thoughtful, and unguarded criticism. I also wish to thank a number of others for their remarks on versions of the complete manuscript—Bruce Russett, Burton Sapin, and Joseph Goldberg—or portions of the manuscript—Ole Holsti, Patrick Morgan, Bruce Blair, Desmond Ball, Jo Husbands, J. Philip Rogers, and Steven Wayne. I am also grateful to Kate Wittenberg for believing in this project and for her useful suggestions as editor at Columbia University Press. There is no question that this is a much better book because of the contributions of these people.

I have also benefited from the support of many at George Washington University. My colleagues in the Political Science Department, as friends, encouraged me when I needed it most—Bernard Reich, Hugh LeBlanc, Burton Sapin, and Robert Stoker—and I owe them more than I can show. Columbian College and the Graduate School of Arts and Sciences assisted my work through a summer research grant.

Finally, I must thank those who have labored in this field much longer than I have, invaluably contributing to our understanding of strategy and its deficiencies—Robert Jervis, Glenn Snyder, and Thomas Schelling, among others. I will not pretend to have moved boldly into uncharted terrain. This book could not have been written without the insights of these intellectual pioneers.

INTRODUCTION

THIS BOOK is about the *failure* of U.S. nuclear strategy. U.S. nuclear strategy has failed because it cannot competently direct arms control, weapons development and deployment, or nuclear targeting. This disjuncture between strategy and practice is widely recognized, but not as a failing of strategy.

This book finds U.S. strategic thought in disarray. The decades since Hiroshima and Nagasaki have contributed much complexity, depth, and nuance to U.S. thinking about the avoidance and conduct of nuclear war. Nevertheless, much of this knowledge has been built upon an untenable foundation. Strategic thought has been refined, but it remains inconsistent, incoherent, and incomplete. The problems of strategy are certainly understandable: "The tensions are so severe and the choices so painful that a consistent position is hard to maintain" (Jervis 1984:53). Unfortunately, the consequences of these deficiencies are not made less severe because they are understandable.

This book argues that the deficiencies of U.S. strategic thought have a recurrent quality. U.S. strategic thought is multifaceted and thus inadequate in seemingly disparate ways; but beyond the substance of these deficiencies, strategy is fundamentally flawed: Strategists, despite their other differences, dwell on the "concrete" at the expense of the "abstract." This conclusion contrasts with the more typical criticism that U.S. strategic policy is ungrounded and overly abstract.[1]

Strategists pose critical abstract questions: Does deterrence presume rational or nonrational behavior? Is a capacity to deny an adversary its gains more crucial for deterrence than a capacity to punish? Can strategic "defense" be treated apart from strategic "offense"? Is deterrence a consequence of rivalry or a policy objective? Is nuclear capability best conceived in absolute or in relative terms?

Strategists also confront concrete questions that are, in some respects, counterparts to those above: Can U.S. nuclear "sufficiency" or the U.S.-Soviet nuclear "balance" be simply measured? Should the balance be assessed before or after a hypothetical nuclear exchange? Should U.S. weapons be targeted against Soviet "value" or Soviet "force" targets? Should some U.S. weapons be "withheld" in time of war and certain Soviet targets avoided in the hope of deescalating a conflict? Should Soviet targets be assessed for their value to the Soviet leadership or for the extent to which the destruction of these targets contributes to the military war effort? Can U.S. policymakers infer Soviet intent from the quantity and character of Soviet weapons deployments? Should the United States rely upon its military capability or upon policy "credibility" to maintain deterrence? (And does the former contribute to the latter?) Can the United States rely upon its strategic nuclear weapons to deter any kind of Soviet attack? Does a "warfighting" capability make war more or less likely?

Yet because abstract logic fails to inform the concrete, strategists fail to ask the right questions or else they contradict themselves in response to questions. Policy can be consistent, coherent, and complete only when structured and guided by an overarching set of principles that exhibit these same characteristics. When the abstract fails to guide, the concrete feeds upon itself: weapons advocacy, targeting changes, and arms control discussions occur within a void; the unfortunate result is that technology emerges to provide its own justification and arms control proposals are contrived to safeguard favored weaponry or to reflect specious strategic arguments.

Strategists argue, identify themselves and others, and seek legitimacy for their doctrines in the abstract, and yet they disconnect from the abstract when they embellish these doctrines. This disconnection leads to unsound strategy. When strategists fail to attend to the abstract, they leave important questions unanswered, they errantly combine inconsistent ideas, they propose policies and abstract principles that cannot be reconciled, and they think in the abstract with the substance of the concrete. Strategists have noted the irony that we can never know if deterrence works until it fails, but if we should be enveloped in a nuclear conflagration, we should not presume that deterrence failed for reasons that were well understood.

STRATEGIC NUCLEAR DETERRENCE

This book centers on the conception of deterrence in U.S. nuclear strategy. All strategists offer their proposals in the name of nuclear deterrence (henceforth *deterrence*). Even those who assert that the United States must be prepared to fight a nuclear war do so by maintaining that preparedness enhances deterrence. The deficiencies of strategy, then, are deficiencies in the conception of deterrence.

Deterrence is most often defined as "dissuasion"—the prevention of an act through the threat of unacceptable cost. But this definition says little about the way in which deterrence is actually conceived in policy. Explicit and concise definitions for political concepts are a rarity in the policy world and even if they were not, these definitions do not translate neatly into policy—the same definition has different practical meanings.

Therefore, this book rejects the search for explicit definitions in favor of a focus on the elements (components, characteristics, or parts) that all definitions of deterrence have in common—elements that pertain to nuclear "capability," "strategic action" ("offense," "defense," "punishment," and "denial"), strategic "objectives," and strategic "processes" ("rationality"/"nonrationality"). This book assesses strategy to show which of these elements is prominent, how each is interpreted, and how these elements are related.

STRATEGY AND INFERENCE

A book about "strategy" (or strategic policy) should certainly start with some discussion of what is meant by this term. As elsewhere, strategy can be thought of as a set of general policy assumptions and prescriptions, but strategy has some unique features here. Strategy is distinct from the views expressed by individual policymakers, U.S. declaratory doctrine, and U.S. operational policy, yet strategy draws from these aspects of policy and reveals its deficiencies through them.

Strategy and Policymakers

Strategy is distinct from the viewpoints of any one policymaker. It can, however, be inferred from the words and deeds of particular policymakers.[2]

Strategy is identified by the essential tenents that all who subscribe to a given strategy share. In the U.S. policy spectrum, three sets of tenets, or rather three distinct strategies, can be discerned: "assured destruction" is based upon the capacity to inflict unacceptable cost upon an opponent in retaliation for an attack and upon a bolstering of the distinction between conventional and nuclear war (thereby distinguishing the strategy from the doctrine of assured destruction); "pure warfighting" is based upon the capacity to deny an opponent its gains; and "political warfighting" is based upon the capacity to engage in a protracted nuclear war that would assume the form of a nonverbal negotiation and upon a multiplicity of potential escalatory rungs (of which the use of nuclear weapons is only one). The essential tenets of each of these strategies combine with other beliefs that all who subscribe to a strategy might not share. The deficiencies of strategy often hinge upon these beliefs and their link to the essential tenets.

This conception of strategy does pose an analytic challenge: strategy must be empirically grounded if coined to aid a policy critique; strategy must record the beliefs of actual policymakers if it is to be more than a logical or normative exercise.

The three nuclear strategies identified here are based upon empirical rather than logical linkages. These strategies do not indicate what policymakers "ought" to say in the public interest, nor even what they "should" say in order to achieve logical doctrine; instead, they refer to the "is." These strategies are based upon distinct sets of premises, but do not assume that all who share premises agree on the specifics. Policymakers articulate the deficiencies of strategy in a variety of different ways.[3] These strategies are about the intellectual nuances and departures of individual policymakers as much as they are about the ideas that these policymakers share.

This analytic effort is not without its problems. Individual policymakers must be correctly linked to the strategies to which they adhere to reveal both the richness and the failings of particular strategies. This task might not seem difficult. Some policymakers seem to fit with a strategy, though with different emphases: McGeorge Bundy, George Kennan, Robert McNamara, Paul Warnke, and Morton Halperin are currently easy to relate to the assured destruction position; James Schlesinger, Thomas Schelling, Bernard Brodie (in one period), Robert Osgood, and perhaps Harold Brown represent the political warfighter perspective; and Herman Kahn, Richard Pipes, Paul Nitze, Albert Wohlstetter, Fred Ikle, and Colin Gray have been among the more powerful advocates of the pure warfighter view. Nevertheless, for three reasons, attribution is not as easy as it may seem:

First, policymakers change strategy over time. McNamara played a critical role in the development of U.S. assured destruction doctrine, and yet McNamara is intimately associated with both the pure warfighter–biased "damage limitation" doctrine and the political warfighter arguments of "city avoidance." Kahn remains the most noted pure warfighting advocate, and yet he also enriched political warfighting by offering elaborate bargaining scenarios in the form of an elongated escalation ladder.

Second, policymakers might not fully articulate their strategies and might actually voice ideas that are common to two or more strategies. Partly for this reason, advocates of the "countervailing strategy" of the Jimmy Carter–Harold Brown years seem to embrace the pure warfighting perspective, while supporting the political warfighting strategy of the previous administration. This complicates analysis. Strategy can appear falsely inconsistent and incoherent when compiled from the beliefs of people who do, in fact, have coherent and consistent beliefs. In aggregating beliefs across people and time to form strategy, policymakers might be made to appear more illogical than they actually are.[4]

Third, a policymaker might adhere simultaneously to two or more strategies, mistakenly believing them to be compatible dimensions of a single strategy. Henry Kissinger, for instance, is known for his nuclear policy contradictions and shifts. It is not always apparent when policymakers do adhere to multiple strategies, since these strategies are not completely exclusive. Whether consciously or not, political warfighters do, in fact, remain bound to principles of assured destruction; and political and pure warfighters share an interest in the military consequences of nuclear weapons use.

These problems of identification require careful attention to the central tenets to which given policymakers adhere—that is, whether strategy is based solely on annihilative retaliation, the potential for intrawar bargaining, or the ability to physically deny the adversary its objectives. These problems warrant an analytic sensitivity but not exceptional measures. Questions about "who said what" are subordinate to whether policymakers, in general, fall victim to the same debilitating intellectual tendencies. The central issue is not whether Harold Brown, as Secretary of Defense, was a misunderstood political warfighter or whether Caspar Weinberger truly departed from the positions of his predecessor. The critical questions are not about individual policymakers per se, their personal ability to develop and argue a coherent position; the critical questions are about the strategies themselves, where policymakers can and have gone with them and whether they should and can possibly be constrained by their logic.

The strategies discussed and developed here loom larger than the beliefs of those who subscribe to them. These strategies have been a permanent fixture of U.S. nuclear policy and the high-level strategic debate for at least the last quarter century. Nonetheless, the story need not end here. New strategies can emerge, rejecting or building upon existing ones. The prospects for strategic innovation appear good in these times of potentially profound Soviet domestic political change.

These strategies balance analytic construction with empirical validity. These strategies do not capture fully the specific "belief systems" of identifiable policymakers, mirroring reality faithfully in all of its complex detail. But nor should they be made to do so. They are designed to improve understanding of the pitfalls and failures of nuclear strategizing —in other words, to catalyze debate and inspire reflection as much as to explain. They connect the detail without getting lost within it.

These strategies rest on critical, identifiable, and distinguishable assumptions that policymakers make about nuclear war. These strategies can be analyzed usefully—their implications, deficiencies, and mutual compatabilities and incompatabilities identified—regardless of whether policymakers equate or misunderstand them.

Strategy, Declaratory Doctrine, and Operational Policy

Strategy is also distinct from U.S. declaratory doctrine and operational policy. Notwithstanding this distinction, declaratory doctrine and operational policy can aid in an understanding of strategy.

Strategy can be drawn from U.S. declaratory doctrine (the general outlines of policy as articulated by high-level Department of Defense officials)—doctrine such as "damage limitation," "limited nuclear options," and the "countervailing strategy"—even if it is distinct from that doctrine. Strategy and doctrine are intertwined. U.S. declaratory doctrine is a hodgepodge of conflicting strategies, and strategy binds seemingly disparate declaratory doctrines.

Strategy can also be inferred and its deficiencies recognized from operational policy (which includes weapons procurement, deployment, employment, and targeting), a policy that traditionally has been distinguished from declaratory doctrine. The distinction between declaratory and operational policy reflects the existence of bureaucratic politics and organizational inertia, but this distinction, unfortunately, obscures an actual link between strategy and operational policy.

For some purposes, operational issues should be treated apart from strategy. Policy is not always implemented in ways that high-level policymakers intend, and policymakers often do not understand the subtleties, complexities, and constraints that determine how policies are implemented. But the distinction between strategy and operations does narrow. First, the division of labor in policy is not clear-cut and high-level policymakers must implement policies. These policymakers work in a variety of capacities to direct programs through the cumbersome Washington bureaucracy, and moreover, policymakers are sometimes forced to address (if only belatedly) the unanticipated consequences of their directives (e.g., during the Cuban missile crisis). Operational policy can thus reveal much about actual strategy. Second, operational policy shows how strategic concepts are practically interpreted. For example, strategists distinguish between "force" targets (those related to military capability) and "value" targets (those that possess a social worth); but operational policy has been based on more concrete sets of concepts—"blunting," "retardation," and "withhold" targets and command and control centers, among other things—that do not fit neatly with the force/value distinction. Third, operational policy exposes the weaknesses of strategy. Illustrative of this, the interpretations given by U.S. intelligence organizations of Soviet weapon deployments reveal the limited manner in which policymakers deal with the issue of Soviet intent. Finally, operations influence strategy. For example, weapons can provide their own justification; strategy can fail to guide and might only ratify deployment decisions.

Without due caution, of course, this conception of a strategy that exists above any one policymaker or doctrine and that can be understood from operational policy could also result in aggregation problems: strategy can also appear falsely inconsistent and incoherent when surmised from operational policy if those who design U.S. security policy have little knowledge or control over policy implementation. In sum, intellectual failings must be attributed properly, and these failings must not be inferred from that outside the purview of policymaking.

STRATEGY AND THEORY

The terms *policymaker* and *strategist* refer here to members of the large community composed of those who have contributed to the strategic policy debate and those who have served in high-level governmental positions. This broad usage is justified in the area of nuclear policy where the influence of academics or "strategic theorists"—those with a more basic theoretical orientation—is apparent. The declaratory doctrine of the United States reflects the influence of these theorists— Thomas Schelling, Bernard Brodie, Herman Kahn, Glenn Snyder, Henry Kissinger, and Albert Wohlstetter, among others. These theorists have dominated serious discussions about the deployment and use of nuclear weapons because existing theory (political realism) and methods (game theory, systems analysis) could be easily elaborated to cope with the dilemmas posed by these weapons—weapons that were perceived widely to be of a new order of destructive magnitude.

As policymakers, strategic theorists have directly and indirectly contributed to the current state of strategy. Nevertheless, these theorists have also served as perceptive critics and skilled architects of U.S. policy and their works on strategy have remained timely. Furthermore, the impact of these strategic thinkers upon policy has not been as great as is often assumed. Their influence can, to some extent, be attributed to their championing of ideas "whose time has come"—ideas that have gained acceptance because they give voice to changes in the physical world. More generally, and in line with the thesis of this book, these ideas can be said to have gained acceptance and to have been given life by a more concrete set of factors—capability measures, available weapons technology, target sets, and concrete sets of policy prescriptions.

OVERVIEW

This book critically evaluates U.S. nuclear strategy as it pertains to deterrence while it reflects upon the role of the abstract and the concrete in policy. Its four chapters on deterrence policy stand on their own as policy critiques. But each chapter also draws upon the arguments that are developed in a single explicitly theoretical chapter that is based on the cognitive psychological and foreign policy belief systems literature.

Chapter 1 argues from a philosophical and psychological vantage point. It maintains that any policy goal can be analytically decomposed into its essential parts and that goals and their parts are conceived in concrete rather than abstract terms.

Chapter 2 introduces two abstract perspectives on nuclear capability —an "absolute" and a "relative" one—and examines the historical development and standing of each. It also assesses the problems and limitations of nuclear capability measurement. The chapter concludes that policymakers are attracted to simple measures of U.S. nuclear force adequacy and attend to simple measures over abstract issues and the complexly interrelated consequences of nuclear weapons use.

Chapter 3 evaluates in historical perspective the four major "action" components of U.S. nuclear strategy—"offense," "defense," "punishment," and "denial"—and assesses their relevance to and conception in strategy. The chapter also examines the concrete counterparts to these abstract concepts as the source of deficient strategic logic; it does this through a critical presentation of three strategies—"assured destruction," "pure warfighting," "political warfighting"—and an assessment of U.S. nuclear targeting.

Chapter 4 examines the abstract assumptions about Soviet "objectives" that are inherent in assured destruction, political warfighting, and pure warfighting and assesses their deficiencies. The chapter notes that most thinking about Soviet objectives occurs at a more concrete level and is concerned with the meaning behind Soviet force deployments. The chapter evaluates this thinking in a critique of two opposing theses—the "arms-race" and "capability-as-intentions" theses—and a historical assessment of U.S. intelligence estimates of the Soviet threat. The chapter thus shows that while Soviet force assessment can reinforce abstract assumptions, much of what is ostensibly an assessment of Soviet intent is disconnected from those assumptions. The chapter also suggests that another concrete factor—U.S. military technology—affects U.S. strategy.

Chapter 5 assesses the abstract "strategic processes" by which assured destruction advocates, political warfighters, and pure warfighters believe deterrence is maintained and therefore undermined—specifically, the "rational" and "nonrational" underpinnings of deterrence. The chapter argues that policy suffers when deterrence is assumed to be influenced simultaneously by the rational and the nonrational. The chapter asserts that policymakers are conscious of the dilemmas that greet attention to these abstract influences on deterrence; but in their attention to the concrete, these policymakers fail to adequately deal with these dilemmas and recognize the flaws in abstract assumptions and end up caught between the rational and the nonrational.

1

THE PSYCHOLOGY OF FOREIGN
POLICY GOAL FORMATION

THIS CHAPTER adopts a cognitive psychological perspective in order to explain why the concrete dominates the abstract in policy. It examines this preponderance of the concrete through a focus on the structure and formation of policy goals—specifically, the foreign policy goal of strategic nuclear deterrence. This chapter presents its argument in two parts and expresses this argument in three formal hypotheses that guide the analysis of subsequent chapters.

First, this chapter examines the structure of policy goals with the assumption that "goals" are also "concepts." Policy goals are indeed often the key concepts by which policymakers and academicians guide their way through the political universe, and these concepts are therefore a vital bridge between academic theory and policy and between political understanding and political practice. The status of goals as concepts is significant for two reasons: first, goals can then be understood by assessing the nature and interrelationship of their key components; and, second, goals can then be typed by their level of abstraction—the relative number of components or characteristics by which goals are defined. These two goal properties shape goal definitions and explain their deficiencies.

Second, this chapter examines the dynamic quality of goals through the process of goal formation—the psychological process that determines how these key goal components are interpreted, weighted, and interconnected. This chapter draws an important inference from two related findings in cognitive psychology: first, that beliefs tend to be simple, stable, and consistent; and, second, that some beliefs are more central (or salient) than are others. This chapter thus asserts that the salience of an idea determines its importance relative to other ideas—that salient ideas color the interpretation and fix the causal priority of less salient ones. This chapter thereby argues that concrete ideas, by merit of their salience, govern abstract ones.

GOALS IN COGNITIVE PSYCHOLOGY

Ideas developed within the sanctity of the ivory tower assume quite different proportions when they emerge as goals within an individual or collective goal hierarchy. Goals are often ambiguous and incoherent; they change too rapidly, or else they survive longer than they should; and their key elements are often inconsistent and exist in uneasy relation to one another. When these goals are translated into action, policy will seem aimless and at odds with itself. Although the inadequacies of goals are thus a critical policy deficiency, they are not explicitly addressed or explained in the current policy literature.

The internal problems of goals are not acknowledged by, and are indeed irrelevant to, the dominant classical or "rational-actor" model in the field of international politics. The rational-actor model assumes that lower-level goals merely minister the ultimate ends of policy—that the relationships among goals are solely instrumental in character. This chapter challenges that view by drawing from the literature on cognitive psychology and foreign policy belief systems. It argues that as concepts, high-, medium-, and low-level policy goals have relatively distinct cognitive properties and that these properties determine the manner in which goals are conceived and how they relate to one another.

Numerous studies acknowledge the role of psychological factors in the conduct of foreign policy. The premise that the subjective world of the decisionmaker provides a filter for the perception and comprehension of the political world is now virtually axiomatic to those who challenge the rationality and state-centered assumptions of the political realists. The realist perspective has spawned alternative models of decision (Lindblom 1959; Cyert and March 1963; Steinbruner 1974), and the terms *cognitive maps* (Axelrod 1976), *images* (Jervis 1976), *operational codes* (George 1969), and *perception* (de Rivera 1968:40) have been used to explain why foreign policy decisionmakers are slow to perceive "novelty" in their political environments and attempt to fit events to their preexisting viewpoints and thus why foreign policy is often impervious to change. Hindsight offers innumerable examples of statesmen failing to adapt their beliefs to the seemingly overwhelming evidence that they were wrong. But even the critiques of the rational-actor perspective unfortunately neglect one of its important assumptions—that is, that the policy preferences of statesmen can be represented as an instrumental hierarchy among goals. Both the traditional view and the cognitive critique are static, the first because it fails to incorporate cognitive factors, the second because it fails to recognize that cognitive factors affect the very conception of goals and hence their relative priority.

The foreign policy psychology literature does address the role of goals in policy. It borrows insights from the study of organizations and shows goals to be disaggregated in practice and sequentially managed. Nevertheless, this literature does not directly assess the structure and substance of goals or the forces that shape them.

Some of the psychology literature actually shares much with the classical model. The influential operational code approach perhaps best illustrates the weaknesses of these cognitive studies. The approach presumes that decisionmakers possess an elaborate, integrated, broad, and enduring set of principles about political life that pertain to "definitions and estimates of particular situations" and provide "norms, standards, and guidelines" that influence the "choice of strategy and tactics." These principles are both "philosophical," i.e., "assumptions and premises" made about "the fundamental nature of politics, the nature of political conduct, the role of the individual in history, etc.," and "instrumental," i.e., "beliefs about ends-means relationships in the context of political action" (George 1969). Further, these principles are hierarchally ordered; some philosophical beliefs serve as "master beliefs" and are more "central" by virtue of the constraints they pose on beliefs of lower levels of generality (George 1979:101; Sjoblom 1982:50).

Despite the rigorousness of the operational code approach, it has three shortcomings: First, it does not examine goals per se. Second, it presumes that the elements of the code are deductively arranged (as are the means and ends of the classical model)—that one set of beliefs logically constrains another (philosophical beliefs guide instrumental beliefs). Third, it presumes that all relevant aspects of the conceptual schema are brought into play when a decision is made; it thereby suggests that the operational code acts as a whole.

In contrast, this chapter focuses on goals and, in doing so, indirectly challenges the above assumptions. First, this chapter asserts that the process of goal formation is largely *inductive*. It therefore emphasizes change. Since no belief system can anticipate all aspects of the political world, goals, like all ideas, must grow and change with experience and levels of understanding and awareness. People do not inherit all of their viewpoints intact from others; nor do they arrive at their thoughts solely through prior reasoning and contemplation. People generalize from their experiences, and as they do, old ideas intermix with and are supplanted by the new. Second, this chapter asserts that hierarchies among goals are not rigidly maintained and that goals are not necessarily interdependent —this because concrete ideas and lower-level goals (viewed instrumentally) can be more central and important to thinking than higher-level objectives.[1] Higher-level goals may languish on the fringes of policy, while low-level goals may be critical to policy formulation.

THE STRUCTURE OF GOALS

An understanding of goal structure facilitates an understanding of goal formation and change. Therefore, this section, first, examines the properties that goals have as concepts and, second, presents the properties goals have by merit of their level of abstraction. As concepts, goals can be shown to be constituted by interrelated components and thus to be redefined with changes in the identity and organization of these components; as concepts that vary in abstractness, goals can be shown to differ in the number of components by which they are defined and thus by other associated properties.

Goals as Concepts

To recognize that psychology plays a part in goal formation is to appreciate the conceptual character of goals. Concepts are the means by which the data of experience are distilled and given meaning in the accumulation of knowledge—whether these concepts are used to construct theory, design a sound foreign policy, or simply cope with everyday life. "They capture the notion that many objects or events are alike in some important respects, and hence can be thought about and responded to in ways we have already mastered" (Smith and Medin 1981:1). People are tempted to "stay close to the facts" and to be as open to experience as possible, but facts never "speak for themselves." Facts are "recognized" only when people are prepared to recognize them, and facts can only be given meaning by preexisting concepts and beliefs.[2]

As concepts, goals are actually explicit and implicit statements of causality (Stinchcombe 1968:40). The concept of gravity in physics encompasses the "law" of gravity; the concept of strategic deterrence in political science embodies the "theory" of strategic deterrence. Each of these ideas contains a whole set of assumptions about how relevant aspects of the world are interrelated. Thus the meaning of a goal is determined by its components, their relative importance, and the implicit and explicit relationships among them.[3] Indeed, just as strategic deterrence means different things to different policymakers, a single goal can have many contradictory meanings.[4]

Definitions of strategic deterrence can be reduced to key elements and their interrelationships. First, the meaning of strategic deterrence changes with the omission and inclusion of elements. Strategic deterrence, most inclusively, denotes a role for components such as nuclear "capability," "credibility," "stability," and strategic action elements like "offense," "defense," "punishment," and "denial," though different definitions feature different sets of these elements. Advocates of "assured destruction" argue that the adversary can be deterred through the threat of "punishment" while some advocates of "warfighting" claim that deterrence requires that the adversary be "denied" gains. Second, the meaning of strategic deterrence changes with the meanings of its elements. For instance, assured destruction advocates conceive of capability primarily in absolute terms while warfighters conceive of it in relative terms —the former suggest that deterrence is dependent on the survivability of a force that can inflict a required minimum level of retaliatory destruction while the latter believe that deterrence rests on the nuclear balance.

Finally, the meaning of strategic deterrence can be altered through changes in the relationships posited among its elements. This can be seen in the posited relationships between nuclear capability and policy "credibility." Some believe credibility to be largely a function of the manipulation of the risk of an all-out nuclear exchange, others believe credibility to be more directly related to capability in the capacity to employ limited nuclear options, and some warfighters go a step further and deemphasize credibility when they treat it as the virtual capability for damage limitation.

Goals and Abstraction

Many of the features of a goal stem from its "level of abstraction." The level of abstraction of a goal is determined by the number of characteristics (components) that it has relative to the diversity of the things to which it applies (on this, see Sartori 1970, 1984). The level of abstraction of a goal, therefore, can be raised by decreasing the number of its characteristics (i.e., raising its generality or lowering its specificity) to increase the number of classes of things to which it applies and can be lowered by the reverse.[5] Arms control is thus a more abstract goal than "nuclear" arms control and deterrence is more abstract than strategic nuclear deterrence.

Low-Level Goals

Low-level goals are the most concrete goals (and their components are more concrete than those of more abstract goals); they thus have the greatest number of defining characteristics and apply to the fewest classes of things. Low-level goals also have important characteristics by reason of their concreteness—"particularity," "tangibility," and "immediacy." These characteristics increase the salience and significance of low-level goals and their components.

Concreteness and particularity are qualities that are distinct but are nevertheless often confused. Concreteness refers to the number of characteristics by which something is defined, and no matter how concrete a concept, it can logically refer to more than a single case; in contrast, particularity refers only to a single instance and therefore requires proper names (e.g., arms control with the "Soviet Union," force commitments to "Europe").[6] One reason that concrete concepts are confused with particular ones is that the two types of concepts co-occur in practice. Policymakers define low-level goals in highly concrete terms—for example, "maintaining air and naval base rights in developing countries experiencing domestic instability"—but this might only mask their particular objectives:[7] The Philippine government is the subject of the base rights example, Arab governments propose peace formulae in general terms that are actually structured around a role for the PLO (e.g., an international forum involving all parties to the conflict), and the Chinese still regard "hegemonial" ambitions to mean "Soviet" ambitions. People tend to think in particularistic terms for the same psychological reasons that they think in concrete terms (see below).

Concreteness is also linked in practice to concept "tangibility" where concepts are defined in "physical" rather than "analytical" terms (e.g., a "weapon" as opposed to "power"). Tangible concepts can be directly experienced and are prominent because of it,[8] serving as referents by which policies are realized and thoughts are translated into action. This is certainly the case in nuclear capability assessment where concrete capability concepts are infused with the characteristics of tangible weapon systems. Policymakers often tie a "first-strike" capability to vulnerable and accurate "land-based" missiles and a "second-strike" (retaliatory) capability to invulnerable and inaccurate "nuclear submarines."

Finally, goal concreteness is linked to goal "immediacy." Abstract goals tend to be "prime" or "ultimate" goals, and concrete goals tend to be immediate or "instrumental." Concrete goals, then, might have recognized and therefore predictable consequences; these goals have trade-offs and relationships to other goals that are better understood.[9]

High-Level Goals

High-level goals, as the most abstract goals, have the smallest number of defining characteristics but, nonetheless, command little attention and elude precise definition. Because high-level goals are not subject to scrutiny, they suffer in clarity.

High-level goals can be recognized by two of their common traits — traits that reflect the deficiencies of these goals.[10] First, high-level goals are often defined through negation. While most people would find it difficult to precisely define "peace" and "security," they "know" what peace and security are not. Part of the reason for this may be that people more easily recognize and define failure than success. They powerfully feel the ramifications of failure in war and death, economic depression and deprivation, and fear and anxiety. They see failure, unlike success, to be intrinsic to the events that signal it.[11] Second, high-level goals are conceived in categorical rather than in quantitative terms. For instance, people view peace and war not as a continuum, but as conditions. Because people have only a limited understanding of these goals, they do not recognize intermediate states between these conditions. At the limit, they might even reduce high-level goals to simple dichotomies: they may juxtapose peace and war, security and insecurity.[12]

Middle-Level Goals

Middle-level goals are distinguished from high-level goals by the greater number of characteristics by which they are defined and the more limited number of things to which they apply (and their components can be similarly distinguished from those of higher-level goals). Middle-level goals, such as arms control, counterterrorism, and a balance of power, are at the very center of the psychological dynamics of goal formation. Strategic deterrence is just such a middle-level goal.

Middle-level goals are abstract enough to direct policy and are thus the subject of political debate: Should the United States reduce or maintain the number of its alliance commitments? Should the United States subordinate human rights concerns to the requirements for arms control?

Yet these goals are shaped by the concrete through the cognitive dynamics discussed below.

GOAL FORMATION AND CHANGE

A goal has been shown to be defined by factors that determine its parts and their meaning, relative importance, and interrelationship. Concrete thinking has just such a defining effect.[13] This section, first briefly presents the insights of the foreign policy belief systems literature and, second, builds upon these insights to account for the effects of the concrete on goal formation.

The Dynamics of a Foreign Policy Belief System

The study of perception in modern psychology is oriented toward an understanding of "cognition," the manner in which subjective knowledge is encoded, stored, organized, and retrieved.[14] The psychology literature suggests that subjective knowledge acts as a filter in the assessment of the external world; it suggests that the "mind's eye" captures little of what the "optical eye" actually "sees." But the metaphor of a "filter" hardly does justice to the dynamic inner workings of a belief system.

Cognitive psychological research and its applications to foreign policy decisionmaking suggest that a belief system has primarily three attributes: it is internally consistent, to the extent that inconsistencies are recognized; it is relatively stable; and it is parsimonious. These attributes suggest, at first glance, an unflattering picture: People are dogmatic, closed- and simpleminded. But these attributes can sound more appealing. Despite mental limitations, people strive to understand the world around them. This requires that people err in the direction of simplicity, so that they can accumulate knowledge and are not lost in a sea of trivia, that people integrate and synthesize worldly phenomena that might always appear unique, and that people adhere to a strict standard of proof, one that rejects change for its own sake and favors conceptual order over intellectual anarchy. These two perspectives represent opposing extremes. Whereas the first perspective too harshly emphasizes conceptual rigidity and stasis, perhaps the latter overgenerously ascribes to rational intent that which is not actually rational. Each perspective contains some truth.

Much of the psychologically oriented foreign policy literature holds human motives constant and focuses instead on the twin notions of "perception" and "attention" (on these terms, see de Rivera 1968:40–

43).[15] Beliefs determine "perception," the manner in which evidence is interpreted and weighted, but through "attention" they also determine what is received from the senses and operate prior to perception. Therefore, beliefs determine the meaning information is given and also determine what information is missed—in other words, what *is* and what *is not* treated as information.

The attention-perception literature highlights an *unconscious* process. This process is one of *unmotivated bias* and explains the consistency, simplicity, and stability of beliefs and thereby suggests the ways in which the concrete affects the meaning of goals: pressures toward consistency and simplicity mean that concrete ideas, like other salient parts[16] of a belief system, will influence goal conceptions.

The literature on unmotivated bias must be distinguished from that on *motivated bias*—a literature that makes many of the same arguments about human cognition but assumes that people are at least partly aware of their cognitive contradictions (on this, see Janis and Mann 1977). This literature draws on Festinger's (1962) theory of "cognitive dissonance," for instance, to explain the stability of beliefs—people find incongruence psychologically discomforting and therefore resist information that is at odds with their beliefs.[17] Thus, when motivated, people employ a diverse set of intellectual tools to discount offending information—for example, they may devalue the source of the information, search for information that will support their own view and/or discredit the information, or downplay the incongruence involved even so as to see the information as confirming their own view. Ironically, then, and at odds with the implications of unmotivated bias, an affront to a belief could strengthen it.

The motivated bias literature contains powerful insights, but is nonetheless limited. It can explain why beliefs remain simple, consistent, and stable but, unlike unmotivated bias, cannot explain the conceptual dominance of the concrete.

Concreteness in Cognition

Concrete ideas are central, in part, because they, along with the tangible, particular, and immediate ideas that accompany them, provide the numerous "cues" by which ideas are "recalled" and the situations in which they are relevant are "recognized."[18] Objects, places, and people can trigger all sorts of mental associations, emotions, and images of the past, just as word combinations and musical melodies are laden with rich connotations and meanings.[19] Similarly, concrete, tangible, and particular "details" account for the interpretations given an analogy as well as its emotive and "sensory" impact (on this, see Nisbett et al. 1982:112).[20] Psychological research has indicated that knowledge is dependent upon context and individual experience (Halff et al. 1976; Murphy 1984; Murphy 1988).

When the details of an analogy fade from memory, the impact and general message of the analogy dim with them. The diverse "lessons" of the Vietnam War are embedded in the symbols of that experience; the lessons about the dangers of the overextension of power, the pursuit of policies regardless of their cost and appropriateness, and the overreliance upon military force are experienced more directly. As these symbols or details disappear from the collective consciousness, so will the so-called Vietnam syndrome. These details, then, provide the referents by which decisionmakers determine the lesson's wider applications.

Psychological research has demonstrated the difficulties people have in recognizing the structural similarities of problems that differ in superficial detail (Simon and Hayes 1976). With the loss of detail, people will lose their ability to apply an analogy. People find it extraordinarily difficult to separate the important from the unimportant, the specific from the general, and the particular from the universal when they apply an analogy. Indeed, evidence shows that individuals treat the concrete as more relevant and meaningful than the abstract. People might not recognize parallels between the U.S. intervention in Vietnam and U.S. intervention elsewhere, and when they do it is because of superficial similarities between the actions. Partly for this reason, they are more likely to oppose intervention in Asia than intervention in general, the use of troops more than air or naval support, and long-term commitments more than quick operations. "Decisionmakers usually fail to strip away from the past event those facets that depend on the ephemeral content. They often mistake things that are highly specific and situation-bound for more general characteristics because they assume that the most salient aspects of the results were caused by the most salient aspects of the preceding situation. People pay more attention to what has happened than to "why" it has happened" (Jervis 1976:228). These observations explain why students only with practice are able to solve mathematical word problems that differ solely in detail from ones previously mastered or, when tested, have difficulty recalling definitions for terms apart from the examples by which those terms are understood. (For related observations, see Kuhn 1970:187–198; Simon 1979:263.)

Cognitive psychological research has also revealed the extent to which people are inclined toward concrete conceptualizing. Some of this research has tested and supported the assumption that people employ "exemplars"—concrete representations for abstract concepts (e.g., a "robin" or "eagle" in the case of "bird")—for purposes of categorization (on this, see Smith and Medin 1981).[21] Other research has worked with the assumption that people are cued to "basic level" concepts that are of a lower level of abstraction (Rosch et al. 1976; Tversky and Hemenway 1984).[22]

All of this is important because concrete ideas influence thinking. Cognitive psychology recognizes that salient entities affect the perception of less salient ones. First, considerable evidence indicates that the "availability" or "accessibility" of information causes a person to exaggerate its significance. Phenomena that are easily brought to mind are judged to have greater importance and a higher probability and frequency of occurrence.[23] What is "conceivable" becomes what is "probable" (George 1980:61) and, by implication, what is "notable." Put somewhat differently, concrete concepts can "bring out" the features of more abstract ones and thereby effectively redefine them.[24]

This finding accounts for the effect that concrete capability measures and weapon systems have on assessments of deterrence requirements: While many speak of an abstract "nuclear balance," policymakers are drawn to the U.S.-Soviet force configuration and often advocate that U.S. forces be made to "match" or "counter" Soviet deployments; other policymakers refer to an abstract level of "sufficiency" or "assured destruction," but then look to actual or projected U.S. force levels to operationally define these abstract terms; and some policymakers might be driven by the sheer desire to acquire advanced technology or to target potential aim points without concern for strategic doctrine.

Second, evidence indicates that salient concepts directly shape the conception of less salient ones. When people compare similar phenomena, they tend to select the less salient phenomenon as a subject and the more salient one as a referent; this is significant because they make the subject consistent with the referent. People use the distinctive characteristics of the salient referent to assess the subject. Americans are more likely to compare Nicaragua with Cuba and Arab-Israeli military deterrence with U.S.-Soviet military deterrence than the other way around, and they are therefore likely to see Cuba in Nicaragua or the potential for stability within the Middle East.

Examples are plentiful. In foreign policy, an abstract entity can be made to resemble a concrete one—as when abstract concepts are personified. Analysts often evaluate foreign policy as if nation-states have distinctive personalities and needs and are calculating, adaptive entities. In nuclear strategy, policymakers more assiduously maintain distinctions among target sets (e.g., urban-industrial, military) than among abstract strategies (e.g., denial, punishment) and their targeting recommendations thus often conflict with their professed strategies. In nuclear capability assessment, analysts emphasize measures over the abstract principles by which they claim capability must be judged, becoming attached to measures that violate those principles.

The "choice" of subject and referent is critical, for detected similarities are not "transitive": " 'A man is like a tree' implies that man has roots; 'a tree is like a man' implies that the tree has a life history. 'Life is like a play' says that people play roles. 'A play is like life' says that a play can capture the essential elements of human life" (Tversky 1977).

Useful insights into the psychological relationships between lower- and higher-level goals can be gained when the former are conceived as referents and the latter as subjects. This because means shape ends through a human tendency to conceive effects through their apparent causes. Michotte (1963), in a classic work on the perception of causality, records that people are inclined to see cause and effect as a process centering on apparent causes. In an example from mechanics, when one object bumps into another and the second object moves off, the impact and the corresponding result are perceived by the observer as an organic whole, based on an "impact-which-launches." The active object is seen to extend itself on to the passive object; one event "appears to be produced as a result of the evolution of the other." "This new event appears 'as a continuation of a previously existing event; it is the earlier event in an evolved form' " (Michotte 1963:217,222). In a word, causality endows objects with "meaning."[25]

This is given added significance by the finding that people have an "irresistable tendency to perceive sequences of events in terms of causal relations" (Tversky and Kahneman 1982:117,126) and that people are inclined to think in "causal" rather than "diagnostic" terms. "A causal schema has a natural course; it evolves from causes to consequences. Hence we suggest that it is more natural and easier to follow the normal sequence and reason from causes to consequences than to invert this sequence and reason from consequences to causes" (Tversky and Kahneman 1982:118).

The formative influence of means on ends is observed in the manner in which an organization's "mission"—the specified responsibilities and activities[26] of an institution—shapes the perspective of its members. As policy problems are "factored" among agencies with specific responsibilities, the organizational means by which high-level policymakers seek

solutions to those problems may loom larger than the problems themselves (March and Simon 1958:152–153). A long-accepted truism of bureaucratic politics is that "where you stand depends on where you sit."
Much of bureaucratic politics can thus be described as "solutions in
search of problems" as members, through self-interest, internalize the
interests of their organizations (albeit some members with more zeal than
others). However, in this context means also determine ends more insid-
iously through the "law of the instrument." As Kaplan (1964:28) aptly
observes, "Give a small boy a hammer, and he will find that everything
he encounters needs pounding." The lesson is not that policymakers "do
with what they have" or even the exuberance with which they go about
doing it, but rather that what policymakers do conditions what they *want*
and what they *see*. The hammer increases the prominence of those goals
to which it is suited (e.g., getting attention, disciplining acquaintances,
"repairing" the unbroken) but also reshapes the conception of existing
goals (e.g., completing a puzzle by pounding ill-fitting pieces). Ends
resemble means because the latter have conceptual priority. For this
reason, corporate managers might conceive a problem of declining prof-
its, market position, and product demand in terms of internal operational
remedies available to the firm, e.g., cost reductions, reorganization (on
this, see Ansoff 1965:10). Also for this reason, policymakers refer to an
"arms balance" as if it were a sine qua non for "stability" or even use
these terms interchangeably as if one implied the other.[27]

HYPOTHESES

The cognitive psychology literature suggests an important insight:
when a salient entity influences a nonsalient one, the nonsalient entity is
made more consistent with the salient one—the result is greater simplicity, for the nonsalient entity loses its individualizing features. These
general conclusions can be reduced to a few simple hypotheses—hypotheses that are predicated upon the assumption that concrete entities
by merit of their concreteness and associated properties (tangibility,
particularity, and immediacy) are more salient than are abstract ones.

*H1: Goal components tend to be conceived in concrete rather than in
abstract terms.*
The parts by which goals are defined tend to be understood in concrete
terms. This applies to all goal components, though the extent of their
concreteness varies inversely with the abstractness of the goals involved.
(By definition, higher-level goals have more abstract constituents.)

H2: Goals tend to be conceived in concrete rather than in abstract terms. Linkages among and with concrete components tend to be emphasized over those among more abstract ones; the former linkages are likely to be more clearly drawn and conceived to be causally prior to the latter.

H3: Higher-level goals tend to be conceived to resemble lower-level ones. The characteristics of more-concrete lower-level goals tend to be projected on to higher-level ones.

In the following chapters, these three hypotheses will be presented in more substantive terms. The first hypothesis will feature heavily in this analysis, because this book is organized around the key components of policy; the other two hypotheses are assessed in the final chapter. The following chapters examine whether and how policymakers disconnect from the abstract—whether they neglect the abstract and fail to use it to guide the concrete. Stated somewhat differently, these chapters will determine whether abstract issues are neglected in policy despite the elaborateness of concrete thought and whether contradictions exist at and between abstract and concrete levels of thought.

These hypotheses are tendency statements. They indicate what might happen, but because human beliefs are complexly determined, these hypotheses do not guarantee that it will happen. Moreover, these hypotheses certainly cannot ensure that in the absence of the influence of the concrete, policy would no longer be deficient.

UNMOTIVATED BIAS AND THE OTHER SOURCES OF STRATEGY

Unmotivated bias could indeed be a preeminent, though not singular, source of concrete thinking in policy. Motivated bias and bureaucratic politics also affect policy concreteness, complicating analysis.[28] In fact, bureaucratic politics is now the most common explanation for the deficiencies of national security policy. The policy effects of unmotivated bias are not distinguished easily from those of these two other factors. Nevertheless, unmotivated bias can account for that which the other two explanations cannot, and as will be demonstrated for bureaucratic politics in subsequent chapters, explanations based upon unmotivated bias are not fundamentally inconsistent with those based upon bureaucratic politics or motivated bias.

Motivated bias shares much with unmotivated bias: Motivated bias can account for the perverse consistency of policy. Motivated policymakers can employ numerous psychological devices to postpone critical choices and maintain their beliefs; they may thus doggedly adhere to flawed decisions, deficient logic, and ill-founded beliefs that are overreliant upon the concrete (e.g, the belief that nuclear dilemmas can be addressed with traditional military instruments).

Bureaucratic politics also shares with unmotivated bias. Bureaucratic politics can account for policy rigidity and can go even a step further and explain the conceptual reliance upon the concrete. Bureaucratic politics is behind much of the hyperattention to weapons—particular weapon systems, capability measures, weapon properties, target characteristics, and so on—within the U.S. government and thus much of the concreteness of U.S. nuclear strategy. Bureaucratic politics has effects that resonate through all aspects of strategy. Government leaders inject the concrete into strategic policy when they manipulate strategy to sell weapons of dubious merit to a sometimes unreceptive legislature; the military services are similarly creative when they alter strategy to support sophisticated and costly weapons that promise an increase in service visibility, importance, and resource share.

Notwithstanding the virtues of these two alternative explanations, motivated bias and bureaucratic politics are less compelling explanations for the deficiencies of policy goals. The reason is simple—unmotivated bias could conceivably explain more with less. Unmotivated bias could not only account for a larger amount of the observed deficiencies, and do so under less restrictive conditions, but could also explain these deficiencies parsimoniously. Unmotivated bias could explain why policymakers, differing in cognitive awareness and regardless of expertise and authority, are drawn to the concrete and do so with greater economy.

Neither of these two other factors has the potential to as completely explain policy deficiencies. Motivated bias says nothing about the attention to the concrete; it explains why and how policymakers resist policy change, but it does not, in and of itself, account for policy content. Bureaucratic politics, in turn, says nothing about the inattention to the abstract; it explains why policymakers attend to the concrete but fails to account for the absence of coherent policy at any level of the policymaking process. The bureaucratic politics perspective does predict that policy will be incoherent, but only in the aggregate—policy is incoherent because it is a conflictual outcome.[29] Admittedly, bureaucratic contenders might articulate incoherent strategy when it suits their political purposes; but if bureaucracies are rational competitors, they might find coherent strategy to be a more effective tool than an incoherent one—an incoherent strategy is a political liability when its flaws are only too apparent to a rational bureaucratic adversary.

In important respects, unmotivated bias can also subsume both motivated bias and bureaucratic politics when the assumptions that underlie the bureaucratic politics perspective are relaxed. This claim cannot be made for either the motivated bias or the bureaucratic politics perspectives.

Under the most restrictive assumptions, unmotivated bias, motivated bias, and bureaucratic politics each apply to a different policymaker. On the one hand, the motivated policymaker is an active policymaker who consciously bolsters or suppresses conceptual deficiencies to avoid attitude or decision change. On the other hand, the bureaucratic politician is an activist and a rationally self-interested one at that—one that can intentionally manipulate strategy to advantage when not steadfastly holding to it. The first policymaker struggles to resolve internal conflict while the second struggles to profit from external conflict. Differing from the other two, the unmotivated policymaker is a passive policymaker, one oblivious to conflict—conflict that exists within his/her beliefs or between those beliefs and reality.

Unmotivated bias can explain some of what is currently attributed to bureaucratic politics and motivated bias. Under a relaxed rationality assumption, the bureaucratic politician becomes a captive, rather than just an advocate, of organizational ideology. This bureaucratic politician is conceptually dependent on weapons sought for the good of the organization—that is, he/she is psychologically bound to organizational means at the expense of national ends. With existing assumptions, unmotivated bias could explain that attributed to motivated bias. This because unmotivated policymakers share with their motivated counterparts a nonrational resistance to change—resistance in the form of, among other things, a suppression of evidence, a failure to recognize decisional alternatives and consequences, and an inattention to conceptual inconsistencies. Even when unmotivated bias is present in degree, policymakers, when motivated, might actually defend those beliefs of unmotivated origin. At the very least, unmotivated bias can coexist with (if not reinforce the effects of) these other policy determinants.

In a nutshell, the strength of unmotivated bias is that it could explain more than motivated bias and bureaucratic politics do either separately or together. This does not mean that unmotivated bias would subsume motivated bias and bureaucratic politics fully, but it would establish unmotivated bias as a critical policy source.

CONCEPTS AS GOALS: THE ISSUE
OF INSTRUMENTALITY

This chapter offers a conception of the relationship between means and ends in foreign policy that is at odds with the classical model. Nevertheless, if concepts are indeed goals, they must somehow be instrumentally tied to policy means. To put it simply, "goals" must be goals.

To determine how goals instrumentally influence policy, it is helpful to draw from the seminal contributions of Herbert Simon, Charles Lindblom, Richard Cyert, and James March on organizational decisionmaking, captured more recently in the foreign policy literature by the "organizational processes" and "bureaucratic politics" models of Graham Allison and John Steinbruner's "cybernetic" model (1974).

Steinbruner's cybernetic model comes close to denying that goals are relevant to the policy process by substituting programmed responses for the classical model's option outcome calculations. The cybernetic model is clearly not a "decision" model. It allows little latitude for choice and maintains instead that people gauge their actions to the values of a limited number of monitored variables (see also Simon 1957:204,219f). For example, this model predicts that procurement decisions will be based upon weapon performance characteristics rather than on the ability of a weapon to conduct certain missions. The cybernetic model posits that people select short-term, simple, and causally proximate solutions because they are more "visible" than long-term, complex, and indirect ones; these solutions produce immediate feedback and do not require that people painstakingly evaluate evidence, broadly interpret problems, or exhaustively consider policy alternatives.

Organizational theorists have been less willing to discard decision from their conceptions of the policy process,[30] but these theorists depict a choice process that is hardly exhaustive.[31] These theorists implicitly support the cybernetic model, though, when they show people to search restrictively for decisional alternatives at first in the "neighborhood of problem symptoms" and then in the "neighborhood of the current alternative" (Allison 1971:77; Cyert and March 1963:120–122.) For instance, a doctor who cannot explain a medical problem may prescribe medication aimed directly at local symptoms; if this treatment fails, his/her likely next step will be to vary the previous method, e.g., he/she might change the prescribed dosage, might try similar medication, or might consider interaction effects and confounding variables. In preferring "conservative" to "aggressive" treatment, the doctor is conceptually bound to the character of the malady (at least as he/she defines it) and the current treatment.

A narrow focus on the symptoms of a problem can be found when those in the policy community contend that the United States must renounce existing arms control treaties to prevent the Soviets from reaping unilateral advantages by violating these agreements. This contention, whatever its ideological foundation, suggests that "symmetry" and "reciprocity" guide policymakers to select solutions in the neighborhood of recognized symptoms. If the Soviets are continuing to arm, then the United States must do the same; if the United States cannot violate a treaty, then it must renounce it. An "eye for an eye" is clearly a more compelling solution than an "eye for a tooth" or a "tooth for an eye." While the former policy can be criticized as an overreactive escalation and the latter can be assailed as ineffectively soft, in fact, policymakers find reactions in kind and of like intensity to be attractive by their very nature.

A similar, narrow focus on problem symptoms is found when policymakers contend that the United States must match or at least counter Soviet weapons deployment or that the United States must bring its nuclear doctrine into line with Soviet doctrine. Inherent within the Soviet threat is the solution—Soviet force improvements must be met with U.S. force improvements, whether in quality, quantity, or mode of deployment.[32]

A preoccupation with problem symptoms might actually center upon currently recognized alternatives. Policymakers might monitor certain symptoms because of their apparent resemblance and causal connection to existing policy instruments.[33] U.S. policymakers may choose to meet force with force, then, because their prior use of force has left them perceptually tied to the military option and a narrow, military conception of the Soviet threat. A policymaker that has been conditioned to see the world in military terms will see military threats where others see economic ones and still others see no particular threat at all.

Although these models depict a policy that does not result from rigorous and exhaustive choice, they suggest ways that higher-level goals can direct policy. One possibility is that these goals guide policy when a system is "set up" to perform certain functions. Consistent with this, the cybernetic model suggests that individuals and organizations only irregularly attend to any higher-level goal and are alert to a goal when it is threatened. Policy is seen to alternate between a state of "inertia" and more rational "crisis management"—though policy change is suboptimally defensive and reactive.

The idea that the foreign policy is "corrected" consistently by externally induced rationality is compelling, but should not be overstated. By definition, crises are periods of high threat, stress, and limited decision time (Hermann 1972). Such conditions reduce decisionmaker abilities to assess the operational environment and explore alternatives and are associated generally with rigid stereotypic thinking (Janis and Mann 1977).

Further, decisionmaking is hampered under all circumstances by an absence of foreign policy performance indicators. Foreign policy goals cannot be easily matched to valid quantitative measures, and it is too easy, then, to fall back on available indicators—Olympic medals, moon launchings, or nuclear warheads, and, as we remember in Vietnam, body counts or percentage of the population in government controlled areas. Even in times of crisis, policymakers employ questionable indicators of success—"they blinked first," "no shots fired," "they didn't cross the line," "the receipt of a complete explanation," the mere presence of agreement, or short-term and even empty concessions.

The problems of decisionmaking transcend the paucity of valid indicators, though. Foreign policy goals elude precise definition, and therefore, not surprisingly, policymakers have difficulty prioritizing objectives, selecting alternatives, and evaluating policy trade-offs and consequences. The reasons the United States was in Vietnam were never clear, so that the issue of measuring success there was always secondary at best. More recently, without a clearer specification of the rationale behind the Reagan-inspired strategic defense initiative (e.g., Is it designed to protect missiles or cities? And at what level of successful warhead penetration?), a program undertaken with deliberation and strong commitment at the highest levels of the government, a high level of rationality appears absent at the top.

Another role for higher-level goals is suggested by Steinbruner (1974: 78), who notes that the cybernetic approach dissects complex problems, in part, by "disaggregated values" ("factoring"). Given the argument of this chapter, the disaggregated values can be assumed to be goal components—components that when in concrete form will influence the selection of feedback variables. The components of deterrence, for instance, suggest numerous concrete feedback variables—weapons targeting, weapons capabilities, levels of superpower tension, and so forth. The selection of concrete feedback variables can also be affected by lower-level objectives (as policymakers search the neighborhood of a current alternative). Deterrence might then be conceived, for instance, as a force balance. In any case, feedback variables determine whether policymakers judge deterrence to be stable or unstable.

To recognize that "goals are concepts," then, is not to abandon the assumption of goal-oriented behavior. People can be goal-directed even when their goals are flawed and pursued haphazardly.

CONCLUSIONS

Cognitive psychology suggests a preeminent role for the concrete in policy goal formation. The concrete, with its abundant cues and its association with the tangible, particular, and immediate, is salient and therefore central to policy. Given its salience, the concrete can define goals through its effects on key goal components and their interrelationship.

The effects of the concrete are captured, here, in three hypotheses that will inform the analysis of subsequent chapters—hypotheses that record the effects of the concrete on goals and their components. These hypotheses are not reintroduced explicitly until the last chapter, where they are shown to be validated by the major conclusions of this work.

The observations here are in keeping with the emphasis on man as a "problem solver" and "naive scientist" rather than a pure "consistency seeker" (on this, see George 1980:58). The prevalence of human nonrationality does not mean that man is hopelessly irrational—slavishly adherent to misreadings of history and outdated conceptions. Human beings are also goal-oriented and adaptive, as demonstrated by scientific achievement and increased technical mastery of the physical environment. Human beings struggle continuously with issues of causality in identifying worldly threats and opportunities and adopting means to advance their interests, even if they do this with intellectual shortcuts and limited reflection.

Perhaps the study of goals can be redeemed from the rational-actor tradition, sparked by the image of man as a "deficient problem solver," but a "problem solver" nonetheless. By joining the rational-actor and cognitive-process traditions, a more exhaustive model that captures the virtues of both of these traditions can emerge.

Policymakers and theorists can both benefit when they recognize that goals are often defective as concepts. Policymakers might be inspired to define more sharply their professed objectives, and theorists might ask whether an academic concept is useful when it means something different to policymakers.

2

STRATEGIC ASSESSMENT

STRANGELY ENOUGH, policymakers and policy analysts (technical specialists) rely upon the concrete and the simple to cope with the intricacies and attending uncertainties of strategic assessment. More specifically, they use simple measures to determine the adequacy of U.S. strategic forces and the consequences of a nuclear exchange; in this they *are only loosely guided by abstract strategic force requirements,* and they *work with abstract assumptions that record the influence of simple measures.*[1] Policymakers and policy analysts are enticed by what can more easily be measured, understood, and predicted.

This chapter investigates the source, extent, validity, and impact of simple measurement. It does this, first, by examining two dominant abstract views of nuclear capability, their deficiencies, and their dependence on simple measures; second, by exploring the popular capability measures and their limits; and, finally, by examining the reasons policymakers and analysts are drawn to simple measures.

ABSTRACT CONCEPTIONS OF CAPABILITY: ABSOLUTISM AND RELATIVISM

At the most abstract level, policymakers view nuclear capability in primarily two different ways—in "absolute" and in "relative" terms. The absolutist and relativist conceptions of capability are quite distinct, but in practice they comingle, and to a large degree the contradictions of U.S. strategic nuclear policy reflect an unwillingness of U.S. policymakers to commit to only one of them. Moreover, policymakers elaborate their conceptions of capability by looking to that which can be measured. This has resulted in a proliferation of overly simplistic and inadequate capability terms.

"Absolutists" recognize a ceiling at which no ends can justify incurring a nuclear attack and beyond which nuclear superiority is meaningful only in a narrow technical sense and cannot be translated into political influence or bestow advantages in combat. At this ceiling, these weapons are solely a means of deterring and avoiding war rather than of fighting it. "They must not do less, and they cannot do more" (Bundy 1969a:11). Absolutists believe their view to be supported by three characteristics of nuclear weapons—their phenomenal destructiveness, their inherent bluntness, and the lack of an effective defense against them. Absolutists are thus greatly concerned with weapons survivability to ensure deterrence and, unlike relativists, are not greatly concerned with accuracy or the degradation of retaliatory power in successive nuclear exchanges, and because they emphasize deterrence over the actual conduct of a nuclear war, absolutists also accept a higher level of uncertainty in performance.

"Relativists," on the other hand, believe that the nuclear "balance"—the distribution of capability among nations—rather than floors and ceilings, determines the utility of weapons. They evaluate the efficacy of weapons in relative terms—the ability of a system or an arsenal to withstand enemy countermeasures (either active or passive) or to perform at levels that match or exceed those of the adversary. Relativists are uncomfortable with the idea of nuclear "overkill," given the tendency for the military balance to change, and they view imposed ceilings as arbitrary or, even worse, a threat to national security.

The Early Years: The Origins of Relativism

The Truman and Eisenhower years were periods of policy ambiguity and inconsistency; in these periods, the conception of capability that was predominant was not always clear and policy appears to have reflected elements of both conceptions. Absolutism is apparent when the atomic bomb was conceived as an "ultimate weapon," a "special weapon," and a "weapon of last resort." On the other hand, relativism surfaced in the belief that the atomic bomb was "just another weapon."

Truman exhibited some absolutist tendencies. He initially pursued international control of atomic weapons, though with quickly diminishing enthusiasm; domestically, he maintained authority over the use of these weapons and resisted attempts by the military to gain control of the nuclear stockpile and production facilities. If nuclear weapons had to be used, Truman apparently planned to employ them "to 'terrorize' his enemies rather than win a specific battle" through attacks on a limited and select group of targets (Halperin 1987:6). Furthermore, Truman sought conventional weapons to supplement the bomb, and his administration was unable to agree upon criteria to govern its use, except that it would be employed "to reduce or eliminate Soviet or 'bolshevik' control inside and outside the Soviet Union" (Rosenberg 1983:11–14).

Truman was not a central figure in the nuclear debate, though. Those active in nuclear planning, the Joint Chiefs of Staff (JCS), the Air Force, and numerous advisory committees were more convinced of the necessity and utility of employing nuclear weapons in a future military engagement (Rosenberg 1979). The Air Force believed that the Soviets could be felled by a "Sunday punch." Plans for strategic nuclear bombardment, however, were based on conventional war experience rather than a belief that nuclear weapons are somehow unique. Moreover, in the early postwar years many were skeptical about whether nuclear weapons could assure victory in war due to the limited size of the postwar nuclear stockpile, doubt as to whether weapons could be delivered to their targets, and the mixed success of WW II strategic bombing (Quester 1970:1–7).

The Eisenhower administration viewed the bomb in even more conventional terms. Eisenhower sought to integrate both strategic and tactical nuclear weapons into defense by reversing civilian control of the bomb (though these weapons had already been integrated into war plans). But even if "Eisenhower was not awed by nuclear weapons . . . neither was he sanguine about them," and he "recognized that they had permanently altered the character of warfare" (Rosenberg 1983:27). Contrary to common belief, Eisenhower did not adhere to the doctrine of "massive retaliation," at least as it was publically promoted. Massive retaliation embodied the conception of nuclear weapons as special and would have required all-out nuclear retaliation against the Soviet Union, the center of world communism, as a response to lesser communist encroachments. Massive retaliation, understood in this way, was more important to campaign rhetoric and early administration attempts to define a strategy than it was eventual policy (Wells 1981).[2] Later "clarifications" of this doctrine (by Secretary of State Dulles) amounted to a "retraction" (Brodie 1959:249).

The Eisenhower administration accepted the idea that nuclear weapons could work in tandem with conventional forces to blunt a Soviet attack and to prevent the Soviets from continuing their war effort, while acknowledging that nuclear weapons were inherently of a distinctively powerful nature. In a sense, the administration was dependent upon a form of "massive retaliation." It showed little restraint in target selection and could have reduced the Soviet Union to nuclear rubble in the event of war and it pushed a "New Look" that reversed the prior conventional buildup. Nonetheless, the Eisenhower administration, like the Truman administration before it, envisioned the purpose of phenomenally destructive atomic power as that of accomplishing traditional strategic missions.[3] Furthermore, the Eisenhower administration was unsympathetic to both the development of limited war options and the replacement of nuclear with conventional forces (even if it rejected the inflexibility of response inherent in massive retaliation doctrine). This reflected the administration's unwillingness to identify "firebreaks" between conventional and nuclear war and between limited and total war or to define war aims short of the traditional objective of "winning" (on this, see, for example, Betts 1987).[4] Ignoring the question of escalation, the Eisenhower administration became increasingly reliant on tactical nuclear weapons when strategic theorists had turned their attention towards limiting the consequences of war.

In sum, it can be asked whether the Truman or Eisenhower administrations could have failed to appreciate a qualitative distinction between conventional and nuclear weapons given the destructive power of the latter. Cautious of the potentially horrendous consequences of a nuclear exchange, both Truman and Eisenhower were judicious and restrained when considering the use of the bomb. Despite this, the Eisenhower administration threatened to use nuclear weapons—albeit reluctantly—in taking both the Korean War and the conflict over the Taiwan Straits to the Chinese mainland, though escalation was avoided when the Chinese chose not to test the sincerity of the U.S. nuclear commitment. In the case of Hungary, Eisenhower was quick to recognize the considerable constraints on the effective use of U.S. military power and refused to risk a nuclear war with the Soviets. But neither the Truman nor Eisenhower administration looked at nuclear weapons solely in revolutionary terms. If a relativist perspective prevailed in the early postwar period, it was because the United States had overwhelming nuclear superiority; the United States enjoyed the luxury of not having to consider the untoward implications of its nuclear threats, the circumstances under which the use of nuclear weapons would be less than propitious, or whether it could retain the ability to retaliate against Soviet targets so as to deter a Soviet attack.

The relativist perspective had its origins in a time in which U.S.

nuclear capability knew no limits and superiority was the policy by default. Deterrence of a Soviet attack did not require hard choices: "Deterrence was easy and uncontroversial, an accident of history not a creature of policy" (Huntington 1961:298).[5] The choices certainly became harder in the Eisenhower years, but not so as to force a fundamental acceptance of the limits of atomic power.

The Sixties: Between Relativism and Absolutism

Absolutism became more dominant in the sixties. By the midfifties, many policymakers had come to recognize that a Soviet first strike could have crippled the U.S. ability to retaliate and that the U.S. could no longer guarantee its immunity from nuclear attack through preemptive war. More optimistic assessments could be offered by the early sixties. By then, the United States was protected from a disarming Soviet first strike by the deployment of elusive Polaris ballistic-missile submarines, the beginning of U.S. reliance on solid-fuel missiles in hardened silos, the placement of bombers on higher-alert status, and the growing Soviet dependence upon inaccurate intercontinental ballistic missiles (ICBMs).[6] With a prompt retaliatory capability, the United States might not have to continuously enlarge its strategic force and could conceivably disengage from the arms competition.

The absolutist conception is clearly found among advocates of "minimum deterrence." Proponents of minimum or "finite" deterrence are serious advocates of the absolutist position. They emphasize the revolutionary consequences of nuclear weapons on war and believe that it is misleading and even dangerous to "think the unthinkable" and to cross the nuclear threshold intellectually. They take guidance from the admonition that "everything about the atomic bomb is overshadowed by the twin facts that it exists and its destructive power is fantastically great" (Brodie 1946:52). At the extreme, they believe deterrence to be virtually "automatic"—a product of characteristics intrinsic to nuclear weapons—and are concerned with operational issues only when they desire a deterrent that will "at least 'look' potentially reliable and effective."[7] Minimalists are distinctive among absolutists in their belief that relatively low levels of destructive capability constitute an adequate deterrent. George Kennan[8] was one of the first to embrace the minimum deterrent (on this, see Gaddis 1982:79–80). The Navy, in the fifties, also turned to the minimum deterrent in assailing the war aims of the Air Force, the dominant nuclear service (even if the Navy also departed from a "pure" absolutist position by offering a promise of nuclear war termination short of an all-out nuclear exchange). The Navy offered a modest alternative to what it somewhat disingenuously claimed was an indiscriminate, open-ended, and even immoral Air Force commitment to nuclear weapons that was rooted in the belief that wars are best deterred by the ability to win them. More recently, McGeorge Bundy (1969b:159) has taken the minimum deterrent even a step further in arguing that "a single surviving submarine, in itself, would be deterrent enough."

Minimum deterrence advocates are more willing than other absolutists are to specify deployment ceilings or the destruction levels that are required to preserve deterrence. The Navy offered such a limit through their commitment to forty-five Polaris submarines. Admittedly, the Navy accepted a conservative limit for bureaucratic reasons. The Navy worked within constraints imposed by restricted funding and resistance from the Air Force. The Navy also had to contend with factionalism (unlike the Air Force, where SAC was the dominant command): Navy factions resented funding a "national" program that was unrelated to the control of the seas without corresponding increases in the Navy budget. Nevertheless, the Navy *did* promote a finite deterrence argument that received support from civilian analysts aloof from the bureaucratic competition.

Absolutists, as a whole, are more confident that the United States can inflict destruction on the Soviet Union than they are that the United States can deter the Soviet Union under all circumstances. For instance, many absolutists fear that a U.S. overreliance upon nuclear weapons opens conventional opportunities for the Soviets or that a U.S. conventional skirmish with the Soviets could explode into a nuclear engagement. In other words, absolutists have some fear of Soviet risk taking. For this reason, absolutists tend to err on the conservative side[9] (if only by default): if the United States cannot manipulate Soviet perceptions of risk, it can affect Soviet perceived payoffs with high levels of potential destruction.[10]

Absolutism is perhaps most closely associated with Robert McNamara and the doctrine of assured destruction. McNamara was the first U.S. Defense Secretary to commit to explicit absolute retaliatory criteria for deterring the Soviet Union. He offered various estimates that established an "assured destruction" range of between 20 to 33 percent of the Soviet population and 50 to 75 percent of Soviet industry. His successors, Clifford and Brown, offered comparable estimates (U.S. Department of Defense FY1970; FY1979; Schilling 1981:59–60). But such estimates are not set in concrete. McNamara adopted criteria that reflected the then current levels of U.S. destructive capability and reflected bureaucratic considerations, technical factors, and ad hocism more than they did a studied assessment of what was required to deter the Soviets. McNamara aimed to establish a strategic defense budget ceiling to counter the escalating force demands of the various services, while avoiding a service revolt.[11] He chose a ceiling at which additional deployments would yield "diminishing returns" in inflictable damage. He eventually somewhat arbitrarily committed to a one-thousand-missile Minuteman force. Although McNamara asserted that the projected size and character of Soviet strategic forces shaped U.S. force requirements, he appears to have been carried by the momentum of prior U.S. production authorizations (Ball 1980:168–177).[12]

The point, then, is that the absolutist has often been a dissenter rather than protagonist in the policy debate. Given the problems of establishing assured destruction criteria and the effective absence of a bureaucratic disarmament constituency, the absolutist has served as a reluctant participant in the arms race and as the guardian of the status quo.

The relativist conception survived the end of the U.S. nuclear monopoly and has persisted to the current day, for despite the rhetoric and deployment ceilings of assured destruction, even McNamara clung to "superiority" in public statements and policy justifications and the United States intended to preserve a margin of advantage over the Soviet Union (Kahan 1975:107–108). Superiority is difficult to reconcile with the doctrine of assured destruction, but fits with a competing set of ideas, termed *damage limitation*, that gained currency in the early sixties (and emerged again, in somewhat altered form, in the seventies) and emphasized the destruction of Soviet retaliatory capability (on this, see chapter 3).

Under McNamara, U.S. declaratory doctrine evolved from a damage limiting to an assured destruction posture (this was apparent, for instance, in the successive annual reports of the U.S. Department of Defense). Some claim that McNamara merely flirted with damage limitation, while others maintain that it was assured destruction that he never fully embraced. The latter argue that McNamara never proposed "that nuclear weapons actually be 'used' in this way" (see Rowen 1979:146) and that "assured destruction defined the 'minimum' capabilities required, not the desirable level of forces" (see Betts 1982:104).[13] This debate points to a fundamental contradiction in the way in which policymakers approach the problem of nuclear war: McNamara and his successors believed that the horrendous consequences of nuclear war made nuclear war less probable, but simultaneously sought to minimize those same consequences should deterrence fail.

The Seventies: The Rebirth of Relativism

Relativist thinking came into its own in the Nixon administration with the adoption of "sufficiency" in place of "superiority." This is not to say that the administration rejected absolutism. The Nixon administration claimed that increases in the size of U.S. strategic forces were of limited practical value and would stimulate an arms race (Freedman 1977:147) and battled congressional forces that demanded that strategic arms control agreements be based on U.S.-Soviet "equality" in intercontinental strategic forces (Barton and Weiler 1976:211). Nevertheless, although sufficiency connotes the absolutist adequacy criterion of assured destruction, it is very much a relativist concept.

Sufficiency was defined by the Nixon administration with a general set of criteria (see U.S. Department of Defense FY1972)—such as an effective retaliatory capability and reduced force vulnerability. Even then these criteria were never made specific and "the precise meaning and relative priority of each sufficiency criterion changed with evolving technical, military, and political circumstances" (Kahan 1975:150). Nixon explicitly rejected a nuclear balance that was disadvantageous to the United States or would leave the United States "inferior" to any nation, but he did not make clear what constituted an unacceptable asymmetry of capability and this criterion "seemed to have no obvious weapon implications" (Kahan 1975:145, 149, 157–158). More generally, a question remained as to whether this standard implied that capability alone was insufficient to deter the Soviets.

Relativism of the seventies gave birth to a jumble of terms that may have meant the same thing or even nothing at all. Sufficiency was equated by some with equivalence. Defense Secretary Schlesinger, however, defining the concept as "elastic," associated it with assured destruction and, at other times, with superiority (as when counterforce was involved) (Ball 1974:6,8). Even existing concepts were not safe. In what seems to be the ultimate perversion of meaning, Schlesinger suggested that assured destruction is a relative concept by asserting that deterrence can be maintained at lower levels of destruction if reductions in destructive capability are reciprocal (Ball 1974:37). Thus Schlesinger's stance as a pure relativist was compromised by his advocating that the United States and Soviet Union maintain an equal ability to "threaten" the other (see U.S. Department of Defense FY1975). His predecessor, Laird, had explicitly rejected assured destruction, yet focused on absolutist notions when arguing that the Soviets should not be allowed the capability to inflict more civil damage on the United States than the United States could inflict on the Soviets (Rowen 1979:152).

Relativism and absolutism blend together then when absolutist criteria, such as the extent of industrial damage, are presumed to be meaningful as a ratio of the damage to one society to that of another; but absolutist assumptions can fuse with relativist reasoning in other ways. For example, some state that deterrence requires that no advantages accrue from a first strike or, rather, that the differences between the outcome of a first and second strike be minimized (on this, see Conover 1977:17). This requirement is often expressed in a preference for single warheads over multiple independently targetable reentry vehicles (MIRVs), since attacks by single-warhead missiles would disarm an attacker more than a defender; this requirement is also expressed in a fear that an attacker might preempt if it anticipates unfavorable shifts in a force balance.[14] This requirement does not rely upon the U.S.-Soviet capability or damage ratios that are more typical of relativism, but nor does it reference an absolutist capability ceiling by which to judge the significance of those differences. In contrast, absolutism argues that differences in outcome are meaningful only when a first strike deprives the defender of an adequate retaliant.

Relativism and absolutism also come together when relativists design strategy around threats to things that the Soviet value, and they, like absolutists, must then determine exactly what it is that the Soviets value. Relativists have addressed this issue in its relative form—"will the Soviets suffer greater or lesser losses than the United States?" But they also deal with the issue in its absolute form and therefore call for "decapitation" by destroying the Soviet leadership, centers of coercion and control, and lines of communication (see Gray and Payne 1980; U.S. Department of Defense FY1982) and a "regionalization" (or Balkanization) of the Soviet Union through the extermination of its Great Russian population and the economic, political, and military isolation of its largest republic (on this, see Cattell and Quester 1986). Putting aside questions of feasibility, they can be criticized for actually misunderstanding Soviet values and for drawing inferences about these values through "reverse imaging." U.S. policymakers sometimes presume that their Soviet counterparts are the exact opposites of themselves: "We are good, they are bad . . . we arm for peace, they arm for war . . . we seek to promote the general welfare, they seek to promote their own power . . . we are self-sacrificing, they seek to 'save their own skins.' "

Despite their incursions into absolutism, relativists obviously cast their argument primarily in relative terms. Indeed, their evaluations of the U.S. and Soviet arsenals have centered on a host of "equivalence" terms—*essential equivalence, strategic equality, true equality,* and an *equilibrium of forces*—though at the cost of clarity. Relativists fail to define the military balance consistently whether they are concerned with existing hardware or its physical effects.[15] This raises basic questions: When they stress physical effects, is damage to enemy society more important than that to enemy military forces? When they stress damage to society, is damage to economic recuperative capability more important than immediate economic damage and human casualties? When they emphasize force damage, should numbers be counted before or after a nuclear exchange? Moreover, relativists fail to reconcile the very different policy implications that exit between a hardware and physical effects emphasis. Equivalence on an effects measure could require superiority on a hardware measure when equivalence is interpreted to mean an equal ability to destroy. A superior force may be required to overcome the force advantages of the opposition, particularly if the "disadvantaged" country does not plan to strike first. Reflecting, and all the while adding to the confusion, policymakers have expressed strategic objectives in the most general terms, embodied, for example, in the Carter directive (PD-18) that called for U.S. forces "strong enough to ensure that any possible nuclear war would end on the most favorable terms possible" (on this, see Ball 1986:76).

We have come full circle. The relativists assail the static nature of assured destruction criteria, yet, in offering empty prescriptions, similarly flounder on the question of "how much is enough?" They find sanctuary in the technical world of force comparisons, but only by hiding from still critical issues: "under what conditions and for what purposes are nuclear weapons likely to be used?" Relativists deal with these issues, but not in ways that neatly translate into measurement criteria.[16]

The relativist inability to establish criteria for effective deterrence means that they cannot specify limits to the useful accumulation of nuclear weaponry. This has led them to adopt two decision rules that have undesirable consequences.

First, relativists (and absolutists as well) have planned for the "worst case." Worst case planning is explicitly and decidedly nonprobabilistic; planning centers on the assumption of a malevolent adversary against whom what can fail *will* fail and for whom what can fail *won't* fail. In this vein, it is argued, for example, that McNamara based force requirements on Soviet capability rather than intentions (Enthoven and Smith 1979:178–179) and aspired to the highest level of security that was achievable and not just probably required (Ball 1980:140). This conservative strategy of planning for the worst case might seem warranted given the stakes involved and the ease of assessment afforded by the presumption of an enemy that "optimizes,"[17] but the result of worst-case planning could be wasteful misallocation of resources and stimulation of an arms race.

Policymakers do not always plan for the worst case, though. For instance, the concept of a greater-than-expected threat was institutionalized in the McNamara Defense Department, but only as a threat that, by its very nature, was unrealistic. The greater-than-expected threat, a threat that fell short of the worst case, was not a criterion for actual deployment and was used instead to guide military research and development and thereby enhance U.S. preparedness should this threat unexpectedly arise (Freedman 1977:85–86). Moreover, despite its insistence that U.S. ICBMs had become perilously vulnerable to a preemptive Soviet strike (the so-called window of vulnerability), the Reagan administration eventually proposed that the newly developed MX missile be placed in existing Minuteman III silos. Furthermore, the intelligence agencies have not necessarily offered overly pessimistic Soviet strategic force projections. Although the U.S. intelligence community still bears the stigma for the missile gap scare of the late fifties and early sixties, the annual Posture Statements of the Secretary of Defense and the annual National Intelligence Estimates, produced jointly by the various intelligence organizations, consistently underestimated the size of Soviet missile deployments in the sixties (Wohlstetter 1974; Berkowitz 1985a).

Second, relativists have often advocated the simple "matching" of the size and character of Soviet deployments. Matching is attractive because "technical inputs are easier to measure than hypothetical outputs" and because many are lured by "symbolic" Soviet gains from bigger ICBMs (on this, see Betts 1982:120–121). Moreover, matching also has a strategic justification. Since the early seventies, U.S. strategic policy has looked again to "warfighting" and such requirements as "escalation dominance," "escalation control," and "flexibility" (see chapters 3 and 5). Strategic policymakers maintain that the United States must position itself to respond to Soviet attacks at any level of provocation and create for itself the largest number of policy options in the event of a nuclear confrontation. Those who accept this argument maintain that the United States must "counter" rather "match" Soviet deployment; nevertheless, they tie U.S. deployments to those of the Soviet Union in a way that is indifferent to the particular historical, cultural, technological, and doctrinal factors that motivate Soviet conduct. To the extent that the United States simply mimics Soviet deployments, it binds itself to an emphasis on land-based missiles and a related counterforce posture; the United

States may unwittingly sacrifice strategic viability, operational effectiveness, and comparative advantage (Betts 1982:121) and thus undermine the very purposes that policy is claimed to serve.

For these reasons, some of the architects of the "new relativism" of the seventies and eighties have rejected the matching approach, and Secretary of Defense Brown thus defined essential equivalence to mean that the United States could offset Soviet force advantages with force advantages of its own and Secretary of Defense Weinberger rejected the suggestion that U.S. forces "mirror Soviet forces according to some superficial tally. . . ." (U.S. Department of Defense FY1983.) Nevertheless, Secretary of Defense Schlesinger supported matching by rejecting major asymmetries in factors that govern the effectiveness of strategic forces—throw-weight, yield, accuracy, numbers of warheads, and so forth. He believed that these factors could affect political influence through the perceived balance of forces. Schlesinger did not think that the involved force disadvantages were real, but believed them important because they could lead the Soviets to miscalculate (U.S. Department of Defense FY1975 FY1976). Brown left the door open to matching when also asserting that the United States must ensure that its forces are not perceived by the Soviets to be inferior (U.S. Department of Defense FY1979), and Weinberger shared this sensitivity.

Policymakers have not carefully considered the abstract capability requirements of deterrence. Absolutists offer ill-founded assured destruction criteria, and relativists offer an ambiguous and open-ended set of terms; neither duly considers what it actually takes to deter the Soviet Union. As a result, neither is fully at ease with its conception of capability; both advocates have allowed that which can be measured to determine what they choose to measure—in the end, the McNamara criteria are as specious as relativist notions of equivalence.

CONCRETE CONCEPTIONS OF CAPABILITY: MEASURES

Strategic assessment is an arcane craft. Its vocabulary, arguments, assumptions, and methods are accessible only to a few, and to the uninitiated it presents a confusing mix of terminology. Nonetheless, strategic assessment is rich in metaphor and reliant upon convention and, even when technically sophisticated, employs simplifications. Strategic assessment is a demanding subject, and its experts make do with measures that inevitably are deficient.

Strategic assessment unfortunately creates a false impression of precision and objectivity. Estimates of the outcome of a nuclear exchange are encumbered by numerous unknowns and incalculable physical interactions. Furthermore, policymakers and analysts cannot determine whether the United States is adequately armed without asking "adequate for what?" They cannot correctly answer the question "how much is enough?" apart from a political context. (At a minimum, they must appreciate diverse U.S.-Soviet force missions and objectives.)

Measures of nuclear capability can be classified in any number of ways. Here they are grouped by their implications for deterrence with a scheme borrowed from Nitze (1976–77) and Richelson (1980). This scheme places these measures into three broad categories—"pre-attack," "retaliatory," and "multiple-exchange" indicators: "Pre-attack" (or "static")[18] indicators show nuclear capability before combat, "retaliatory" indicators measure capability after an attack, and "multiple-exchange" indicators emphasize relative advantage after various strikes and responses, and present the greatest analytic challenge.

Pre-Attack Indicators

Consistent with existing practice, pre-attack measures are distinguished here by whether they relate to soft-target or hard-target destruction. Contrary to existing practice, the subsequent section addresses whether these measures should assume a probabilistic form.

Soft-Target Destruction

Some pre-attack indicators measure "soft-area destruction" capability. These indicators, such as "throw-weight"[19] and "megatonnage," are most appropriate for measuring the scope of potential destruction of unsheltered targets (e.g., urban/industrial destruction); they would seem to mesh most closely with absolutist concerns. These indicators emphasize explosive yield and thus a capability to subject an area to a minimum level of overpressure.[20] They are inadequate for measuring the potential destruction of hardened targets, such as missile silos, for these indicators do not acknowledge the large disparities in the ability of different weapons systems to deliver their payloads with the level of accuracy required for hard-target destruction.

Various proposed mathematical adjustments to raw megatonnage more realistically portray the destructive potential of a nuclear explosion. These adjustments, expressed in the notion of "equivalent megatonnage," reduce the stated effects of higher-yield weapons and lower the apparent

Soviet megatonnage advantage over the United States. Needless to say, the use of megatonnage data is not without controversy. But it must be noted that the United States deliberately reduced the yield of its strategic arsenal in the sixties because, at the same time, the United States was increasing both the accuracy and number of its warheads[21] and was becoming less reliant on the bomber force and its higher-yield weapons.

Measures of soft-area destruction center on the effects of blast. Blast is a major source of target damage and its effects are largely known,[22] yet blast cannot account for all potential soft-area destruction. Thermal and ionizing radiation effects would account for a large percentage of prompt fatalities, and these effects change nonlinearly with the extent of blast.[23]

A more serious problem with these measures is that they emphasize "prompt" damage and fail to consider long-term physical effects that will be distributed widely. The long-term effects of fallout, in the form of genetic defects and the taxing of available medical care and safe food and water supplies, could well be horrendous. Mounting evidence suggests that the use of even a fraction of the Soviet and American nuclear arsenals will lead to massive and synergistic interruptions of delicate ecological systems. Sun-obscuring dust and smoke (particularly that ensuing from the direct incineration of cities or resulting firestorms) could lead to the onset of a "nuclear winter"—devastating winterlike effects on the world climate. The effects of nuclear winter, in combination with toxic chemicals and residual radiation, could disrupt the food chain, creating, among other things, tremendous food shortages. Nitrous oxide produced by the intense heat of rising, radiating fireballs could deplete the stratospheric ozone layer, increasing surface exposure to harmful ultraviolet radiation (see Office of Technology Assessment 1979; R. P. Turco et al. 1983; Ehrlich et al. 1984).[24]

Standard measures also ignore long-term social effects. To measure these effects, the analyst must consider the interdependence between the various elements of modern industrial society under catastrophic conditions (an analytical problem that plagued recent attempts to predict U.S. and Soviet postwar economic recovery rates) and must be as much a social theorist as a physicist. Analysts cannot presume that these effects are merely additive or that all of them are known (Ball 1981:29).

In all, severe long-term effects might not enter into either absolutist or relativist calculations. For absolutists, prompt damage assures the floor level of destruction necessary for deterrence: U.S. planners and decisionmakers are purportedly risk adverse and willing to count only that damage that can be estimated with a high level of certainty (on this, see Steinbruner 1976:226–227; Blair 1985:30). (Those who focus on absolute capability, however, often refer to long-term effects, arguing that even severe cuts in the nuclear arsenal would leave a capacity for over-kill.)[25] For relativists, long-term effects are irrelevant to a core concern —the destruction of various military targets.

"Number of warheads" can be used to measure "soft-target coverage capability" (Brown 1977:489–490)—the number of unsheltered "points" (e.g., government control centers, petroleum installations) and "areas" that can be targeted and thus also the number of weapons that are available to cover single targets. This measure does not take account of weapons accuracy or yield. This measure provides a more favorable picture of U.S. relative nuclear capability than does megatonnage, but the Soviets have closed the warhead gap, and the number of warheads is now constrained by the SALT II agreement.

Hard-Target Destruction

Pre-attack indicators can also be used to measure hard-target kill capability. These indicators are preferred by relativists, even if pre-attack indicators are not, in construction, relative measures. These measures of "counter-military potential" or "lethality" exist in a great number of forms (Baugh 1984:129–133), though the best known is developed in Tsipis (1974, 1975) and appears as a ratio of equivalent megatonnage to warhead accuracy (more specifically, the square of circular error probability).[26] These indicators measure the vulnerability of land-based silos to direct hits and blast,[27] though they are most sensitive to changes in precision (given the susceptibility of silos to destruction with accurate hits at low-yield and the rapid decreases in overpressure with distance from the point of impact).[28]

Hard-target measures suffer from design deficiencies. These deficiencies are found, for instance, when accuracy and yield are combined to form a single indicator that implicitly assumes that accuracy can substitute for yield. Arsenals might not have the silo-killing capacity that calculations suggest. The yield of a weapon may be too small to take out a target even with a direct hit (a bullet fired from a gun), and accuracy will not benefit yield beyond a point. Ironically, at the point where high levels of accuracy make "improvements" inconsequential, further increases in accuracy most affect standard lethality measures by inflating apparent weapons performance.[29]

Hard-target measures also misrepresent conditions through simplifying assumptions. Among other things, they might ignore the time urgency of hard-target destruction and include weapons like cruise missiles, which have the accuracy for destroying ICBM silos (and can be used to thwart their reloading) but are slow to respond and potentially vulnerable to countermeasures. Moreover, hard-target measures generally ignore the variable hardness of targets and further assume that the nth warhead is as effective as the first and neglect the important problems of the timing of blasts (discussed in the next section), empty silos, and the declining marginal utility of hitting targets that have already been "killed" (a problem that could disarm an attacker faster than a defender).

Measures of soft-target destruction might show different results than those for hard-target destruction. In fact, a tradeoff exists between soft-target and hard-target destruction: Airbursts can spread immediate soft-target damage over a large area but are not as effective against hard targets. However, surface bursts are required against extremely hard targets and these bursts could extend the area inflicted with fallout, because they kick up large amounts of radioactive debris (Drell and von Hippel 1976).

These two different sets of measures also appear to support competing conceptions of strategic capability. Soft-target measures seem to fit with absolutist concerns, and hard-target measures seem to go with relativism. The reality is not that simple. Relativists are concerned as well with soft-target destruction, even if they express this concern in the form of relative measures (e.g., the throw-weight gap).

Weapons Accuracy, Reliability, and the Unknowns of an Initial Attack

Some of the problems of pre-attack measurement can best be understood in the probabilistic terms of weapons accuracy, the likelihood that warheads will land at a given proximity from a target. Because even a small and inaccurate force can create high levels of soft-area destruction, these problems are of concern to relativists interested in hard-target damage. Nevertheless, pre-attack measures usually fail to allow for the probabilistic nature of hard-target destruction.

Within limits, proximity enhances the probability of a hard-target kill, but the commonly used measures assume that the probability of destroying a target is the same within a given "lethal radius" (Davis and Schilling 1973:215). In other words, measures offer a "cookie cutter" approach to the problem that distinguishes only between warheads that fall inside and outside a specified target area and, within this area, take no account of either the probability of a warhead landing at various distances from the target or the probability that this will result in a target kill.

The standard accuracy assumption is that arriving warheads operate independently and will distribute randomly around the target so that each successive warhead increases the overall probability (even if only slightly) of a kill. However, actual error is likely to be "systematic" as well as "random," because warheads are more likely to fall in a place other than the target. Systematic bias can occur at the missile prelaunch, boost phase and free-fall stages, although error induced upon reentry is the most severe (Tsipis 1984: 390,396).[30]

The problem of blast timing, related to the problem of "fratricide," the neutralization of one warhead by another, is a key source of systematic bias. Nuclear explosions create a hostile environment for incoming warheads; fantastic levels of radioactivity and heat, violent atmospheric disturbances, and a massive cloud of debris will lower the accuracy of warheads,[31] if not destroy them. Nevertheless, fratricide effects are not often accounted for (except to the extent that the attacker is thereby presumed to limit the number of warheads it allocates to a target),[32] and even under normal conditions, weather and atmospheric factors do not enter into accuracy calculations.[33] Nuclear explosions could reduce the probability of a kill when they force warheads to distribute over a wider area,[34] but they could also systematically bias their distribution, creating unpredictable effects on accuracy.

Accuracy estimates also do not consider system reliability (the extent to which warheads are actually deliverable) and thereby overlook a host of possible system disabling problems ranging from human error to electromagnetic pulse (EMP) (where the radiation effects of a nuclear explosion disable incoming warheads). System reliability reflects the multiplicative effects of system unreliability at all stages of launch and flight (Davis and Schilling 1973: 216–217); the probability of failure at any one stage may be small, but failure at any stage will prevent a weapon from successfully completing its mission. System reliability could thus be a more serious problem than warhead accuracy.

Better accuracy and reliability parameters cannot be offered without improved understanding of the physical forces that affect them. Even if it were theoretically possible to develop better estimates, practical considerations intervene:

Intercontinental range missiles are so expensive, politically provocative, and inherently dangerous that there is much about their operation which we cannot learn by experiment or experience. The

United States has never fired a strategic missile on 15 minutes warning from an operational silo randomly chosen, and has never fired more than a very few missiles simultaneously or in close coordination.

As a result of these altogether desirable restrictions, calculations about overall force performance under actual combat conditions must be projected from data on single components under highly unrepresentative test conditions. What must be projected, moreover, is the overall technical performance of a missile force *the first time it is used*—not the performance which might result after many iterations. (Steinbruner and Garwin 1976:141).

Information on Soviet missile performance must be evaluated with even less confidence.

Given these information deficiencies, analysts are tempted to ignore probabilities altogether. This has obvious costs. When analysts fail to consider the probabilistic nature of destruction, they implicitly support a best-case analysis of friendly forces and a worst-case one of enemy forces.

Despite the negative tone of these remarks, analysts can compensate for information deficiencies. By positing a variety of scenarios and experimentally modifying key estimates, analysts can gauge the sensitivity of findings reliant on "soft" data. They must realize, though, that a change in a key value could significantly alter conclusions about such things as the effectiveness of U.S. and Soviet counterforce capability (Brown 1976; Richelson 1982:278)—indeed, current nuclear weapons "barely possess the combination of accuracy and explosive yield which is necessary to destroy a silo with high probability" (Tsipis 1984:383).

In all of this analysts must not forget that a nuclear exchange is inherently a competitive relationship. They must examine the "vulnerability" of targets to numerous well-timed blasts, but behind ostensible targets are opposing groups of analysts addressing the issue in terms of the "survivability" of launchers. In other words, analysts can assume a passive environment for analytical purposes, but in the nonanalytic world the United States would have to engage an adversary capable of removing targets (e.g., launch-on-attack or launch-on-warning) and of shooting back.

Analysts, then, must confront a host of unknowns and contingencies and cannot use simple measures to measure accurately the effectiveness of an attack. For this reason, analysts have designed measures to account for fratricide effects, to match weapons with target characteristics, and to determine the effects of attacks optimized for any number of purposes

(Baugh 1984:134).[35] Accordingly, the Department of Defense offered the Relative Force Size (RFS) index to measure the number of times an arsenal can destroy a specified fraction of selected urban-industrial and military targets. This measure appears in Carter-era Department of Defense annual reports and allows for a wide variety of technical considerations, attack plans, and methods of warhead allocation. In practice, though, this measure is no better than the data of which it is composed, and the measure is highly dependent on the speculations and judgments of the analyst. The measure is sensitive to assumptions made about weapon accuracy, reliability, survivability, and penetrability, to specified changes in the number of targets, to damage objectives, to aggregate measures used to establish force size (e.g., warheads, equivalent megatonnage), and to tolerance for the diminishing marginal utility of increasing the number of times a force objective must be achieved to assure the success of an attack (Richelson 1980:794; Bennett 1980:79–81).

Retaliatory and Multiple-Exchange Indicators

"Retaliatory" indicators measure strategic capability after an attack. Because they focus on second-strike capability, they are consistent with both absolutist and relativist criteria. These measures of residual force characteristics could, for instance, combine a target-coverage index with weapon survival probabilities (see Payne 1977).

Despite the analytical advantages of retaliatory indicators, they combine the uncertainties of pre-attack indicators with those of retaliation. With respect to the latter, EMP could blind early warning systems and leave missiles vulnerable to attack, penetrate silos and disable missiles, and, in combination with the effects of blast, seriously impair command and control and thereby thwart coordinated retaliation. Outgoing missiles are subject to the same fratricide problems as incoming warheads,[36] as well as to "pindown," in which the attacker uses its warheads at high altitude to neutralize and destroy these missiles.[37]

Retaliatory indicators also suffer when they measure effects against enemy targets. For instance, the effects of the destruction of "nuclear threat" targets cannot be evaluated apart from ultimate war outcomes; indeed, implicit within counterforce is the idea of a multiple exchange. Nor can these effects be considered apart from the diverse quality of the targets involved: One U.S. warhead could destroy one Soviet single-warhead missile, but it could also destroy a multiple-warhead missile or incapacitate a substantial portion of the Soviet retaliatory force through a well-designed command and control attack.

Retaliatory measures thus betray a fundamental weakness of virtually all strategic capability measures: they fail to assess targets for their military importance or value to the adversary. More generally, both pre-attack and retaliatory measures direct attention to the characteristics of weapons at the expense of the properties of targets and thereby treat potential rather than actual or effective capability. Indeed, even the RFS index is calculated by evaluating U.S. and Soviet force performance against a common set of targets. (Perversely, this amounts to comparing the capability of both sides to destroy the Soviet Union.) As a result, capability figures for the United States cannot easily be compared to those for the Soviet Union in order to determine whether the U.S. arsenal meets a standard of "sufficiency."[38]

Finally, "multiple-exchange indicators" assess the relative position of the United States and Soviet Union after an attack and response and are more consistent with the idea of a "warfighting" than an "assured destruction" capability. These indicators aggrevate the problem of assessment by requiring further subjectivity and analytical complexity.

Multiple-exchange indicators are highly sensitive to assumptions made about alert rates, enemy target selection, and attack levels, and they are easily biased by compounded error that results from the interaction of misestimated parameters and from the repetitive analyses required to simulate a multiple exchange. For example, a widely cited Defense Department study (Schlesinger 1975) concluded that a Soviet counterforce attack will produce a relatively small number of casualties, but these conclusions have been shown to be highly influenced by small modifications of its assumptions (e.g., the level at which the population is protected, height of bursts) (Drell and von Hippel 1976; Daugherty et al. 1988), creating doubt as to whether a "pure" counterforce exchange can be "limited" in any meaningful sense. Therefore, the numeric value of multiple-exchange indicators changes with suppositions about the exchange, reflecting implicitly the policy preferences of those who use them.

The compounding of error in multiple-exchange assessment parallels the compounding of physical effects that would occur in a protracted nuclear conflict; the complexities and uncertainties of assessment and the intricacies of the physical reality of nuclear combat could send predicted and actual outcomes in any number of opposing directions. Analysts can easily predict the loss of time-urgent capability in a nuclear war since, for instance, bombers cannot be indefinitely sustained in flight, but they have considerably more trouble assessing the effects of a nuclear exchange on such things as the continuity of government, postwar economic recovery, and the global environment.

Despite the complexities involved, the United States is critically reliant upon multiple-exchange assessment for operational planning. Such assessment is used to develop the Single Integrated Operational Plan (SIOP), the U.S. plan for the conduct of a nuclear war. The SIOP methodology goes beyond the static measurement and aggregate modeling techniques described above and attempts to incorporate the myriad of factors that operate in the "real world" in order to generate "expected outcomes." SIOP planning incorporates weapons arrival and survival probabilities, the matching of weapons characteristics to targets based on established damage criteria, routing and timing of weapons, and wargaming to assure the plan's viability under various conditions (Mariska 1972; Walker 1983). Multiple-exchange assessment, in the form of mathematical models, would also be required to process information obtained during actual nuclear hostilities. This assessment would be needed to generate damage estimates (Bracken 1983:111–112), compensating for the inability to assess damage more directly.

RECONCILING THE ABSTRACT AND THE CONCRETE

Each abstract conception of capability suggests its own approach to measurement. This is not to imply that policymakers adopt appropriate measures. Despite their sophistication and technical expertise, even specialists invoke simplistic indicators, and policymakers often shy from more complex computations in favor of measures offered in the popular literature.

A number of examples show this practice to be widespread: McNamara touted number of "warheads" as a nuclear capability measure, a rather simple measure of target-coverage capability, even though he had access to more complex measures and was highly involved with nuclear strategy.[39] Like others in the seventies, Nitze (1976, 1976–77) assailed unfavorable postexchange "throw-weight" differentials that he claimed gave the Soviets a coercive *countervalue* advantage even though he assumed that a nuclear war would at least start with disarming *counterforce* attacks (on this, see chapter 3). Furthermore, Department of Defense reports (the annual statements of the Secretary of Defense and the Joint Chiefs of Staff) have not included estimates of U.S. second-strike countervalue capability in almost two decades and have never included estimates of U.S. second-strike counterforce capability despite the doctrinal centrality of this capability; these reports have largely rested on less revealing comparisons of the U.S. and Soviet strategic weapons inventories (e.g., ICBMs, SLBMs, nuclear warheads, and so on) and estimates of post-attack force size.

Despite the numerous, complexly interrelated factors that would influence the outcome of a nuclear exchange, and the vagueness of the abstract criteria that supposedly guide judgments about the adequacy of U.S. strategic forces, the strategic debate centers on simple measures. Both relativists and absolutists use these simpler indicators as surrogates. These advocates do not necessarily make rational choices among measures. This is important because conclusions will vary with the indicators employed (Richelson 1982).

The more literal minded argue that relative damage assessment requires complex computations and counterforce indicators, that absolute capability, as the capability to punish, requires countervalue retaliatory indicators, and that static indicators most appropriately measure first-strike or launch-on-warning capability. But, in practice, absolutists and relativists gravitate toward that which can be measured simply and away from that which cannot. Accordingly, relativists compare the pre-attack and postretaliatory position of the United States vis-à-vis the Soviet Union on the crude aggregates (e.g., megatonnage and throw-weight), and they often use pre-attack measures as an ad hoc baseline for assessing the effectiveness of a preemptive Soviet attack.[40] Absolutists also look to simple indicators and use pre-attack measures when assuming that a good portion of the U.S. strategic force (e.g., submarines) can survive a Soviet first strike.[41]

The relationship between ease of measurement and usage is demonstrated in table 2.1. Logically, absolutists and relativists should be concerned with a wide range of measurement issues; in practice, though, they are not.

Logic dictates that absolutists be concerned with warhead availability, weapons yield, weapons reliability, and the characteristics of soft-targets, as well as those post-attack factors that would ensure a short-term U.S. capability to retaliate for a Soviet attack. In practice, though, absolutists are concerned with the more easily measured of these factors at the expense of the less easily measured, such as the short-term survival of U.S. command and control (the U.S. capability to communicate the necessary launch orders to surviving U.S. forces).[42]

Relativists are intellectually more diverse, and they should have a

Table 2.1. Indicators, Uncertainties, Ease of Measurement, and Concerns in Strategic Force Assessment

Indicator	Uncertainty	Susceptibility to Measurement High (+) Moderate (+/−) Low (−)	Concern Main (A and/or R) Conditional (?) Poorly addressed (??) Neglected ( ) Of: Absolutists (A) Relativists (R) Expected	Actual
Static (in absolute or in relative form)				
Soft-area	yield	+	A/R?	A/R
	height of burst	+	R?	
	warhead target coverage	+	A/R	A/R
	atmosphere or terrain	−	R?	
	weapons reliability/ penetrability	+/−	A/R	
Hard-target	weapons accuracy:			
	dispersion	+/−	R	R
	systematic bias:			
	fratricide	−	R	
	weapons deficiencies	+/−	R	
	warhead target coverage	+	R	R
	weapons reliability/ penetrability	+/−	R	
	target mobility or time-urgency	+/−	R	R
	target hardness	+/−	R	R
	target military value	−	R	
Retaliatory	short-term vulnerability:			
	forces	+/−	A/R	A/R
	C³I	−	A/R	R??
	specific survival issues:			
	targets/scale of initial attack	+/−	R	R
	warning time	+/−	R	R
	attack timing	+/−	R	R
	coordination of response	−	R	
Multiple-Exchange	long-term vulnerability:			
	forces	−	R	R??
	C³I	−	R	R??
	post-attack society and governance	−	R	

NOTE: Static indicators are used in pre-attack, retaliatory, and multiple-exchange indicators, and retaliatory indicators are used in multiple-exchange indicators. Biases in one set of indicators thus pervade others.

greater number of concerns. Relativists include those described (in the following chapters) as "pure warfighters" and "political warfighters," and have different strategies and capability preferences.

Pure warfighters should stress hard-targeting requirements, i.e., weapons accuracy and reliability, and target coverage, mobility, hardness, and military value — that is, factors related to the long-term survivability of strategic forces and command and control for combat. They should also be interested in the effects of nuclear combat upon the postnuclear world, since they maintain that a nuclear war can be won or lost. Nevertheless, in practice, pure warfighters emphasize easily measured factors that relate to weapons accuracy and force survivability over less easily measured factors such as the effects of nuclear war upon command and control, warhead accuracy, and postwar society.[43]

Political warfighters should be concerned with long-term force and command and control survivability and the nature of postnuclear society — that is, the requirements of a protracted war fought within observed limits. Political warfighters would also seem predisposed toward absolutist concerns with soft-area destruction: Political warfighting requires (or at least presumes) the capacity to inflict unacceptable destruction upon the Soviet Union as well as the capacity to limit this same destruction — capacities determined by how weapons are employed, weapons yield, characteristics of soft targets, and so on. In practice, though, political warfighters look to crude aggregates, such as relative throw-weight, for the coercive advantages offered (as do pure warfighters), emphasize the characteristics of weapons (e.g., accuracy, yield) over those of targets, tend to promote hard-targeting requirements as a virtual end in itself, and underplay physical conditions that would foil attempts to limit urban-industrial destruction, i.e., the collocation of targets and fallout.[44]

The following discussion demonstrates: first, that while simple measures have their analytic virtues, they are often incomplete; second, that simple measures are often employed precisely because they are biased and can then be used to garner support for a desired policy; and finally, that measures that are simple have an allure by which they can shape policy.

The Convenience of Simplicity

Simple indicators are justified in some circumstances. They can ease the task of measurement when they substitute for other indicators. Nevertheless, they are not without significant drawbacks.

Advantages of Simplicity

Simple measures are justified to the extent that simple expressions of capability are related to more complex or less easily measured ones. For instance, because of its relationship to explosive payload, missile throw-weight is used (if only implicitly) to indicate countervalue capability, but throw-weight can also be used to indicate counterforce capability (Lehman and Hughes 1977:1048). Although throw-weight is inherently distinct from the major determinant of counterforce capability, warhead accuracy, it can be used as an "indirect" measure of counterforce capability or, alternatively, as a "direct" measure of "potential" counterforce capability (assuming that for any given amount of throw-weight the United States or the Soviet Union will optimally combine warhead accuracy, quantity, and yield).[45]

Quantity, then, can be used to measure quality. This was a reason for the "success" of the SALT II negotiations. The SALT negotiators agreed to crude quantitative restrictions, such as those on numbers of warheads and on allowable modifications of missile dimensions and weight. These restrictions proscribed some potentially destabilizing qualitative improvements[46] and glossed over qualitative differences between "same-type" U.S. and Soviet weapons.[47] The negotiators also agreed to limits on number of launchers without having to limit what could be done with them; in other words, the United States and the Soviet Union negotiated on the means of arms control without having to agree on its objectives. The negotiators also found quantitative limits that eased the task of verifying treaty compliance. For instance, under the rules, any missile of a type that had been tested with a MIRV was counted as a MIRVed missile (with the number of warheads fixed by the number tested) regardless of whether it was actually MIRVed. Eventually even un-MIRVed SS-11 missiles were counted as MIRVed SS-19s when these two types of missiles were mixed together in Soviet missile fields (Talbott 1980:111–114, 138–140).[48]

Disadvantages of Simplicity

Simplicity does have drawbacks, though. Simple measures are often invalid or incorrectly applied.[49] Indeed, simple measures are used by analysts who are not fully aware of measure deficiencies, mistakenly assume that measures of one thing will account for another, or despair of "hopeless complexity" and fall back on measures of convenience.

For instance, analysts might presume that fallout effects are determined by weapons yield[50] and ignore the host of factors (e.g., the proximity of explosions to populated areas, wind speed, direction and height of burst) that actually determine these effects. The determinants of fallout are so numerous, variable, and difficult to measure that the analyst may choose not to contend with them and may downplay the importance of fallout by focusing only on the short-term consequences of a nuclear war (e.g., the destruction of military targets), or the analyst may presume for the sake of expedience that fallout is a simple linear function of other measures, redundant in that it "kills" that which has already been killed, or low because the adversary purposefully minimized fallout (e.g., through airbursting its weapons) or because populations are sheltered.[51]

Similarly, analysts generally acknowledge C³I (command, control, communications, and intelligence) survivability to be a serious problem, but one of largely unknown dimensions. Network survival is dependent upon a large number of poorly understood physical principles (such as EMP) and a complex set of components that differ in centrality, criticality, and nature and degree of vulnerability. Network disruption could have any number of contradictory effects (both temporary and permanent) that include system paralysis, an inability to override measures that preclude unauthorized or accidental weapons launch, spasmodic or uncoordinated weapons launch, and a mechanical execution of war plans. Command and control vulnerability has long been recognized to be a problem, but it still does not enter into standard calculations. The omission is a significant one. Analyses have shown that even in the so-called golden age of U.S. nuclear supremacy that ended in the midsixties, the U.S. Minuteman force was far more vulnerable to command disruption than to missile-silo attacks and could possibly have been disabled by the direct and indirect effects of nuclear blasts upon the command system. Even today, putting aside various indirect (e.g., electromagnetically induced communications disruptions) and collateral effects, "half the 400 primary and secondary U.S. strategic C³I targets could be struck by Soviet missile submarines on routine patrol" (Blair 1985:88–89, 189). And "fewer than 100 judiciously targeted nuclear weapons could so severely damage U.S. communications facilities and command centers . . . that the actions of individual weapons commanders could no longer be controlled or coordinated" (Steinbruner 1981–82: 18). These vulnerabilities render command and control "the most sensitive dimension of the strategic balance" (Steinbruner 1978:411); put even more strongly, "deficiencies in U.S. C³I systems have been so severe for so long that

developments in the size and technical composition of the superpowers'
arsenals have been practically irrelevant to the nuclear confrontation"
(Blair 1985:4).[52]

By merit of their convenience, simple measures are found at the
highest levels of policymaking, but they too have significant drawbacks.
This is the case with measures inherent in proposals for arms reduction.
Some of these proposals, by merit of their simplicity, could have unde-
sireable consequences, and others have complicated the task of future
arms negotiators:

Both the Carter and Reagan administrations offered arms reduction
proposals, based on simple counts, that could be counterproductive.
Despite their apparent equanimity, these proposals do not address the
problem posed by targets that provide an incentive for preemption, a
problem created in the seventies by the introduction of MIRVed missiles.[53] Indeed, the 50 percent force reductions that were anticipated
toward the end of the Reagan term could aggrevate the problem of "crisis
stability" (i.e., the extent to which one or both parties have an incentive
to preempt during periods of high tension); these reductions would make
the United States reliant upon a smaller, and thereby more vulnerable,
strategic submarine and land-based missile force (see Kissinger 1988).

Experts who design and support these proposals might be aware of
their deficiencies, but cannot easily assess the benefits of these proposals
against their costs. Experts are impeded in assessment by the absence of
a common unit of utility. They measure the benefits of an agreement in
the relaxation of tension, momentum for further arms reduction, resource savings, and effects on current target-coverage capability and
measure the costs of an agreement in decreased crisis stability and the
potential to redirect arms competition toward more expensive, sophisticated weaponry.

Simple solutions have also increased the problems of negotiating future arms agreements. First-round negotiators have settled upon simple
limits that have redirected arms competition into new technology and
other weaponry not constrained by agreement (Berkowitz 1987:50). This
redirection was apparent, for instance, in the aftermath of the signing of
the INF treaty as the Reagan administration moved to extend the capability of NATO nuclear forces (e.g., air-launched cruise missiles, artillery
shells, short-range ground-launched missiles) and conventional forces
(e.g., precision-guided weapons) to cover the gaps left by the removal of
intermediate-range systems (Wilson 1988; De Young 1988) and as the
Soviets could do the same by retargeting and augmenting their strategic
nuclear forces (Berkowitz 1988).

Subsequent-round negotiators must cope with weapons properties that are less easily controlled, create problems for verification of treaty compliance, are controversial because they suggest U.S.-Soviet force asymmetries, and are not as legitimate as existing weapons currency. The SALT I negotiations showed restrictions on launchers to be more easily negotiated than limits on allowable warheads, while the SALT II and START negotiations showed restrictions on missile warheads to be more easily dealt with than limits on multipurpose cruise missiles (e.g., conventional/nuclear, air-based/sea-based). Subsequent-round negotiators must grapple with properties that are a less compelling basis for agreement.

The Deceptiveness of Simplicity

A wide variety of strategic measures are employed in both public and internal governmental assessments of U.S. and Soviet strategic capability. Sometimes these measures are used deliberately by policymakers to deceive, but these measures always present problems of interpretation.

Strategic Deception

Policymakers often select indicators for their persuasive appeal. A simple chart or trend line based on crude aggregates, such as number of missile launchers, weapons yields, or number of warheads, is likely to have greater influence in the public debate than the computerized results of hypothetical nuclear exchanges that vary greatly by scenario. Proposals for strategic arms limitation and reduction that are based on crude aggregates (e.g., throw-weight), equal reductions, and round numbers have been sold and have acquired adherents because of their simplicity. For instance, many in the Reagan administration promoted the so-called zero-zero option, by which the Soviets would dismantle their intermediate-range missiles in Europe in exchange for a U.S. commitment to forego deployment by arguing that any deviation from this simple and thereby compelling option would shift the negotiation focus to more onerous Soviet-supported provisions.

Policymakers do not always use numbers to inform or to facilitate negotiated agreement; they employ numbers in deceptive ways to justify weapons procurement, to argue for arms control and disarmament, or to sensitize Americans to the "Soviet threat." Policymakers often use numbers in a public relations game. Both sides in the domestic debate present only the numbers that support their position—"doves" refer to U.S.-Soviet similarity in numbers of warheads and U.S. advantages in weapons accuracy, and "hawks" emphasize U.S. throw-weight disadvantages. Both groups fail to acknowledge the conditions under which their measures are valid and the varied qualities of units forced into crude aggregates. Further, they do not acknowledge that their data can be interpreted differently:

> Does the bigness of Soviet systems indicate greater capability, or a Soviet inability to design lighter and more compact missile payloads, and more efficient rocket engines, as some analysts suggest? Does the large numbers of Soviet systems indicate a Soviet force of greater diversity and strength, or does it demonstrate a Soviet political incapacity to prevent Soviet design bureaus from deploying samples of their less successful products? Does the number of new Soviet systems suggest Soviet strategic momentum, or an inability to modernize efficiently by upgrading existing systems, as the United States has done (for instance, with Minuteman III)? (Salman et al. 1985)

Numerous techniques are available to those who seek to manipulate and misinform through statistics. Relativists selectively present numbers. For instance, they argued that the United States faced a "window of vulnerability" in the eighties by focusing solely on ICBMs and warned about Soviet throw-weight advantages that take no account of weapons accuracy. Relativists also posit unlikely scenarios. For instance, they might presume that an alert Soviet nuclear force will catch U.S. forces at a low state of alert, therefore, among other things, rendering U.S. B-52s inoperative or ineffective. Moreover, relativists present trends without considering the absolute level of capability involved. The accelerated pace at which the Soviet ballistic-missile force grew in the sixties can look ominous, but the rate of increase is partly explained by the miniscule size of that force at the beginning of the decade. Relativists use trends to portray an unfavorable and ever widening absolute or relative gap between Soviet and American nuclear capability and interpret trends to show that the United States has remained passive in the face of accelerated Soviet weapons deployments. Relativists present disparities in the quantity of similar-type weapons systems as if qualitative differences did not matter and falsely imply that these disparities will prevent U.S. systems from successfully completing their missions.[54] On the other hand, absolutists provide capability figures without reference to how that capability will be used: many absolutists are distressed by the awesome destructive power of nuclear weapons and express this power in terms of tons of TNT per person on earth, number of cities that can be leveled by a single submarine, or the power of the payload of a single bomber as compared to tonnage dropped in a previous war.[55] However, the United States and the Soviet Union cannot freely allocate these weapons, and besides, the United States and the Soviet Union would not use these weapons solely to maximize human fatalities and collateral destruction.

The Counting Problems of Military Data

Numbers have a variety of meanings. Military data are no exception, and users face difficulties in interpreting data on strategic nuclear forces and the more general figures on military expenditures. Policymakers disagree over what to count and how to count it.

Strategic Force Data

Counting is a problem even when U.S.-Soviet strategic force assessments are based on weapons type. Counting problems occur because strategic forces are composed of incomparable weapons systems. Submarines are cherished for their invulnerability, and ICBMs are valued for their prompt, highly accurate attack capability, and it is difficult to determine the trade-offs between SLBM and ICBM deployment (though SLBMs will soon have the hard-target kill capability of ICBMs). Counting is also made difficult when the same system can be used toward different ends. ICBMs can be used aggressively to disarm an opponent or defensively for damage limitation (limiting the damage that an enemy can inflict in turn).

Counting problems are bound to arise in U.S.-Soviet discussions because of the asymmetries between the United States and Soviet force structure—the Soviets have relied upon ICBMs while the United States has deployed most of its warheads in SLBMs. Even if the United States and Soviet Union philosophically agreed on the "worth" of various systems,[56] negotiators would continue to devise counting rules that shift the burden of force restructuring to the opponent. The SALT II, START, and INF negotiations show that the issues of what to count and how to count it cannot be separated from the intentions and judgments of the negotiators—whether the negotiators want to limit weapons with destabilizing effects and what weapons they believe to be destabilizing.[57]

The SALT negotiators were able to overcome some of their differences by setting the lowest numerical sublimits for MIRVed ICBM launchers. Nevertheless, the negotiators were often apart in their positions. They disagreed over whether and how cruise missile deployment should be limited,[58] whether special restrictions were necessary on Soviet heavy ICBMs, what constraints were needed on new-type ICBM deployment, how to count MIRVed missiles, how to treat "multiple protective shelter" systems,[59] and what number of warheads should be permitted on a single missile (Talbott 1980). The United States and the Soviet Union continued to disagree on the extent to which cruise missiles should be constrained and on whether the Soviet deployment of an intermediate-range bomber (the Backfire) should be limited without similar constraints on U.S. forward-based aircraft. These issues would combine with others to slow the START negotiations as old questions were resurrected[60] and new questions were posed.[61] While the START negotiators were stimied initially by how weapons systems would be grouped for negotiation,[62] toward the end of the Reagan term the negotiators differed over how to translate into practice the large cuts in strategic forces that had been agreed upon. The INF negotiators addressed similar issues in whether to include in the negotiations Soviet SS-20s and U.S. aircraft located outside the European theater, British and French strategic forces, and short-range with intermediate-range systems, whether the Pershing II poses a greater threat to the Soviet Union than slower-moving ground-launched cruise missiles and how these latter two single-warhead missiles should be counted against the three-warhead SS-20, and whether to base counts upon systems capability and geographic region of deployment or upon a weapons intended use.[63]

Counting practices obviously also remain a matter of internal dispute. For instance, static measure force assessment, a practice prejoratively dismissed as "bean counting," is under assault. Some maintain that less easily measured factors that relate to force effectiveness, such as the redundancy and survivability of command, control, communication, and strategic forces, are more important now that the United States and the Soviet Union have established parity on traditional force measures (see Burt 1980:38). Analysts might be compelled to "keep up with the times" and to modify counting rules to accommodate weapons innovations and new strategic concerns and priorities, but they must recognize that particular policy biases and preferences are reflected in any set of rules. A shift toward force survivability measures substitutes "warfighting" criteria that relate to preparedness for a protracted nuclear war for those associated with assured destruction.

Military Expenditure Data. Those who create and use military expenditure data also disagree on what to count and how to count it.[64] Among other things, they disagree over how to divide military from civilian spending and whether to include expenditures for internal security, appropriations or actual expenditures, or figures expressed in constant prices or nominal amounts. In sum, they disagree over what constitutes a military expenditure.

The problems of comparing U.S. and Soviet military spending are monumental (for a discussion of different Soviet expenditure estimation practices, see Cockle 1978). The Soviets include military research and development within their reported "science" expenditures and exclude procurement, civil defense, foreign military assistance, and some personnel costs (such as pensions) from their "defense" budget. More severe problems of comparison are posed by fundamental U.S.-Soviet economic dissimilarities—U.S.-Soviet differences in factor costs, production efficiency, technological sophistication, and government control of production cloud the actual significance of any given dollar figure. Problems persist even when comparisons are restricted to either military hardware or manpower because the relative costs of capital and labor differ between the two countries (Lee 1977): A dollar assessment of Soviet military spending will produce inflated Soviet expenditure figures just as a ruble account of U.S. spending will overvalue U.S. military expenditures (see Holtzman 1980; 1982).[65]

The choice among military expenditure measures, like choices among other military measures, is not simply a matter of adopting the most "correct" measurement procedure. Wohlstetter (1974b) could be right, then, to argue for a disaggregation of the defense budget in analysis, for each part of the defense budget could be controlled by forces peculiar to it. The size of some parts of the budget is actually negatively related to others: "overhead" or "support" costs might vary inversely with direct costs, negotiated arms reductions could force an increase in intelligence costs for verification of compliance and costs for the increased vigilance required of remaining forces, some "defensive" expenditures might increase with "offensive" reductions, and operation and maintenance costs rise with the age of a weapon system. In any case, correctness is related to the purposes and perspective of the analyst.

Measures, then, are only valid conditionally; they are not inherently right or wrong. This has important implications for at least one military expenditure controversy—the method by which the CIA calculates Soviet defense spending. The CIA has been criticized for expressing Soviet defense expenditures in terms of U.S. costs if dollars were similarly expended. This practice can be made to sound absurd (e.g., Soviet soldiers receive a "pay raise" whenever American soldiers do) and is somewhat inappropriate when the purpose is to evaluate the sensitivity of Soviet military spending to U.S. expenditures (the measures of

Soviet and U.S. spending would not then be independent of one another). At best, this practice has limited validity. Because of U.S.-Soviet economic asymmetries, the measures that result can say little about Soviet objectives: The Soviet Union can field a soldier less expensively than can the United States, given the costs to the United States of a volunteer army and the Soviet soldier's greater tolerance for a lower standard of living, but the Soviet Union must cope with production inefficiencies and a smaller GNP and therefore might accept higher opportunity costs than a U.S. dollar accounting reveals (Lee 1977:120–124). However, the CIA practice remains useful. The procedure expresses U.S. and Soviet military expenditures in a common unit of utility by accounting for differences in purchasing power between the two economies. The CIA method can be used as one measure of the arms race and accretions in national military strength.

Numbers require judgments. Monotonic, unfavorable force trends and numerical expressions of the absolute destructiveness of nuclear weapons are frightfully compelling, but these numbers are always open to interpretation. No method of data presentation is more "natural" or inherently more valid than any other.

The Allure of Simplicity: The Reification of Capability

At the highest levels of policy, a number of factors influence the selection of capability measures, and their effects are not readily distinguished. Choices determined by political considerations and motivated bias are not easily separated from those due to unconscious bias and lapses in reasoning—that is, the psychological allure of the concrete and the simple.

Nonetheless, even at the highest levels of policy, the distinctive role of unmotivated bias upon capability measurement is apparent. Policymakers themselves acknowledge this when they refer to measures of the "psychological balance."

The Standards of Force Assessment

The effects of unmotivated bias upon one aspect of measurement are particularly apparent—the measurement standards used in strategic assessment.[66] These standards are little more than simple decision-rules and are often based upon false assumptions:

The "matching" of U.S. with similar-type Soviet forces is just such a standard—but it is hardly the only one. For instance, a general policy consensus exists on the need to maintain the integrity of the U.S. strategic force "triad" (composed of air, land, and sea forces). This consensus, however, largely reflects the legitimization of existing practice. The redundancy and complementarity of the legs of the triad are assumed essential with little consideration of force survivability or the expendability of force missions involved (e.g., a prompt hard-target kill capability). The inviolability of the triad thus remains an operative principle despite the onetime sole U.S. nuclear reliance upon bombers and the increasing difficulty and financial cost of maintaining an invulnerable land-based missile force.

A similar consensus underlies standards used to identify various weapons classes. Because of these standards, many feared the deterrent gaps that would be created in the absence of "intermediate-range nuclear forces" and resisted proposals for their dismantlement (that were eventually codified in the 1987 U.S.-Soviet INF agreement). Nevertheless, the standard that underlies the designation of a force "class" is an imposed one and does not merely reflect the properties of the weaponry involved. For many purposes, long-range, intermediate, and short-range forces, like strategic, theater, and tactical weapons, are not easily distinguished; indeed, intermediate forces are diverse and their physical function can be assumed by other weapons in the U.S. arsenal.

Other standards for force effectiveness are more controversial. This is certainly true of the standard that distinguishes "time-urgent" from non–time-urgent targets. Proponents of a time-urgent attack capability—that is, secure communications for a prompt second-strike attack against Soviet military targets (hardened command centers, ICBMs, submarine bases, airfields, and so forth)—herald the flexibility offered by such a capability, but with disregard for its limited operational relevance. A U.S. prompt-attack capability is of little consequence after a Soviet first strike if, then, Soviet submarines are dispersed and aircraft alerted, the Soviet leadership is sheltered, Soviet ICBMs are to launch-on-warning, and Soviet launch instructions have been received, because even the destruction of a substantial part of the Soviet air- and sea-based strategic force would have a relatively insignificant effect on Soviet retaliatory capability and because attacks upon the Soviet leadership would negate their political value as a hostage or would vastly complicate bargaining (a "decapitated" adversary cannot bargain effectively, since bargaining requires the involved parties to be coherent and effectively in command of their forces).[67]

The standard that underlies the triad and other functionally based classification schemes implies that each designated weapon type serves a uniquely valuable purpose, but these standards can also affirm the special properties of a single weapon type. This is apparent in the extent to which land-based missiles and their capabilities dominate assessments of the U.S.-Soviet force balance.[68] Indeed, this ICBM emphasis suggests a larger assessment problem that is associated with a preoccupation with a single weapon type—assessment concentrates simplistically on weapons features at the expense of sound analysis. When policymakers type heavy Soviet ICBMs as first-strike weapons (due to their accuracy, responsiveness, and multiple-warhead capacity), they could presume that a Soviet first-strike capability follows virtually from the existence of these weapons. The "window of vulnerability" argument of the early eighties was predicated upon this leap in logic; the argument required only a simple count of accurate Soviet ICBM warheads relative to U.S. missile silos. A "theoretical vulnerability" came to be regarded as "accomplished fact."[69] Policymakers concentrated on ICBMs even so as to discount completely U.S. air- and sea-based forces; they treated ICBMs as the key means by which a nuclear war could be won or lost and as virtually the only means by which to obtain limits to nuclear escalation.[70] Moreover, a weapon preoccupation has induced policymakers to avoid unfavorable balances within a force class, irrespective of the actual military utility of those imbalances. Accordingly, policymakers have sought to bolster U.S. theater nuclear war capabilities with little regard for whether nuclear weapons use would vitiate U.S. military advantages,[71] magnify U.S. strategic disadvantages,[72] and be generally self-defeating.[73] (on this, see Kaufmann 1983; Jordan and Taylor 1984:263–264; Cimbala 1988:166–171).

A weapons preoccupation might also lead policymakers to exaggerate the invulnerability of a weapon system, as when assured destruction proponents champion submarine-launched ballistic missiles (SLBMs) as the cornerstone of the U.S. strategic deterrent force. These proponents presume correctly that impediments to antisubmarine warfare would render a large percentage of the U.S. SLBM force invulnerable to Soviet detection and destruction within the short time frame in which they expect a nuclear exchange would occur. However, these assured destruction proponents are less sensitive to potential devastating Soviet attacks on U.S. command and control targets that could impair U.S. retaliation and devote little thought to the number of U.S. submarines that are necessary to deter a Soviet attack.[74]

Unconscious Bias vs. Deliberate Deception in Assessment

Policymakers must employ measures by which they can sell policy, but even then, these policymakers may not be fully cognizant of the deficiencies of the selected measures. The same can be said of arms negotiators: negotiators are constrained by domestic interests, considerations of strategic advantage, and the need for negotiated compromise in devising arms reduction formula, but these negotiators are also subject to unconscious bias when they weight unduly the benefits of a formula relative to its costs, particularly when the costs are to be realized only in the long-term (e.g., SALT I and the failure to restrict MIRVs). As a formula gains adherence and is legitimized through practice, it can continue to bias thinking about the utility, distinctiveness, and numerical requirements of various weapon systems (e.g., the "special" status of strategic weapons, the relationship between offensive and defensive weapons).

When policymakers adhere to questionable indicators and stances, it is easy to attribute this to politics. Policymakers certainly could employ different indicators in private than they do in open debate; they could fear that public disclosure of "actual" U.S. military weaknesses would compromise U.S. security. However, to assume that any public stance is politically motivated is to argue that high-level government policymakers and negotiators rarely believe what they say and that they understand completely the complex issues and policy trade-offs with which they work. These individuals can hardly be expected to understand that which has been shown here to elude even technical specialists. Moreover, most of the technical information required for detailed assessment is available in unclassified sources, and policymakers have not been afraid to voice fears of U.S. vulnerability.

This is not meant to imply that policymakers are oblivious to or merely distort the contributions of the all-knowing strategic expert. Mountains of studies have been conducted within the Washington bureaucracy or through direct government sponsorship that offer new methods, equations, and statistical techniques for assessing force potentials and vulnerabilities and the short- and long-term social, economic, and political effects of a strategic nuclear exchange. Yet, in excess, information does not clarify and may actually stultify, and policymakers, moved by unanswered questions raised by those studies, may fall back on their existing prejudices and policy prescriptions.[75] Much of strategic assessment is simply noncumulative. Because of the peculiar set of assumptions employed, the implications of a methodological "innovation" or the knowledge contribution of any one study might not be apparent. Ironically, the most painstaking, deliberate analyses might be the ones that assume a wide variation in possible outcomes. Interpretation is further impeded by complex interactions among nuclear effects and between these effects and attack scenarios, and findings must be predicated, then, upon a host of conditions and assumptions.[76]

Studies could indeed have a cumulative impact when, despite their differences, they reach similar conclusions or reinforce a prevailing strategic assumption. The numerous studies that point to the vulnerability of U.S. land-based missiles could have such an impact. Nevertheless, the force of these findings is diminished with an awareness that the Soviets could act with restraint in an initial counterforce attack, that a wide range of uncertainty exists in Soviet attack performance, that assessments of the adequacy of U.S. retaliatory forces require judgments about how U.S. forces will be used, that the United States retains the option to launch its forces before they are destroyed in an attack, and that a significant number of U.S. nuclear-armed bombers and submarines will survive a Soviet attack.

The Acknowledgment of the Psychological

Policymakers could be inclined to dismiss simply measured disparities in the nuclear balance, but may find the magnitude of these disparities too much to ignore. Policymakers often acknowledge this seemingly illogical state of affairs by distinguishing the "psychological advantage" from the physical advantage gained from a capability gap.[77]

Policymakers who make this distinction are in the seemingly paradoxical position of acknowledging the inadequacies of static measures of the nuclear balance while arguing that "to deny the importance of static measures in the world of international politics is to refuse *to recognize reality* [italics added] and to ignore the importance of political and subjective factors in the effective operation of nuclear deterrence and strategic forces" (Kahan 1975:240). That which is not militarily useful is said to be of political use. For this reason, Nixon defined "sufficiency" as roughly an assured destruction capability and yet added that these forces must also be "adequate to prevent us and our allies from being coerced."

Recent administrations have stressed the importance of considering the perceived balance—a balance that they maintained is linked to bargaining or coercive capability. Policymakers have claimed Soviet coercive advantages to reside in Soviet superiority in total numbers of missiles, missile throw-weight, and overall megatonnage. They have also alluded to these advantages to sell a hard-target kill capability and, in particular, the ICBMs (the MX) that can provide it. Moreover, strategic analysts have been attentive to coercive advantages when measuring the destructive capacity of U.S. and Soviet weapons with warhead targeting and allocation assumptions that are different from those that actually guide U.S. policy.

Those who make the case for the "psychological balance" argue that U.S. policymakers cannot be sure that their Soviet counterparts do not take these measures seriously. The psychological edge, then, is essentially one of relative confidence—"*We* don't believe these advantages to be real, but unfortunately, *they* do." The Soviets may be emboldened by the belief that they enjoy meaningful superiority, and the United States may be inhibited by the belief that such advantages are illusionary. The Soviets might push and the United States might be forced to retreat to avoid catastrophe.[78]

Missing in all of this, though, is that psychological edges are given and not taken. The Soviets will possess these edges only when U.S. policymakers allow supposed Soviet psychological advantages to become real ones. Indeed, the Soviets might be the beneficiaries of a "self-fulfilling prophecy": policymakers, through publically expressed fears of U.S. force vulnerabilities and disadvantages, could conceivably promote Soviet assertiveness.

Those who extol the psychological balance do not claim that it is unrelated to the "actual" balance; U.S. concerns that the Soviets might not recognize the actual existence of a force balance rose markedly in the seventies with a closing of the gap on a number of strategic nuclear dimensions. Nevertheless, despite its objective referents, deterrence could be essentially psychological and symbolic, "a generalized sensation rather than an entirely rational conclusion based on any elaborate set of calculations" (Friedberg 1980:64). The CIA has made this argument and has employed measures of residual destructive capability in the National Intelligence Estimates that reflect rather artificial conditions (e.g., no launch-on-attack or C^3I attacks) (on this, see Lebow 1982). Analytic simplicity could be an asset, then, in the detection of strategic threats. In this regard, experts of the fifties asserted "that the very ease with which one could perform calculations to demonstrate the potential threat posed to US bombers by possible Soviet ICBM deployments was in itself a source of instability that could lead to a failure of deterrence" (on this, see Kahan 1975:70).[79]

The importance of the perceived over the actual balance is further supported by psychological research that demonstrates that decisionmak-

ers fail to think in complex terms, responding to the evidence possessed
and not to that lacking. Decisionmakers ignore information and work
with "won'ts" and "wills" rather than "coulds," "shoulds," and "mights";
they are more impressed with what can happen than what is likely to
happen; and they concentrate on payoffs rather than on probabilities
(Jervis 1979:310). Decisionmakers do not consciously choose to ignore
probabilities, but are not pressed by their absence (Heuer 1981:302);
decisionmakers can interpret numbers without them. This explains the
popularity of the "worst-case scenario," but also has heartening implications for the stability of deterrence: decisionmakers will not risk high
costs for small gains.

CONCLUSIONS

Policymakers and analysts hold abstract beliefs about the political and
strategic impact of nuclear weapons upon warfare. These beliefs are
ambiguous, deficient, and inconsistent in a number of important respects. No one knows what it has taken or will take to deter a Soviet
nuclear attack. No matter how large the U.S. nuclear arsenal, doubts will
remain about its adequacy for the task. Thus, despite the phenomenal
destructive potential of nuclear weapons, every postwar administration
has at least toyed with using these weapons to accomplish traditional
military missions or has fallen back on more traditional notions of what
constitutes an adequate deterrent. Abstract confusion has led to contradictory policy, resulting in an inefficient expenditure of resources and
posing a threat of ill-conceived nuclear weapons use.

The conceptual confusion has enhanced, if not reflected, the importance of nuclear capability measures. Although concepts should control
measurement, abstract conceptions of capability suffer from neglect and
are even shaped by measures. With ill-defined concepts, policymakers
and analysts inevitably invoke indicators that are questionable or belie
the complexity of the subject with which they work.

It has been observed that in defense systems engineering the "conflict
elements" are "not in the center of the analysis" and are "treated by
assumption or suppressed" (Wohlstetter 1964:193). Policy analysts give
prominence to technical elements that are more calculable and better
understood. Policymakers are also seduced by the technical: they combat
knowledge deficiencies with technological solutions (e.g., the matching
of Soviet deployments), propose nuclear capability measures that do not
square with concepts, and opt for simple measures over more complex
ones.

3

STRATEGIC ACTION

THIS CHAPTER finds that both abstract and concrete thinking about the "action" components of U.S. nuclear strategy have suffered because of the failure to attend to the abstract. This is particularly ironic because abstract thinking about these components has been central to the writings of strategic theorists. Concrete thinking substitutes for the abstract at all levels at which strategy is conceived. This substitution leaves critical holes in strategy: the abstract follows when it should lead and remains on the periphery when it should be central to strategy.

This chapter scrutinizes the action components of nuclear strategy and demonstrates that the problems of strategy stem from concrete thinking. To this end, the first and second sections explore respectively the changing meaning of four abstract strategic concepts and their relationship to their concrete strategic counterparts. The third section further probes the relationship between the abstract and the concrete by examining the operational concepts of U.S. strategic targeting. The last section returns to abstract strategic issues and assesses the implications of recent proposals for strategic defense.

THE ABSTRACT ELEMENTS: OFFENSE, DEFENSE, PUNISHMENT, AND DENIAL

Abstract thinking about deterrence currently centers on four interrelated strategic concepts—"offense," "defense," "punishment," and "denial." Opinions divide in the contemporary nuclear debate on which of these ideas deserves greater prominence and on how they are most effectively paired. But it has not always been that way. Punishment did not become important until deterrence of a Soviet nuclear, rather than conventional, attack became a principal objective of U.S. strategic policy, and offense was initially championed with little regard and even a healthy disdain for defense. In sum, the significance and very conception of these "strategic elements" changed with technology and beliefs about the consequences of a nuclear exchange.

The Formative Years: Offense and Defense

Offense pertains to damage inflicted upon an adversary and defense the safeguarding against the same. Offense and defense are related, but the distinction between them grew important with the development of strategic airpower and nuclear weaponry and hence with the primacy of offense; these elements previously "were embodied, more or less, in the same weapons." The separation of offense and defense occurred because the development of a long-range delivery capability meant that a nation could inflict damage on the enemy heartland without directly affecting the course of battle and the control of territory (Snyder 1961:8); these effects were, of course, magnified by nuclear weapons.

Primacy of the Offensive

Documentary evidence and historical events can reveal the relationship between offense and defense in the first nuclear decade, though the temptation is to recast early strategy in terms of the arguments and conditions of latter years. Truman and Eisenhower administration strategies (despite the input of the strategic theorists) did not fully anticipate the strategies that would become prominent in the sixties.

U.S. nuclear strategy in the early postwar years featured the "dominance of the offensive" (Freedman 1983:170). The Air Force made the offensive a basic tenet of their organizational ideology: the SAC war plan called for a single massive attack on the Soviet Union and required the delivery of the most nuclear destruction on the Soviet Union in the least amount of time. Nevertheless, their conception of the offensive remained incomplete. Its objectives were unclear and megatonnage requirements and optimal weapon uses could not then be determined. Policymakers seldomly indicated whether the A-bomb was primarily a terror weapon designed to instill maximum shock, fear, and hopelessness in the Soviet population and was thus ultimately aimed at undermining national morale and will or whether the weapon had a more strictly military purpose;[1] they seemed to presume that the Soviet governmental and military structure would simply collapse through nuclear bombing.

WW II left a legacy of doubt over the wisdom of dependence on strategic bombing. The extravagant claims for the effectiveness of strategic bombing often seemed little more than a rationalization for its indiscriminateness, if not also Air Force self-promotion. The nuclear bombing of Hiroshima and Nagasaki might have precipitated the Japanese surrender, but most policymakers could not forget that Japan had also suffered a conventional military defeat. The limits of strategic bombing were identified by the U.S. *Strategic Bombing Survey;* aerial attack by itself seemed incapable of undermining adversary public support or of slowing critical war production.[2] The influential 1949 Harmon Committee report[3] echoed this theme—strategic bombing might not generate desired psychological effects and could even be psychologically counterproductive, Soviet industrial losses were recoverable, and nuclear bombing would do little to halt a Soviet conventional advance into Europe. Key government officials, most notably within the State Department, argued for a balanced defensive posture that gave more equal weight to U.S. conventional capability; their concerns eventually led to a major intragovernmental policy review that produced a blueprint for a large-scale U.S. conventional (and nuclear) military buildup (NSC-68). But the strategic offensive still remained central to policy.[4] The buildup envisioned by NSC-68 was resisted, and even the Harmon report offered no alternative to urban-industrial bombing and argued instead for the acquisition of the means to deliver an increased number of atomic bombs against the existing target set (Rosenberg 1979:73).

Offensive thinking survived the development of thermonuclear weapons. Under Truman, the issue of whether to deploy the hydrogen bomb generated considerable tension among concerned U.S. government agencies because it was debated in the wake of the first Soviet A-bomb test and involved phenomenal increases in destructive capability. But the H-bomb issue reinforced existing organizational positions and did not force a fundamental rethinking of strategy (Schilling 1961; Stein 1984). The JCS "presented the bomb as a logical extension of existing weapons programs that neither offered great advantages nor posed new dangers" (Rosenberg 1979:83).

The early to midfifties brought a recognition of the significance of defense. This came in the form of concern over the vulnerability of U.S. strategic forces to a Soviet surprise attack. By the close of the decade, this concern would be "identified as the surprise-attack problem, and indeed as 'the' problem of nuclear war" (Schelling 1985–86:221), portending concerns of latter decades over the problem of "crisis stability" —whether either side might preempt because of the potentially unacceptable consequences of waiting.

Despite vulnerability concerns, defense was incorporated into offense. The persisting primacy of offense was reflected in beliefs that the United States must retain offensive superiority, that the United States must "preempt" and seize the initiative with the approach of war (a war that presumably would be slow in developing), and that, in war, the United States should massively attack the full range of Soviet military and urban-industrial targets. The predominance of offense was partly due to the inadequacy of defense, and anything less than a full employment of U.S. bombers would have left the remaining force vulnerable to a Soviet retaliatory attack. Vulnerability concerns thus prompted calls for offensive force increases and improvements and meant that defensive deployments were generally aimed at increased warning time rather than directly limiting the damage that could be inflicted in a Soviet attack.

The influence of offense resounded in arguments for preemptive and preventative war. Nevertheless, the "bomber gap" scare of the midfifties signaled that preemption was increasingly an ineffective means for thwarting a Soviet attack. Preemption appears to have remained U.S. operational policy, but Eisenhower at least eventually believed that national traditions and practical impediments proscribed a U.S. first strike (Rosenberg 1983:40). Offensive thinking was more pronounced in the argument that given the unremitting Soviet threat, the United States should take advantage of the existing favorable balance in nuclear capability and attack the Soviet Union sooner rather than later. Eisenhower consistently rejected these arguments for preventative war even though they were actively considered within high-level policy groups in the first half of his administration (Trachtenberg 1988).

The incorporation of defense did not proceed smoothly. Defensive concerns were explicitly rejected in warnings against a "Maginot-line mentality" (see Knorr 1956:95). Contradictory assertions were also voiced. Eisenhower simultaneously argued that "there is in reality no defense except to retaliate" while insisting that "we must not allow the enemy to strike the first blow" (Rosenberg 1983:47). He consistently emphasized the importance of a quick military response (Rosenberg 1983:63), even though he recognized the need to reduce weapons vulnerability and appreciated the declining benefits of a U.S. first strike. Even Naval advocates of minimum deterrence argued that it was necessary for the United States to retain the initiative in the event of war.

Origins of the Second Strike

Defensive concerns centered on the vulnerability of the U.S. strategic bomber force. The exact dimensions of the bomber vulnerability problem were not clear, for it is unknown how much residual nuclear capability was thought necessary for deterring a Soviet attack, but a surprise Soviet attack would have severely crippled U.S. retaliatory forces. Into the fifties, the United States depended on the intermediate-range B-29 and the intercontinental-range (part-jet) B-36 for nuclear attacks on the Soviet Union, but these aircraft were believed to lack a viable defense penetration capability and were eventually replaced by the (all-jet) B-47 of only intermediate range. The distance limitations of SAC bombers forced a reliance on overseas bases that were within the combat radius of Soviet lightweight and medium bombers.

The United States deployed its forces with little regard for defensive requirements. The positioning of bombers in proximity to the Soviet Union was regarded to be an offensive advantage rather than a vulnerability. Supplies, parts, and repair centers were not dispersed or sheltered from blast (for reasons of efficiency and cost-effectiveness), nor were serious efforts taken to limit the time bombers spent abroad on the ground. Moreover, even by the late forties bases and critical war production and storage facilities within the United States were potentially vulnerable to conventionally armed Soviet bombers on one-way missions, and they were to appear even more vulnerable in the midfifties with the Soviet deployment of long-range bombers. While the latter led to fears of a bomber gap, the reaction to these developments fell well short of a reorientation toward defense. SAC could not launch mission-ready bombers in time, even with "tactical warning" from radar[5] (because, for one thing, bombers did not carry bombs) and was dependent on a longer-term and less-direct "strategic warning" obtained from other intelligence sources (Kaplan 1983:133). (Not until the late fifties was a system in place that was capable of providing "distant early warning" and of guiding the interception of Soviet bombers at distances from their targets.)

The distinction between a first- and second-strike capability grew out of the work of RAND studies of the problem of reliance on overseas bases,[6] bomber and war material dispersal, the adequacy of tactical warning, and the strength of post-attack U.S. nuclear forces. Albert Wohlstetter at RAND managed to turn the vulnerability issue into the "preoccupying issue, the virtual obsession, of strategic analysis" (Kaplan 1983:122). But the military command, for its part, seemed little concerned that U.S. air bases were vulnerable to a Soviet attack and continued to focus on the penetration of enemy defenses and the destruction of enemy targets (Rosenberg 1982:16); "the vulnerability of air bases was viewed as just another in a series of things that might go wrong, as perturbations that might require some minor adjustments in the analysis, but certainly nothing that should attract center-stage attention" (Kaplan 1983:93–94).[7]

The RAND studies led to significant modifications in Air Force basing policy, and much of the opposition that they did generate was narrowly bureaucratic in origin (Smith 1964).[8] Nevertheless, the SAC leadership recognized the vulnerability problem as an opportunity for offense. Its leadership was not only convinced that preemption was essential (even to the extent that its war plans were at odds with official U.S. policy), but implied that offensive threats required offensive solutions in arguing for the expansion of the U.S. strategic bomber force and the deployment of more advanced bombers with intercontinental range (the B-52).

The primacy of offense was also apparent in the U.S. decision to deploy intermediate-range missiles (IRBMs) in Europe (Thor and Jupiter) toward the end of the decade. These missiles certainly had defensive advantages over the bombers that were based abroad. Their wide dispersal created timing problems for a Soviet surprise attack, since anything less than a synchronized Soviet attack against a full range of target sets would leave a residual U.S. retaliatory force. Nonetheless, the United States spurned mobility and concealment in deployment[9] for a more rapid response capability and a reliance upon weapons that were better suited for first use than retaliation. Furthermore, the United States shunned a more defensive approach by choosing instead to increase the number of offensive systems that could survive and hence retaliate for a Soviet attack (Armacost 1969:147–150, 183–185).[10]

The important government-sponsored strategic studies of the period also looked to offense. The RAND studies and the Killian and Gaither reports[11] of the fifties were the most prominent and articulate voices of concern over U.S. vulnerability to a Soviet nuclear strike. They spoke with varying emphases, but they all clearly argued for a defensive posture that would assure the efficacy of the offense and displayed little sympathy for a deterrence-only posture. The 1956 Killian report on "meeting the threat of surprise attack" argued for defense of both the U.S. population and nuclear strike capability, but it also provided impetus to the U.S. ICBM, IRBM, and Polaris submarine programs, as "it added scientific legitimacy to the general feeling among many in government that the arms race must be continued and accelerated at all costs" (Kaplan 1983:131). It rejected what would become the very essence of deterrence in the sixties in recommending that the United States attempt to maintain, among other things, "a very great offensive advantage" relative to the Soviet Union because a condition in which "an attack by either side would result in mutual destruction" was "fraught with danger to the US" (Killian 1977:73–75). The Gaither committee was able to broaden its mandate in the area of civil defense and to examine seriously, in comprehensive terms, the issue of security in the nuclear age.[12] The 1957 committee report (U.S. Congress 1976) stressed the importance of maintaining a viable second-strike capability rather than the building of fallout shelters, and it defined the problem of deterrence "in terms of the vulnerability of the force rather than its initial destructive capacity" (Halperin 1961); it therefore argued for the hardening and dispersal of missiles and air bases and the deployment of submarine-launched ballistic missiles. Even then, the report reflected the influence of traditional offensive thinking. It failed to distinguish adequately between a Soviet attack upon the U.S. in which the "ability to strike back is essentially eliminated" and one in which "civil, political, or cultural life are reduced to a condition of chaos,"[13] saw in short-term military preponderance a unique opportunity for the United States "to negotiate from strength," and foresaw nuclear weapon technology and destructiveness potentially leading to a "period of extremely unstable equilibrium." As it too fell short of embracing what would become the retaliatory deterrence arguments of the sixties—that retaliating U.S. forces must only be capable of destroying Soviet society while denying that US society could be protected—the report not surprisingly recommended accelerated ballistic missile deployments and was even believed by some committee members to justify preventative war (Rosenberg 1983:46–47).

The general civil and military effects of a Soviet nuclear attack on the United States were also scrutinized within the U.S. government. Eisenhower struggled with the implications of the staggering casualty estimates issued during his term (Betts 1986–87:14–18). High government officials recognized by the early fifties that the Soviets could deliver a substantial percentage of their arsenal on target, and the military services had warned years earlier that only a few nuclear bombs could severely debilitate U.S. war mobilization and execution. One NSC study conducted in the first year of the Eisenhower term determined that by the midfifties a Soviet surprise attack could destroy about one-third of the U.S. nuclear retaliatory capability, at least temporarily paralyze two-thirds of U.S. industrial production, and cause many millions of deaths (Betts 1986–87:8–9). Damage projections would continue to grow into the sixties even with the deployment of a defensive warning and interception system, a continued recognition of the technical impediments to a Soviet attack, and Kennedy-era counterforce deployments directed at damage limitation.[14]

U.S. policymakers of the fifties were apprehensive about the projected increases in Soviet promptly deliverable nuclear capability and believed the growth in Soviet capability to be destabilizing. Their preoccupation with offense was at a minimum a desire for nuclear superiority. Their concerns about the Soviet arsenal would, of course, increase enormously with the Soviet launch of *Sputnik*—a veritable symbol of the Soviet entrance into the missile age—and the "missile gap" scare that helped bring in the Kennedy administration, bearing a different set of priorities and concerns.

Cultivation of Offense: Denial and Punishment

With a secure U.S. retaliatory force and reduced Soviet force vulnerability, the sixties brought a refinement of offense. Offense was no longer conceived to require strictly or even primarily the defeat of an opponent through the direct use of force. The strategic debate came to center on two competitive offensive concepts—"denial" and "punishment."

The strategic debate of the fifties showed that offense can be extended to include defense when the offense inflicts damage upon the enemy, aiding defense. But viewed apart from the strategy of the period, the "best offense" could be a "good defense" when this means that a defense directly protects and weakens resistance to an offense. Therefore, the link between offense and defense is the concept of "denial," which refers to "a capacity to deny territory to the enemy, or otherwise to block his aims" (Snyder 1961:9).

Alternatively, denial and "punishment" can be thought to have offensive and defensive components, with punishment pertaining to "pain" or "costs" that are inflicted (either in retribution or for bargaining), which might or might not affect military position.[15] Just as offense and defense overlap, so do denial and punishment. Denial "can mean high direct costs, plus the risk that the war may get out of hand and ultimately involve severe punishment for both sides," and punishment "may foreclose territorial gains, and limited reprisals may be able to force a settlement short of complete conquest of the territorial objective" (Snyder 1961:15). Thus the link between denial and punishment is offense.

The interaction of offense and defense with denial and punishment suggests the two-by-two or four-celled table presented in figure 3.1. The two dichotomous strategic dimensions, offense/defense and denial/punishment, join in four possible combinations—offense/denial, offense/punishment, defense/denial, and defense/punishment. The denial row and the offense column are highlighted, for they connect offense and defense, and denial and punishment, respectively. This row and column intersect at the offense/denial cell, graphically illustrating the centrality of offense/denial in strategic thinking.

Offense/denial is more commonly conceived as a "counterforce" posture in which a nation deploys its weapons to weaken physically or to incapacitate its opponent.[16] A counterforce posture treats nuclear weapons as military rather than political instruments. This posture assumes that weapons promote deterrence only to the extent that the adversary recognizes that weapons use will produce insufficient gains (that the adversary would be denied its objectives); it therefore values inflicted losses only when they deprive the adversary of potential gains, e.g., the destruction of adversary offensive missiles.[17] This posture supposes that even the most malevolent adversary will not attack when its goals cannot be realized, for such an attack would serve no useful purpose.

Offense/punishment, on the other hand, centers on the imposition of

Figure 3.1. Elements of Abstract Strategy

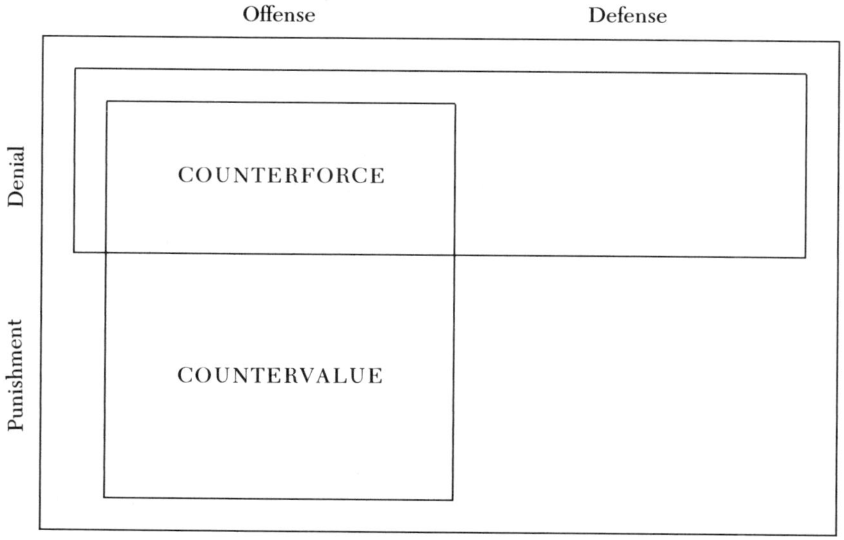

cost and is commonly associated with a "countervalue" posture and an indifference to gains. A countervalue strategy is logically a retaliatory posture, for it does little to limit the damage that the recipient of the retaliation can inflict in turn. Offense/denial and offense/punishment are featured in two competing, contemporary nuclear strategies. These strategies are referred to here as *pure warfighting* and *assured destruction*, respectively.[18]

The more general term *warfighting* has been used in practice to describe a variety of doctrines. Secretary of Defense McNamara proposed a strategy for "damage limitation" upon the United States, and it rivaled assured destruction as declaratory doctrine during his tenure (and was U.S. operational policy throughout this period). Secretary of Defense Schlesinger directed the development of "limited nuclear options" that would allow the United States to limit its engagement by the type and geographical location of targets, the nature and launch site of delivery systems, and the amount of force employed. The Carter administration, in turn, introduced the "countervailing strategy" as a more explicit and comprehensive statement of these prior policy themes,[19] but the strategy fueled new concerns and justified the acquisition of a vast array of sophisticated technology.

These doctrines were shaped by the conditions of the time periods in which they were articulated. Nevertheless, all of these doctrines contain elements of both the "pure warfighting" and a "political warfighting" strategy. These doctrines have been articulated by advocates of each of these two strategies as well as by advocates torn between them.

All warfighters stress the need to disable physically or incapacitate an opponent in time of war and argue that deterrence resides in preparedness for combat. They adopt a "relativist" view of nuclear capability (see chapter 2). In contrast, assured destruction advocates claim that given the devastating destructiveness of nuclear war, nuclear weapons are useful only when they promote nonrecourse to war and that deterrence is achieved by increasing the costs that can be inflicted in nuclear retaliation. They adopt an "absolutist" view of nuclear capability.

Assured destruction advocates accuse warfighters of "conventionalizing" the nuclear arsenal with a false presumption that nuclear weapons can be employed in a controlled, flexible, and precise manner to accomplish various hierarchally arranged traditional military objectives—that is, that these weapons can be used in a conflict in which military tactics can be meaningfully distinguished from strategy. On the other hand, warfighters charge that since assured destruction rigidly presents no nuclear options short of a suicidal war, it will actually undermine deterrence because adversaries will perceive the threats upon which it is reliant to be irrational and thus empty. But as Brodie (1983:20) notes, "the rigidity lies in the situation, not in the thinking." Most warfighters do not deny the practical and physical possibility of a nuclear holocaust, a fact lost in what can (least generously) be thought of as an intellectual "sleight of hand" whereby warfighters focus on the means of nuclear combat rather than on its ultimate outcome. Because warfighters are presented with a U.S. nuclear arsenal short of a first-strike capability, they cannot avoid the dilemmas of assured destruction. But they do try, and in attempting an escape *they inconsistently combine the arguments of the denial and punishment strategies or else they borrow from one or both with little regard for the strategic implications.*

In the end, warfighters of all types may be consoled by the punishment that the United States could inflict upon the Soviet Union in nuclear retaliation. When warfighters recognize the abstract implications of their strategy, they often exhibit a love-hate relationship with punishment—they prefer denial, yet respect the value of coercion.[20] The public record provides ample testimony to warfighter ambivalence toward denial and punishment. While warfighters promote their strategy by arguing that it is necessary to deny an opponent its objectives, "sometimes both deterrence by denial and deterrence by punishment are seen as necessary, sometimes only the former . . ., and sometimes the latter is seen as sufficient, even without the former." Secretary of Defense Brown is not alone in arguing that U.S. forces must assure that the Soviets be "frustrated in their efforts to achieve their objective *or* suffer so much damage that they would gain nothing by their action" while simultaneously arguing that these forces be "in a position to deny any meaningful objective to the Soviets *and* impose awesome costs in the process" (on this, see Jervis 1984:77–78; emphasis added).

Assured destruction advocates and warfighters also disagree on the role for defense. Assured destruction rests on the assumption that there is no defense against nuclear weapons and that defense serves only the ancillary role of safeguarding the offense. Warfighters, on the other hand, more greatly respect the utility of defense (see, for example, Gray 1979:84). However, pure warfighters do not always make the purpose of defense clear and equivocate on whether the defense has or can usurp offense; and political warfighters, as will be shown, fail to recognize significant counterintuitive defensive implications of their proposals.

THE CONCRETE ELEMENTS: THREE STRATEGIES

The dilemmas of warfighting can be missed when strategy is presented at an abstract level. The strategic debate and indeed much of operational policy has narrowly focused on a more concrete set of concepts, though at the expense of policy consistency and coherence.

"Pure" Warfighting vs. Assured Destruction

Offense and defense are more commonly conceived in terms of targets that require "attack" or, conversely, "protection"—terms that are without the open-ended and overlapping meaning of their abstract counterparts. These terms are not inherently more concrete than their counterparts, and in fact, they are often used abstractly.

Attack and *protect* are made more concrete by their association with other concrete concepts when denial and punishment are replaced by "force" targets (broadly defined to include Soviet nuclear, and other military, targets) and "value" targets (associated, at least by assured destruction advocates, with urban-industrial targets), respectively. The distinction between these two types of target sets is highly problematic, and as is demonstrated in the subsequent section on targeting, one target set is not easily separated, in practice, from the other. The attack/protect and force/value dimensions combine to produce a four-celled table that is roughly analogous to the previous one.

Figure 3.2 juxtaposes the "pure" warfighting and assured destruction strategies. These strategies profoundly differ in choice of second-

Figure 3.2. Elements of Concrete Strategy: "Pure" Warfighting and Assured Destruction

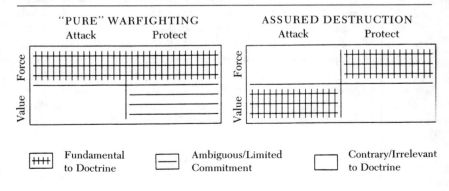

strike targets. Pure warfighting promotes disarming "counterforce" attacks, while assured destruction stresses spasmodic "countervalue" attacks.[21] Assured destruction advocates devote little attention to how nuclear weapons *would* be used and rely more on enemy recognition of how these weapons *could* be used—massively and indiscriminately against urban-industrial targets. Nevertheless, the "attack" is central to both strategies.

Advocates of both assured destruction and pure warfighting stress the need to protect retaliatory capability, but warfighters (in general) are more concerned than are assured destruction advocates with the protection of counterforce weapons, e.g., ICBMs. Furthermore, warfighters are clearly more willing than are assured destruction advocates to protect value targets (even if warfighters do not explicitly acknowledge them to be value targets) such as urban-industrial areas;[22] assured destruction advocates regard city protection to be contrary to the very foundation of their doctrine (that is, that there can be no such defense against nuclear weapons).

The rudiments of pure warfighting can be found in the early writings of Kahn (1961), where the decided emphasis is on military contingencies and tactics and counterforce exchanges are assessed and valued for their military effectiveness. Kahn professes a desire to limit conflict, but he promotes limits that ensue from an ability to disarm an adversary or to force compliance through military preponderance.

The pure warfighter perspective was implied when McNamara introduced a damage limitation strategy by arguing that "military strategy should be approached in much the same way that more conventional military operations have been regarded in the past" and that the "principal military objectives, in the event of nuclear war . . . should be the destruction of the enemy's military forces."[23] Similar reliance upon force is found in the Carter administration's countervailing strategy, as it called for, among other things, the capability to "deny" the Soviets a military advantage and to "defeat" aggression at a variety of levels of exchange (see Slocombe 1981:21–22). It has been said that "the distinction between 'countervailing' and 'prevailing' is, accordingly, a very thin one" (Tucker 1984:10). Thus the administration sought a highly survivable ICBM force for counterforce strikes despite the fact that a large number of U.S. ICBMs could survive a limited Soviet counterforce strike and that an unlimited Soviet counterforce attack would reduce the need for a U.S. hard-target capability (Soviet missiles would have already been fired).

Related arguments underlie the official Reagan administration pronouncement that in a strategic nuclear war "the United States must prevail and be able to force the Soviet Union to seek earliest termination of hostilities on terms favorable to the United States."[24] The Reagan administration's conception of nuclear war as, above all else, a military engagement was witnessed in its unwillingness to forego the deployment of more accurate intercontinental ballistic missiles (the MX, the Trident II) and warheads with a greater hard-target kill capability or to accept Soviet-proposed prohibitions on cruise missiles, its desire to extend US military target-coverage capability, its often expressed concerns about a Soviet ability to reload and refire strategic launchers and about the vulnerability of U.S. land-based missiles (the so-called window of vulnerability), its decision to commence deployment of Pershing II (intermediate-range) ballistic missiles in West Germany, which could be employed in prompt attacks against Soviet military command and control centers, its resistance to the deployment of small, mobile missiles that lack the counterforce capability of heavier ICBMs and that could complicate U.S. counterforce targeting when deployed by the Soviets, and its fear that the Soviets might eventually "break out" of an arms control agreement that failed to limit missile throw-weight and translate their superior throw-weight into a large relative advantage in numbers of warheads (on the Reagan administration, see Talbott 1985).

The pure warfighter emphasizes the military utility of nuclear weapons and thus, it would seem, their denial function. However, even these warfighters are not free of contradiction. While they promote a denial strategy at an abstract level, their concrete proposals are generally more equivocal: Pure warfighters, though they challenge the idea that deterrence is enhanced by mutual vulnerability (see Ikle 1973, 1985), often shy from advocating the U.S. acquisition of a first-strike capability (and might concede that a U.S. first-strike capability could lead the Soviets to attack first in a crisis, inducing strategic instability). Nevertheless, these warfighters promote a first-strike posture through the back door by advocating what amounts to a disarming second-strike counterforce capability.[25] This was the tendency in the McNamara period (Rosenberg 1986:46–47).[26] It was also exhibited in the seventies when limited nuclear options were advanced as a means "to prevent the enemy from achieving his immediate military objective," "to gain control over the future conduct of the war," "to destroy the attacking force early," or "to restore the military balance" (see Davis 1976) and when the countervailing strategy was claimed to provide the United States with "escalation dominance" so that the United States could establish military superiority after responding in kind to any level of Soviet attack.

An abstract justification for this amassing of counterforce capability is offered in the claim that the denial strategy requires a capability to achieve "victory," to "defeat" the Soviet Union, or to "prevail" in a nuclear war.[27] It has been argued that a requirement "to deny victory to the Soviet Union" and one "to avoid defeat itself . . . add up to a requirement for the capability to win wars" (see Gray 1984:11).[28] But warfighters leave critical terms like *victory* and *defeat* largely undefined. For instance, they do not specify precisely whether and to what extent such victories require destroying military, leadership, or economic targets. The justification for a second-strike counterforce posture, then, could be no different from one for a first-strike posture, and a second-strike counterforce capability could become a first-strike capability.

Some unashamedly promote such a dual capability and believe U.S. nuclear superiority to be both necessary and feasible.[29] Most adopt a more ambiguous stance. The United States has not renounced the preemptive use of its strategic forces or its near practical equivalent in the form of a launch-on-warning or launch-under-attack posture, and warfighters have certainly not been among the vanguard arguing that it do so. Launch-on-warning and launch-under-attack have been incorporated into U.S. strategic nuclear war plans, and the Reagan administration actively considered these options as a potential solution to the ICBM vulnerability problem (Lebow 1987:174). Moreover, the distinction between a strategic "first strike" and "first use" of nuclear weapons remains blurred. This is important because the United States has relied upon the latter to extend deterrence to the European continent and has long stated its intent to use nuclear weapons to arrest a Soviet conventional advance in Europe. The blurring of the distinction between a first strike and first use suggests that strategic weapons, like tactical ones, could be employed solely for their military utility and, hence, in a preemptive mode. In the final analysis, warfighters could recognize that if nuclear war can in fact be won militarily, a massive preemptive strike provides the best chance of securing a victory, whether such a victory requires the destruction of the Soviet retaliatory capability or simply a higher relative level of Soviet destruction.

Some pure warfighters are concerned about Soviet values and covet nuclear weapons for more than just their military effects. These warfighters often promote the targeting of sites that they believe to be of value to the Soviet leadership, e.g., political control centers, in the hope that U.S. retaliation would inflict prohibitive costs. They propose a targeting strategy based on the logic of counterforce that would allow nuclear war to be fought "rationally" with the assumption that "war at any level can be won or lost," yet they lean toward "countervalue" thinking when they sell this strategy for its "coercive" potential or advocate leadership targeting because it poses the "most frightening threat to the Soviet Union" (see Gray and Payne 1980:14, 21). Pure warfighters thereby waffle in their commitment to a denial strategy. The failure to fully commit to a denial strategy explains why proponents of the countervailing strategy even sacrificed the concept of a "value" to a "force" target when they justified attacks against critical *force* targets (e.g., political and military leadership and control centers, nuclear and conventional forces) by emphasizing their high *value* to the Soviet leadership.[30]

Pure warfighters also stray from military concerns when they fear nuclear weapons for their political repercussions, to remain at odds again with the fundamentals of their strategy. Pure warfighters cannot be consistent and evaluate weapons and selective strikes for their military effects, believing the Soviets to do the same, and yet fear that inflicted collateral damage will escalate a conflict towards catastrophe (see, for instance, Wohlstetter 1985). If pure warfighters are correct in saying that nuclear use is governed by calculations of advantage, they should not be worried about irrational war outcomes.

"Political" Warfighting

Kahn's ideas contrast with those of "limited war"[31] theorists of the period—suggesting that warfighting actually encompasses at least two schools of thought. The perspective of these limited war theorists is captured in the assertion that force serves to "symbolize" intentions to keep war limited, but that "within these limits the objective should be to inflict heavy and continuing costs upon the enemy's forces," for such wars "perform a function midway between the abstractness of a show of force and the terrible concreteness of annihilative conflict" (see Kaufmann 1956:113–118).[32] This perspective suggests a second view of warfighting—one with a more (but not exclusively) "political" coloration.[33]

The political or bargaining version of warfighting records the most significant contribution of the strategic theorists upon policy. The contributions of Schelling (1960, 1966), Brodie (1966), and Kaufmann, among others, provide the inspiration and a sophisticated justification for the political warfighter perspective. This perspective has had a recurrent hold upon U.S. strategic policy.

Political warfighting may incorrectly appear to subsume pure warfighting. Political warfighting offers more options than does pure warfighting —and this is in *addition to* and not *instead of* the two pure warfighting options of "attack" and "protect." But political warfighting rests on assumptions that are quite different from those of pure warfighting even if political warfighting contains elements of pure warfighting. The inclusion of these elements does not enrich political warfighting but instead confounds it.

The political version of warfighting is found in figure 3.3. It also assumes the primacy of offense, has offensive and defensive components, and distinguishes between force and value targets.[34] But here each of these components is conceived in terms of the interplay among competing parts.

Offense

On the offensive side, political warfighting assumes that nuclear strikes serve both as "challenges" to the adversary and signals of "avoidance." Because these strikes have limited military utility (otherwise an attacker would launch a single, disarming strike), they are important when they convey intent. Political warfighting, despite its interest in force, views offensive actions as signals with implicit meanings; strikes against force targets are important not for the damage inflicted per se but because their military effectiveness conveys a message to the adversary that is one of both resolve and restraint.[35] An offensive strike is important not only for what it is but for what it is not; a strike against force targets is an implicit challenge to value targets and possibly to still other force targets, while it also communicates a desire not to hit them (so as to avoid retaliation).

Figure 3.3. Elements of Concrete Strategy: "Political" Warfighting

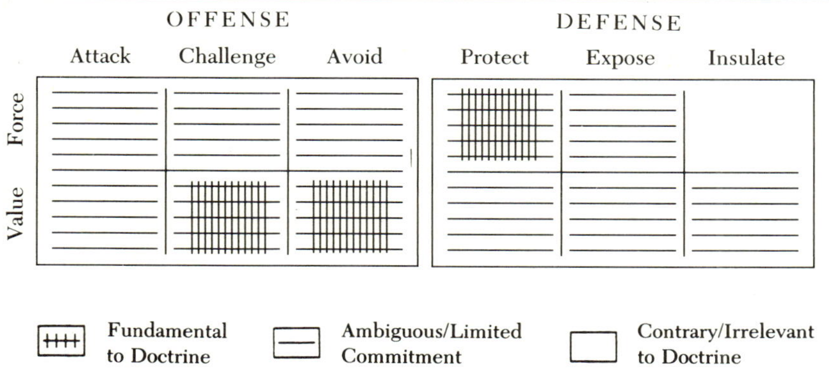

Pure Warfighting Bias. One problem with the bargaining version of warfighting is that it does not provide useful planning guidelines for U.S. offensive strikes. Thus it may not be true to either a denial or punishment strategy. Political warfighters conceive of nuclear war as a form of negotiation; nonetheless, they often judge strikes by their military effectiveness (and hence their denial function).

The paucity of guidelines was particularly apparent with the limited nuclear option proposals of the early seventies, and it was never clear what the United States should do in any given situation or why it should do it. Proponents of limited options argue that U.S. nuclear responses must be proportionate to Soviet actions so as to avoid provocation and terminate conflict "at the lowest possible level of violence." But they suggest an opposing standard when they claim that the conditions of termination must be "consistent with US objectives," that U.S. nuclear attacks could be militarily advantageous, and that enemy attacks might require more severe retaliation if intrawar deterrence is to be maintained or if there is to be a return to prewar conditions (see Schlesinger 1975; U.S. Department of Defense FY1975; Davis 1975). Caught between these competing standards, they emphasize the symbolic virtues of militarily effective strikes (and thereby pull away from pure warfighters).[36] They acknowledge that the enemy may have to be significantly "hurt" to curtail hostilities and that anything less than this may "leave the initiative with the enemy" and demonstrate "timidity rather than courage" (see Davis 1975:16). It should be noted, in this regard, that Schlesinger coupled his limited option proposals with efforts to improve the accuracy of U.S. warheads for a hard-target kill capability.[37]

In the late seventies, the absence of guidelines gave policy an even greater military thrust. As observed already, the countervailing strategy seems an unhealthy composite of political and pure warfighting notions. As such, this strategy can be viewed as a political warfighting strategy with a strong military bias.[38] Like other political warfighters, Brown denies that nuclear weapons are of ultimate military use or that "victory" in nuclear war is possible and yet he defers to military conceptions: "The capabilities of U.S. strategic nuclear forces and the relative balance with the Soviet Union are still important, even if the destructiveness of these weapons sharply limits, and perhaps eliminates for practical purposes, their usefulness in an actual conflict" (Brown 1983:51). Brown also argues that counterforce capabilities are necessary to deny a Soviet postwar advantage in the military balance (Department of Defense FY1982).

When political warfighters support improvements in hard-target capability they work at cross-purposes with themselves. Threats to the survival of Soviet ICBMs in their silos create an incentive for massive Soviet preemption or retaliation. Although limited option advocates downplay hard-target damage when they recognize that only a massive and even preemptive attack will significantly impair Soviet retaliation, they are still not fully sensitive to the political repercussions of the tactics that they propose. They focus on tactics (e.g., the destruction of bridges, petroleum installations, airfields, and missiles) rather than their political effects and concentrate on the qualitatively distinct or "limiting" characteristics of various launchers, targets, and weapons to the exclusion of the political context within which they claim nuclear conflict will occur. They spend little time thinking about whether the Soviet Union and the United States have different ideas about what constitutes a "limited" conflict or whether what appears to be limited to an attacker will appear unlimited to a defender.

The Soviet Union and Limited Nuclear War. Limited nuclear options should not be proposed without due appreciation of the underpinnings of Soviet nuclear doctrine. Soviet doctrine explicitly rejects U.S. thinking about limited nuclear war, and while the tendency in the United States is to reject Soviet doctrine as primitive and backward, Soviet doctrine is firmly grounded in the Soviet organizational structure, security considerations, and historical experience.

Admittedly, the Soviets now accept the possibility of a limited nuclear exchange, just as they now acknowledge the possibility of a strictly conventional war between the superpowers. Soviet doctrine no longer dictates preparation for an all-out nuclear exchange as a sole contingency (Meyer 1985a:183). However, this is not to say that Soviet doctrine accepts or converges with a bargaining strategy: "The evidence that Soviet military doctrine now incorporates the possibility of control, selectivity and restraint in a strategic nuclear conflict is actually very fragmentary." Indeed, this evidence is in the form of muted statements that are largely uncharacteristic of Soviet doctrine—statements that mean something different to the Soviets than they do to the United States (Ball 1986a:12).

The Soviets distinguish between conventional and nuclear warfare and between strategic and nonstrategic nuclear weapons use, but these are not primary distinctions to the Soviets, nor are they distinctions that the Soviets think will be upheld in warfare: "For the Soviets . . . the key threshold is not nuclear employment but war itself . . . the fundamental question of whether or nor to go to war in the first place" (Lambeth 1984:71–72). With a decision to go to war, Soviet forces will be engaged to the level that Soviet decisionmakers believe Soviet security is jeopardized—Soviet forces will be employed to minimize risk, limit damage, and accomplish defined offensive objectives.[39] Soviet doctrine recognizes the "homeland sanctuary" and allows for an engagement limited to Europe, but only if Europe is defined so as to exclude the Soviet Union. Once the Soviet sanctuary has been violated, Soviet doctrine anticipates an imminent, all-encompassing assault on Soviet vital assets and thus preaches an expeditious, decisive launch of the Soviet arsenal against the full range of U.S. strategic targets. Even if the Soviet homeland remains untouched, "the weight of evidence from Soviet military writings, force structure, and exercises suggests that any NATO use of nuclear weapons is likely to unleash a massive and devastating Soviet theater nuclear strike against all NATO military facilities" (Meyer 1985a:185–186, 201).

Limited option advocates expect Soviet doctrine to eventually "catch up" with U.S. doctrine, as if U.S. strategic thinking were more in touch with the fundamental realities of nuclear weaponry than Soviet thinking.[40] Soviet doctrine, however, is nested in a different context than U.S. doctrine, and thus neither of these doctrines can be regarded as more advanced than or as an evolved form of the other: First, Soviet doctrine, more than its American counterpart, is a creature of the military establishment and has not been shaped as significantly by an inflow of ideas from independent civilian political analysts (Meyer 1985b). It is therefore likely that the Soviets are even more loath to reject a nuclear strategy that has been honed for military effectiveness. Second, Soviet doctrine reflects strategic interests that differ from those of the United States. The Soviets have not needed to consider limited uses for nuclear weapons to compensate for inferiority in conventional forces. Third, Soviet doctrine reflects the greater proximity of Soviet value and force targets to the European theater. The United States and Soviet Union cannot similarly assess the threat that any conflict limited by geography will pose, for initially localized conflict stands a greater chance of accidentally or intentionally spreading to engulf Soviet than U.S. strategic targets. But even if this were not the case, the physical size of the nuclear battlefield may not be regarded by the Soviets to mark the difference between a limited and an unlimited war. The Soviets probably believe the U.S. distinction between theater and strategic nuclear war to be specious. Both levels of warfare can involve the same weapons (e.g., strategic missile submarines) and targets. In a war in which "strategic nuclear weapons have been employed, strategic nuclear weapons have come under attack, and strategic nuclear weapons have been landed on the sovereign soil of the enemy . . . few distinctions would remain to be drawn" (Blair 1985:223).

Fourth, Soviet doctrine records the distinctive lessons of Soviet history in the importance of seizing the initiative and of taking the war to the adversary, even if it now seems to be shifting to defense and away from a war-waging capability. The Soviets fear that anything less than a full military commitment could result in another destructive war on Soviet territory. (On these points, see Snyder 1977; on recent changes in Soviet doctrine, see Garthoff 1988.)

U.S. policymakers tend to think of flexibility as an absolute good, but from the Soviet perspective a profusion of options could well be irrelevant. Soviet decisionmakers might even view flexibility as a liability because it makes advance planning more difficult, jeopardizes the control of the military over doctrine, and creates operational problems when implementation cannot follow a set of well-established and well-rehearsed procedures. An insensitivity to the Soviet perspective has allowed U.S. strategy to be shaped more by military considerations than political considerations.

Options and the Problems of Choice. To the extent that warfighters recognize the political implications of their strategy, they are unable to commit in advance to a course of action. Because of the uncertainties attending any option, they opt for flexibility as a virtual end in itself. Warfighters present the advantages of graduated changes in the nature and scale of a nuclear response to make it either more or less severe than the initial attack, stress the importance of communicating to the adversary a willingness to fight and yet a desire to deescalate the conflict, and present strictly demonstration attacks along with others limited to the battlefield or war theater (see SRI 1971; Davis 1975). Warfighters thus present a menu of opposites as tactics and emphasize options over choice; they therefore fail to reveal whether nuclear conflict is best controlled and defused by moving up, down, or sideways on the escalation ladder. Their tentativeness is most apparent when they address the option of U.S. first use of nuclear weapons. Wary of the escalatory potential of any action, warfighters recommend nuclear strikes that "approximate" levels of Soviet provocation. But this does not help them here. The "appropriateness" of U.S. actions cannot be gauged without prior Soviet use, and any first use of nuclear weapons is likely to be seen by the country under attack to be a grievous escalation of hostilities.

Another problem with this political version of warfighting is that it accepts the reasoning of the punishment strategy without a full understanding or acceptance of its link to assured destruction. It is the U.S. fear of "assured destruction" that motivates its bargaining stance, and without the specter of a nuclear holocaust there would be no reason for the United States to issue military challenges or exercise restraint. Paradoxically, those (like some pure warfighters) who argue for rapid escalation and massive counterforce attacks are most indebted to the principles of assured destruction: these warfighters aim to promote deterrence by convincing the adversary that even its limited attacks will be treated as a near total commitment and that nuclear conflict will escalate precipitously and is therefore *not* subject to control.

Various scenarios confirm that behind warfighting lurk the rationale and dilemmas of assured destruction.[41] Warfighters have consistently justified their strategy with the claim that "the Soviets could envision a potential nuclear confrontation in which they would threaten to destroy a very large part of [the U.S.] force in a first strike, while retaining overwhelming nuclear force to deter any retaliation [the United States] could carry out" (see U.S. Department of Defense FY1984).[42] They argue that the Soviets will enjoy psychological and bargaining advantages when they place the United States in the unwelcome position of having to initiate strikes against cities (since the United States would be deprived of the forces necessary for a counterforce option). However, no matter what warfighters may think, they have not escaped the dilemmas of assured destruction. If it is assumed that the Soviets will avoid attacking cities because they fear retaliation (rather than because they are benevolent), Soviet restraint could correctly be seen as "timidity." With the depletion of nuclear arsenals, the belligerents would then face the assured destruction standoff in which each threatens but neither dares attack the other's cities. Even if the preempting country retains a "superior" residual force, it might be deterred from further action by the threat of unacceptable costs when the "weaker" country brandishes a "minimum deterrent." The logic of political warfighting is therefore (by implication) in fundamental respects the logic of assured destruction. (This is more obvious when assured destruction advocates argue for limited (counter-value) options for "demonstration" attacks; see, for instance, Jervis 1979/80).

Just as deterrence based on assured destruction can fail, so can intrawar deterrence. McNamara donned the hat of the political warfighter when he stressed "city avoidance" over damage limitation,[43] but he was not sanguine about the Soviet willingness to cooperate in city avoidance: the paucity of Soviet weaponry meant that the Soviets could ill-afford to go "tit-for-tat" with the United States in counterforce exchanges and, lacking a reserve force, would have to resort to attacks on U.S. cities (Kaufmann 1964:93). His successors have shared his pessimism. Ironically, the political warfighter can even use the logic of assured destruction to offer a way out of this quandry: the combatants can engage in "city trading" (urban strikes that are limited in scope or intensity) in the hope of avoiding an unrestrained nuclear exchange.[44] Nevertheless, such city trading could inevitably lead to a wholesale exchange, and political warfighters must recognize then that they have succeeded only in prolonging the period in which destruction is assured.[45]

Political warfighters do not explore the political context in which nuclear bargaining would occur and thus cannot attest to whether a country that would willingly launch strategic nuclear weapons believes that it can avoid a nuclear conflagration or whether it would even seek to avoid one (on this, see also chapter 4). Furthermore, political warfighters place too much hope in a bargaining process that will inevitably involve misperception and miscommunication (see chapter 5).

Defense

On the defensive side, the political version of warfighting emphasizes the need to protect retaliatory forces, but it could also focus on a defensive counterpart to target avoidance: The defender can encourage attacker restraint by limiting collateral damage through the "insulation" of value targets or the "exposure" of its force targets. The defender could passively (e.g., fallout shelters, population evacuation) or "lightly" defend (e.g., the Johnson administration's "thin" ABM system)[46] against indirect damage to urban-industrial targets or somehow make military targets more inviting objects of attack (e.g., by increasing their vulnerability), even if none of these actions would provide effective defense against direct enemy countervalue attacks. Warfighters, though, do not fully embrace this logic. If they did, they would be more supportive of Soviet civil defense efforts. "In fact, however, the dominant analysis sees Soviet civil defense planning as both an indication of aggressiveness and a threat to the efficacy of American retaliatory strikes" (Jervis 1984:121).

Warfighters of all persuasions have been more attentive to the offensive than the defensive implications of their strategy. While the Kennedy administration promoted civil defense as part of a damage limitation strategy and, like other administrations, recognized its value for the insulation (over the protection) of cities,[47] bombers were dispersed to civilian airfields during the Cuban missiles crisis (Quester 1970:246).[48] Such instances could indicate that warfighters accord the defense (e.g., dispersion) of force targets greater priority than the defense of value targets, but they may also more generally reveal that warfighters are attentive to the requirements of target attacks and challenges above the requirements of defense. It is not surprising, then, that SAC, in the late fifties, opposed plans to headquarter the North American Aerospace Defense Command (NORAD), the center for processing information warning of a nuclear attack, within a hardened facility (Bracken 1983:187); that the Air Force, in the late sixties and early seventies, was not among the strong advocates of anti–ballistic missile defense of ICBM silos; that initial recommendations within the Carter administration for C^{3}I improvements to fight an extended nuclear war were resisted by the JCS and, in particular, by the commander of SAC, who claimed that it was more crucial that the United States acquire weapons that could destroy hardened Soviet targets (Powers 1982:96); or, more recently, that the JCS opposed the immediate deployment of ground- and space-based rockets partially to defend U.S. ICBM silos because it feared that defense systems would encroach upon the offensive budget (Smith 1987).

It is important to note, though, that the two schools of warfighting have significantly different implications with regard to defense. In order to decrease an adversary's incentive to strike, the political warfighter could opt to increase the exposure, rather than the insulation or protection, of urban-industrial areas by extending the collateral damage that would ensue from an enemy strike against military targets (on this, see Jervis 1984:121). This could be done by placing military targets in proximity to cities and by leaving populations exposed to all of the direct and indirect effects of nuclear explosions (this could be a reason that the military employs civilian airfields [Snow 1979:474]). Indeed this ostensibly defensive tactic serves effectively to "challenge" the adversary by considerably narrowing its options. But even if warfighters do not have inhibitions about constraining enemy options through physical incapacitation, warfighters may reject the above tactics because they clearly draw upon the logic of assured destruction—these tactics, in essence, say to the adversary, "If you punish me, I'll do the same to you." Warfighter resistance to these tactics is further evidence that they fail to appreciate fully the abstract implications of their strategies.

Finally, just as warfighters have a tendency to design the offensive around military criteria, their enthusiasm for the protection of force and value targets may be tempered only by their reservations about its technical feasibility. Pure warfighters are buoyed by the technological prospects for improved protection of urban-industrial areas and thereby imply that a denial strategy requires the defense of value targets and, thus, at least by implication, the defense against punishment. Furthermore, political warfighters could once again exhibit insensitivity to the requirements of a bargaining strategy. They propose offensive tactics with the intent of keeping war limited and yet might accept defensive tactics that presume that enemy strikes will be unlimited.[49] Warfighters can be said to even encourage devastating assaults by requiring that the adversary increase the scale of an attack in order to overcome the defense and assure a level of destruction (on this, see Scoville 1974:167).

In all, abstract discussions of the relative merits of a denial and/or punishment strategy have added little to the quality of strategy. The inconsistencies and ambiguities of warfighting are graphically illustrated by the shaded areas in figure 3.2 and, in particular, figure 3.3. Fundamental questions remain: To what extent should only limited attacks be undertaken against force targets? Should value targets be hit or avoided? Should a defender attempt to ease or confound an attacker's efforts to limit collateral damage? Warfighters may be sensitive to the classical dictum that "war is politics by other means," but they offer few meaningful guidelines for policy.

The abstract fails to guide the concrete. The result is that both pure and political warfighters have developed strategies that thrive on the mechanics of warfare.

Pure warfighters are convinced that the worth of tactics must be measured by their military effectiveness, but they may hedge on the more fundamental issue of the precise meaning of "victory," "denial," and "prevailing" in nuclear combat. These terms can mean any of a number of things, but still fail to define limits by which the adequacy of U.S. nuclear capability can be judged—they fail to differentiate meaningfully the requirements of a first from a second strike.

Political warfighters also get lost in a tactical forest. In offering an intriguing variety of symbolic actions, these warfighters lose touch with the fundamentals of their strategy. Political warfighters are thus inclined toward the military tactics of the pure warfighting strategy, a strategy with quite a different purpose. These warfighters fail to recognize that it is assured destruction and not pure warfighting that provides important philosophical underpinnings of the bargaining strategy. In other words, political warfighters lose touch with the peculiar requirements of a punishment strategy. This is most obvious when political warfighters ignore the Soviet perspective on nuclear warfare, failing to see that a punishment strategy can work only if both sides are playing by the same rules. Political warfighters also ignore the requisites of punishment when they turn to the issue of defense and thereby fail to grasp the important counterintuitive implications of their strategy.

The problems identified might seem to result from the method of analysis. A logical retort to the conclusions offered here is that strategy is incoherent and inconsistent only when strategy is fragmented artificially —that the elements of assured destruction (as strategy or doctrine) and political warfighting and of political warfighting and pure warfighting can certainly coexist in a single strategy. Put differently, the retort is that pure warfighters are also political warfighters and, in turn, that political warfighters are in essence assured destruction advocates who reluctantly (and even pessimistically) look to political options only for added insurance. This is a compelling argument, particularly since policymakers seem to draw inspiration from multiple sources and appear largely indifferent to the apparent weaknesses of their strategies.

Nevertheless, assured destruction, pure warfighting, and political warfighting are combined only with peril. Some of their resemblances are superficial and, in any case, these strategies lead in different directions.

Political warfighters fail to see that a resort to war either signals the effective demise of assured destruction (in its more limited doctrinal sense) and that deterrence conditions no longer prevail or else that the intrawar bargaining that they foresee is nothing other than assured destruction. Some political warfighters offer their strategy as a replacement for assured destruction (again in a limited sense) and others offer it as a refinement,[50] and in the latter case it assumes a mild and cautious form.[51] (They present assured destruction as more a "reality" than a "policy"). Nevertheless, in essence, all political warfighters can offer only a recreation of assured destruction—"an extension of the American theory of deterrence [assured destruction] into war itself" (on this, see Gray and Payne 1980:19). Political warfighters only succeed in muddying the logic of assured destruction, and to the extent that they are misled to act provocatively by their conception of limited nuclear combat their strategy is not without serious risk and cost. Therefore, it is a fallacy to argue, as does Osgood (1988:105), that "the burden of proof should lie with those who insist categorically that there is no possibility of significantly limiting nuclear exchanges, not on those who believe that the only responsible course is to make every reasonable effort to hold open the possibility."

For their part, pure warfighters create severe intellectual problems when they appear as political warfighters. Pure warfighters suggest that tactics should be judged by their military rather than political effect, a stance that cannot be reconciled with a bargaining strategy. Beyond this, pure warfighter digressions into political warfighting must respond to an unanswerable question: "If nuclear weapons are militarily effective, why are a political strategy and limited war necessary?" Pure warfighters cannot answer this question, for to do so requires that they shed their military pretentions, if they are unwilling to dispense with the political altogether.

OPERATIONAL POLICY

It would not be wise to rely too heavily on operational policy to draw inferences about nuclear strategy and deterrence. Decisions about the acquisition and use of nuclear weapons (e.g., targeting, methods of delivery) are ideally guided by broadly based high-level decisions, but the ideal is not approached in practice. In fact, high-level policymakers within both the Kennedy and Nixon administrations expressly sought to divorce declaratory from acquisitions and/or employment policy when they recognized the budgetary implications of their strategies. Administrations have not actively sought to assure the implementation of strategic proposals, and often they have made proposals that lacked practical implications. Decisions affecting weapons use are thus made at low levels in the bureaucracy and reflect technical constraints and standard operating procedures more than they do the broad generalities of U.S. declaratory policy.[52] To quote one source, "military planners do not waste their time pondering ultimate national goals or the purpose of nuclear war; they concentrate on the details of executing it" (Arkin and Fieldhouse 1985:84).

Nevertheless, much can be learned from operational policy even when it is not used to infer strategy. A study of targeting, in particular, reveals that the above concrete policy concepts are not firmly grounded and can be applied to the real world only at the cost of further inconsistency in strategy. (In fact, it is targeting that is behind the common charge that nuclear strategy is overly abstract.) These findings are important because the strategic debate often centers on the issue of targeting, and even major policy directives (e.g., NSDM-242 in the Nixon years) focused on targeting at the expense of more general and complex strategic issues (on this, see Sloss and Millot 1984:23). Targeting issues are likely to be even more critical to strategy in the event of an actual nuclear confrontation.

Targeting

Urban-industrial areas were the targets of choice in the early postwar years. The prevailing strategy required that nuclear weapons be used to inflict the greatest amount of damage in the shortest period of time. Even if nuclear planners had desired to deliver weapons in a more discriminating fashion, the state of technology and the modest size of the U.S. nuclear arsenal precluded it. Atomic weapons were most effective against urban-industrial targets. The scarcity of the nuclear supply inhibited the use of the bomb against relatively small and widely scattered military targets, deficient reconnaisance hindered the detection of military targets, and aerial defenses hampered bombers from operating in the manner necessary for destroying these targets (e.g., target searches, low-altitude and daylight attacks).

The military created target categories and rank-ordered them by importance and time priority. By the fifties (with the Soviet acquisition of a nuclear capability), targets were classified as "blunting" targets, i.e., Soviet nuclear capability, "retardation" targets, i.e., "fleeting" targets critical to the war effort, and "destruction/disruption" targets, i.e., major industries (such as fuel and power). Destruction/disruption targets were in the majority, blunting targets were deemed time urgent (their mobility and threat potential required that they be hit first in any offensive), and retardation targets were only a secondary concern (Rosenberg 1983:16–17). The quantitative distribution of targets, then, reiterated the preference for urban-industrial targeting.[53]

The Eisenhower years were marked by a reevaluation and yet a reaffirmation of policy. The blunting mission retained time priority, military installations were heavily targeted, and, by the midfifties many argued for a pure counterforce doctrine, but urban-industrial targets continued to compose the majority of "designated ground zeros" (Friedberg 1980:40–47).[54] By the late fifties, planning centered on the "optimum mix," the combination of military, industrial, and government control center targets, the destruction of which would be militarily decisive. The optimum mix was justified by the argument that a surviving Soviet economy could eventually replace destroyed weapons and that a surviving Soviet military force could retaliate against the United States and seize the economic resources required for revitalization (Lambeth and Lewis 1983:130). It was hardly a dramatic departure, though, as targeting had never been an "either-or" proposition.

The Navy, despite its earlier protests against indiscriminate urban targeting, joined the Army in arguing for a deterrence-oriented targeting of government control and population centers. But SAC established de facto control of target selection, as the other services lacked the intelligence resources to compete with SAC or to even to challenge its selections (Rosenberg 1983:37–38, 53).

Eisenhower expressed misgivings over the emphasis on urban-industrial targets, and he urged that insignificant industrial targets and the overlapping of targets be avoided, along with the targeting of population per se (Rosenberg 1983:43). In this limited sense, Eisenhower's view converged with those of RAND analysts and senior Air Force staffers who were then arguing for a "no-cities" strategy. But the prevailing strategy virtually dictated urban-industrial targeting, and it was reinforced by a SAC war plan that was presented in the name of tactical efficiency: urban-industrial targets required fewer weapons, and to the extent that their destruction was militarily decisive, they limited the time bombers must spend over targets and reduced the need for follow-up strikes (Rosenberg 1983:35). The Eisenhower administration explored the implications of alternative targeting strategies, keyed to the objectives of deterrence and warfighting, but Eisenhower ultimately, though grudgingly, chose to retain the existing targeting emphasis (Rosenberg 1983:55).

The emphasis of targeting policy changed with events, and these changes were institutionalized with the formulation of the first Single Integrated Operational Plan (SIOP) for conducting a nuclear war. The SIOP was initiated in 1960 to centralize the targeting process because of the Secretary of Defense's concerns that the various nuclear services were unable and unwilling to coordinate their target selections. These concerns went largely unanswered. The Air Force used the integration process to attempt to establish control over strategic nuclear operations and to ensure that target lists would not ultimately constrain weapons procurement. The SIOP failed to halt the overlapping of targets, for it adopted inflated kill probability requirements and deflated weapons reliability estimates to justify a high weapons/target ratio (Kaplan 1983:263–268). Moreover, the SIOP only reinforced the disarray in target selection by indiscriminately incorporating the aim points of the various services and by not imposing limits on what had become a wholesale proliferation of prospective targets. The number of targeting points had increased enormously with the tremendous expansion in the U.S. arsenal and weapons delivery capability and a significant improvement in U.S. reconnaissance capability, and despite the deployment of high-yield thermonuclear weapons. The impact of target expansion was to increase vastly the number of military targets (Rowen 1979:134), as priority urban-industrial areas had never been difficult to target and change only at an exceedingly slow pace.

The first SIOP was "a highly inflexible plan for massive retaliation" and reflected an "extraordinarily rigid and mechanical approach to war" (Sagan 1987:23; Sagan 1989:24–26). The Kennedy administration thus

98
STRATEGIC ACTION

sought to introduce multiple options into the SIOP, which were made possible by a number of technological developments. With improved reconnaissance and deployed missiles the United States could locate and more quickly destroy Soviet nuclear targets on land (which at the time were unhardened and thereby also unconcealed). Moreover, the United States was no longer faced with the choice of either "using" or "losing" its weapons. With U.S. offensive versatility, Soviet air defenses could not impair a limited U.S. strike, and U.S. early warning and airborne alert capabilities, passive defense measures, and low Soviet capability limited the vulnerability of forces that would be withheld. Accordingly, the Kennedy administration made a clear distinction between nuclear threat, other military, and urban-industrial targets, and urban-industrial targets were given the status of "reserve targets," to be attacked only if the Soviets were to attack U.S. cities.[55] U.S. warplans had presented only a single option that would include a devastating attack on cities, but Kennedy administration revisions permitted variation in the severity of attacks and escalation from more strictly military to military-industrial targets. Nevertheless, restrictions in the capability to target independently or rapidly retarget missiles, aircraft reliance on fallout generating ground bursts, high weapons yield, and limited missile accuracy, as well as the military's desire to "plan" the offensive, constrained U.S. targeting flexibility.[56]

The Kennedy administration had a lasting affect on nuclear targeting. Indeed, it is claimed that since the Kennedy administration there have not been marked alterations in "the overall structure of the SIOP, the basic categories of targets the SIOP contains, the general priorities established for the allocation of warheads to these target categories, the techniques and procedures by which warheads are actually allocated to specific targets, and the machinery developed for the provision of basic national strategic guidance to inform the strategic nuclear target planning process" (Ball 1986b:57). However, the Nixon administration brought a renewed emphasis on selectivity and flexible targeting in a shift to limited nuclear options (reflecting the relaxation of previous technological constraints, i.e., reduced weapons yield and improved accuracy). While contingency plans were drawn up outside the SIOP, not until 1974 was the military directed to develop truly limited options (Rowen 1979:154); until 1977, U.S. war plans still consisted solely of massive counterforce and combined counterforce/countervalue attacks (Friedberg 1980:55),[57] and various options differed in emphasis rather than in kind (Rosenberg 1986:45–46). The Nixon and Ford administrations distinguished among a wider range of targets and shifted the focus from war-supporting industry to a "broader set of industrial and related targets" (Richelson 1986:159). This was articulated in 1974 in National Security Decision Memorandum 242 (NSDM-242), directing the priority targeting of "economic recovery assets." This new emphasis upon urban-industrial targets, with its attending complications and complexities, would consume military planning for years (Sagan 1989:44–48). Moreover, NSDM-242 also directed that population per se no longer be targeted. But the major innovations of this period were also in the sequencing and magnitude of proposed attacks as well as in target selection, and in this regard the Nixon administration formally introduced the idea of reserve or "withhold" targets (e.g., economic recovery assets).

The Carter-Brown years brought a major presidential directive (PD-59) and a related new "Nuclear Weapons Employment Policy"[58] to guide the SIOP that rejected economic-recovery targeting and refocused on war-supporting industry. Economic targets, however, remained one among many target sets (though they continued to account for the plurality of targets). The Carter administration's most significant policy contribution was the countervailing strategy. PD-59[59] definitively articulated this strategy and put new emphasis on Soviet military (e.g., ICBM silos) and political targets (e.g., Communist party and KGB headquarters, leadership relocation centers) as it directed the development of a capability that would enable the United States to respond flexibly in a protracted nuclear war.

NSDM-242 had been predicated upon the belief that the United States lacked the capability to destroy a substantial number of hardened Soviet military targets (Powers 1982:106). Capability improvements altered this belief. The United States by the midseventies was acquiring the capability for prompt hard-target attack: Minuteman III missiles had been retrofitted with more accurate, higher-yield warheads and more sophisticated guidance systems and a future silo-kill capability was enhanced by the development of the MX (ICBM) and Trident II (SLBM) missiles. The Carter administration was attentive to military targets when it sought to improve the endurance and flexibility of U.S. forces through a survivable basing mode for the MX missile and upgraded C^3I.[60] The Reagan administration added further significance to these targets through an explicit reaffirmation of Carter administration strategic initiatives and by commencing, continuing, or accelerating deployments for all three legs of the strategic triad.[61] The Reagan administration emphasis on military targets coincided with shifts in naval military strategy toward the

use of U.S. attack submarines to destroy Soviet ballistic missile submarines even at the start of conventional war (on this, see Mearsheimer
1986; Quester 1988).

Implications for Strategy

Targets, then, have been distinguished operationally by their respective "execution" and "allocation" priorities. The story of targeting can be
told around the growing importance of this distinction.

The first SIOP brought a clearer distinction among the various targeting tasks (Friedberg 1980:42), and the importance of urban-industrial
targets, for example, was registered in the number and high yield of the
weapons that were targeted against them to assure their destruction.
Nevertheless, it can also be argued that the effect of the SIOP was to
erode the distinction among target types as its "bomb as you go" system
(Pringle and Arkin 1983:45) virtually called for a simultaneous attack
against all of the different target groups (Rosenberg 1983:7).

The emphasis on execution priority (or time urgency) has increased
with the vulnerability and the phenomenal numerical growth in military
targeting points, and policymakers now desire the capability to limit the
attack capability of the Soviet Union through the immediate destruction
of nuclear threat and other military targets. The decades-old trend towards
smaller and highly mobile systems, e.g., cruise missiles, "Midgetman,"
could reduce the interest in counterforce targeting (Berkowitz 1985b),
but it could also have the opposite effect by reinforcing a desire to assure
prompt attack against counterforce targets and by increasing the interest
in decapitating C^3I attacks. Nevertheless, urban-industrial targets remain
salient due to their allocation priority. The United States has always
sought the capability to destroy specific sets of urban-industrial targets
with high confidence, and "cross-targets" its weapons to this end (Rowen
1975:220).[62] Most policymakers will concede that U.S. security ultimately requires that the United States be able to inflict unacceptable
costs and hence unacceptable levels of urban-industrial destruction upon
the Soviet Union.

Despite targeting priorities and assorted targeting changes, fads, and
trends, the distinctions among target types have never been firm. First,
distinctions among target sets have not been well grounded. The term
urban-industrial implies that the terms *urban* and *industrial* are complementary, but these terms are used interchangeably. In promoting industrial destruction, Air Force planners of the forties rhetorically asked
"what was a city besides a collection of industry?" (Rosenberg 1983:15.)

Often target sets are ill-defined so that targets that conform to one set of criteria most assuredly conform to another; target sets end up as distinctions without a difference. Warfighters argue that deterrence and a "theory of victory" require the destruction of targets that, rather than merely imposing costs, could "defeat" the Soviet Union. This recommendation has no practical implications, though, when it requires a broad-based assault on the "essential assets" of the Soviet state (see Gray 1979).

While explicit distinctions are maintained among target sets, the current policy emphasis on flexibility and multiple options has implicitly fostered an erosion of these distinctions. The current SIOP is structured upon tailored sets of options based on, among other things, target type (i.e., Soviet nuclear forces, general purpose forces, Soviet military and political leadership centers, and Soviet economic and industrial sites), general nature of attack (e.g., major, selected, limited, regional), and contingency (e.g., preemptive attack, launch-under-attack) (Ball 1986b:80–82).[63] But the line between target types dissipates when options require cross-cutting sets of targets, when weapons with hard-target kill capability are to be used in "surgical" urban-industrial strikes (by merit of their accuracy and low yield), or when targets are linked through "threat multiplier" strikes (Gray 1986b:190), where, for example, strikes against air defenses and ABM systems are harbingers of attacks on urban areas.

Second, target sets may overlap. It may be difficult to separate a military from an economic target, let alone one type of industrial target from another. The overlapping of U.S. targets is clearly seen in the integration of the land-line communication system for U.S. strategic command and control with the national telephone system (Carter 1987b:250–252). The Soviet military-industrial complex is even more tightly interconnected than that of the United States, so that even if it were possible in principle to precisely distinguish among target sets, the reality is that within the Soviet complex there is a tremendous amount of substitution among economic sectors, certain industries serve a multiple function (i.e., civilian and military), and as "bottlenecks" some industries are central to all forms of economic performance (e.g., petroleum, electric power, steel). This practical coincidence of targets also accounts for contradictory attitudes toward the targeting of political control centers and the Soviet leadership. These targets are critical to both governance and military operations. As interest has turned to intrawar deterrence they have become important "withhold" targets, hostage to the threat of nuclear punishment, but they are also central to the warfighting thesis as "decapitation" targets, vulnerable points of military command and control. Their conception as both "value" and "force" targets[64] explains why proponents of the warfighting thesis can argue for the selection of targets with an eye to restraint while they simultaneously justify the prompt destruction of government control centers.[65] It also explains why the SIOP treats some command targets as time urgent and yet others as "withholds".[66]

Finally, it can be argued that the inseparability of targets resides not so much in their nature, but in their geographical proximity. Despite inhibitions against targeting population per se, all large Soviet cities are targeted "simply by virtue of associated industrial and military targets" (Ball 1986b:27–28), and the distinction between urban and industrial targets "had in reality disappeared in the 1950s with the advent of high-yield weapons" (Rowen 1979:148). Those Soviet targets that are isolated (those whose destruction would produce no collateral damage), e.g., some radar, industrial, and transportation facilities, are in fact of limited military value (Ball 1981:27), and critical Soviet targets (including ICBMs and bomber bases) are found in heavily populated areas. Similarly, U.S. submarine support facilities and many bomber bases are found near major cities and while U.S. ICBMs are located in sparsely populated areas, attacks against U.S. Minuteman bases will have direct and indirect disruptive effects on U.S. command and control (Blair 1985:226–228) and could also produce high fatality rates. Whether the problem is identified as one of "collocation" of targets or of massive weapons yield, hydrogen weapons are best regarded as blunt instruments.[67]

Despite the increased public emphasis on limited nuclear options, policymakers have not sought to minimize collateral damage at all costs. Indeed, the opposite has been true. Military planners emphasize targets over nontargets to the point that they may be alert to collateral effects only to the extent that they can meet their targeting objectives with available weapons (Richelson 1983:136). Moreover, the very ambiguity of target status has led planners to promote "bonus effects." Even when targets can be distinguished, the temptation may be to choose targets so as to maximize destruction and disruption. Without firm target distinctions and in the absence of an emphatic and exclusive commitment to one set of targets over another, "it would not be facetious to suggest that present strategic planners would be perturbed if weapons systems could be developed that eliminated collateral damage" (Richelson 1985:5).

In short, existing target distinctions are not a sound basis for strategy. Target groups ultimately rest on ad hoc categorization, and target distinctions are neither grounded in actual patterns of target incidence or rigorous thought. Thus when policymakers focus on targeting over strategy policy inconsistencies inevitably result.

THE DEFENSIVE "REVOLUTION"

The offense has dominated U.S. nuclear strategy, but defensive deployments and thinking have been an ever-present part of the continuing controversy over U.S. nuclear strategy. The Kennedy administration considered the deployment of the Nike-Zeus defense system, the Johnson administration paired an improved Nike-Zeus (the Spartan) with a short-range interceptor (the Sprint) and a more sophisticated phased-array radar in proposing the Sentinel system for a thin defense against a Chinese attack on U.S. urban areas, and the Nixon administration transformed this defense into the Safeguard system in recommending that it be used instead to protect Minuteman silos. Each of these proposals aroused intense debate over the technical and strategic merits of anti–ballistic missile systems, though controversy temporarily culminated in the ratification of the 1972 Anti–Ballistic Missile Treaty. The Reagan administration rekindled the debate in arguing for a strategic reorientation toward defense.

The defensive debate is an anomaly because it testifies to the power of the abstract in nuclear strategy. The peculiar position of defense can be attributed largely to the Reagan administration and its uncommon willingness to challenge the prevailing wisdoms of the period—to venture into a conceptual world and outdistance the defensive technologies available at that time (on this, see Brooks 1986). Nevertheless, *even defense suffers from the abstract maladies that have been identified in other areas of strategy—incompleteness and inconsistency and a failure to inform the concrete.* Furthermore, the exuberance for the Reagan vision faded with time—and defense appears to have resumed its prior position astride existing strategic concepts and to have been overtaken by more concrete bureaucratic and technological concerns.

The "Perfect Defense" and Its Detractors

Reagan presented a revolutionary vision of a world in which defenses would render nuclear weapons "impotent and obsolete." Many seized upon the Reagan initiative to promote less ambitious policy changes, and still others were more convinced of the futility of any major redirection of strategy. The Scowcroft commission[68] made only passing reference to strategic defense and was not optimistic about its successful deployment. The Hoffman panel,[69] appointed by Reagan to assess the strategic implications of defense, narrowly focused on the contribution of defense to a secure retaliatory capability and a more favorable nuclear balance and assumed that the defense would work in conjunction with the offense to promote U.S. security objectives (FSSS 1983; for a discussion, see Hafner 1986). Even the military posture statement of the JCS (FY1987) promoted strategic defense by acknowledging its contribution to retaliatory deterrence.

Toward the end of the Reagan term, the perfect defense became less than a compelling vision. The highest officials in the Defense Department had relegated defense to a more modest role, and the Pentagon had accepted warhead penetration levels and technologies that were only appropriate for missile defense (Smith 1988a, 1988b).

The advocates of a "perfect defense" have launched a frontal assault on the premises of deterrence and offered defense as an escape from the dilemmas and even immoral implications of deterrence (the latter reminiscent of the Navy argument of the early fifties). They present a technological solution based on a multitiered defense that requires a vast assortment of weapons that are reliant on a variety of physical principles (e.g., X-ray lasers, chemical lasers, neutral particle beams, kinetic energy weapons). They believe that the perfect defense is now possible because exotic technologies operating in space will permit the interception of Soviet weapons in their boost phase,[70] meaning that the defense could be employed against enemy missiles when they are under launch and most vulnerable (because they present a larger and softer target, are more "visible," and have not yet released their numerous warheads and deceptive devices). Therefore, they believe that defense systems have an advantageous "cost-exchange ratio"—the defense costs less than the offensive changes required to offset it—and can surmount traditional problems related to the interception of warheads at low altitudes (e.g., radiation, numerous incoming warheads overwhelming the defense) and a problem of "preferential defense" where an attacker reallocates its weapons to capitalize on defensive coverage deficiencies. Moreover, they can then maintain that defense systems can provide protection for cities, which because of their number and vulnerability cannot be protected effectively at the terminal phase.[71]

In public debate, the perfect defense appears as a deus ex machina because it runs counter to prevailing professional judgments and wisdoms and because the defense is now offered with a fervor and a promise that was uncharacteristic of prior debate.[72] The perfect defense even assumes "magical" proportions when, for example, Reagan promoted it as a virtual panacea and a secret that can be shared with the Soviet adversary for lasting mutual benefit. He failed to acknowledge that dual-purpose applications could render a "defensive" weapon an "offensive" one (e.g., antimissile technology can be used against satellites) or that military technology is susceptible to countermeasures so that the technology would be undermined if it were shared and must be consistently modified and upgraded if it were to remain effective (on this, see Bundy et al 1984–85:272–273).

The advocates of perfect defense are resisted by proponents of assured destruction who argue that the defense of urban-industrial areas is impossible (though they might also argue that it is destabilizing to deterrence).[73] Advocates of the assured destruction position and others (see, for instance, Brown 1985) argue against the perfect defense by claiming that such a defense " 'really would' have to be perfect, not just very good" (see Rathjens and Ruina 1986:244). They base their assessments on the exceptional vulnerability of urban-industrial areas, placing exceptional demands[74] upon costly (and still undeveloped) computer and exotic-weapons technology that can never be tested under actual battle conditions.[75] They argue that military targets can be protected through hardening and permit the defender the luxury of time to discriminate warheads from decoys (when they separate in the atmosphere), of not having to destroy weapons that are at best "near misses," and of selectively protecting targets because only a finite number of them need to survive an enemy attack. They assert that U.S. cities, on the other hand, cannot be protected because of the peculiar geographic distribution of the U.S. population[76] and because high fatality levels and widespread destruction will result if only a small fraction of the Soviet arsenal were to hit near them.

The "Less-Than-Perfect" Defense and Its Detractors

The two extreme positions—no defense and perfect defense—dominate much of the public debate on the subject, but fail to do justice to the more sophisticated arguments of policy specialists. Even the most committed advocates of strategic defense recognize that defense is not an instant and total solution to the strategic problems of the United States and that defensive deployments must coexist with certain offensive realities.

More sophisticated advocates address the strategic, as well as the technological, implications of defense.[77] At an abstract level, they recognize that the offense and the defense are interdependent, though they differ in their assessments of whether the U.S.-Soviet strategic relationship could foreseeably be dominated by the defense. At a concrete level, advocates of assured destruction and of the "less-than-perfect" defense differ in their assessments of the likely effects of defense on both the "arms race" and "crisis stability."[78]

The Arms Race

No matter how a defensive system operates, critics assert that its viability ultimately rests on whether it is more cost-effective[79] than enemy countermeasures (as well as means of passive defense). Defensive deployments will inevitably induce adversary offensive deployments when the defense is competing at an economic and technological disadvantage.

Critics argue that a defense system that does not betray its strongholds might still be overwhelmed with ease and that a defense system with visible preferences could lead an adversary to reallocate its weapons accordingly, for targets that the defender deems important enough to require a disproportionate share of defensive resources might warrant an increased investment by the attacker. They further state that since neither side has thus far had to compete against an active defense, it stands to reason that defenses could be circumvented easily through available means.[80] Moreover, they argue that no matter what the features of a defense system, the initiative remains with the offense—that an effective defense must be able "to overcome the full range of possible countermeasures" and that "this asymmetry means that defenses may always be at a disadvantage" (see Glaser 1984:111–112). For example, the advantage of "preferential defense" can be offset by "preferential offense targeting," whereby the attacker concentrates its forces against targets of its choosing and the defender must defend all of its targets against the range of adversary attack scenarios (Rathjens and Ruina 1986:243).

Therefore, while defense advocates believe that defense can actually reverse the offensive "arms race," advocates of assured destruction believe that defense will fuel an arms race with defensive and offensive dimensions. Space-based defense systems could be combated through a host of countermeasures (e.g., attacks on ground stations or space mines), leading to offsetting defensive countermeasures against those countermeasures, and so on, and if the advantage remains with the offense, then defensive deployments will inspire quantitative and qualitative offensive responses. In this regard, it should be noted that it is claimed that McNamara chose to expand the number of U.S. warheads to counter the Soviet anti–ballistic missile system (Schlesinger 1985:3) and that despite intense Soviet defensive efforts, "the offensive remains the linchpin of Soviet strategy" (Lambeth and Lewis 1988:764).

Rejecting warnings of an arms race, defense advocates argue that defense can actually lead to offensive disarmament. These advocates maintain that defense destroys the incentives for arms control treaty noncompliance at low force levels where even small violations could be militarily or politically significant (see Brennan 1969:115–116; Payne and Gray 1984:838).[81] However, defense critics respond by arguing that an incentive to obtain offensive forces remains even when the defense enjoys the advantage, because small absolute increases in the ability to penetrate enemy defenses are still significant at low levels of urban-industrial target vulnerability (see Glaser 1984:110).

This does not mean that defense advocates believe that defense can perform all tasks with equal facility. Proponents of a "less-than-perfect" defense recognize that a highly effective defense system is not immediately feasible, believing that defenses can most usefully protect retaliatory capability (and collocated population centers) (see Payne and Gray 1984). These proponents maintain that force protection can be enhanced by a multitiered defense.[82] But they are also optimistic about the viability of terminal-phase defense or a "point-defense" (i.e., defense of a small, well-defined area) of military targets: They argue, for instance, that a preferential point-defense can compel an adversary to economize by attacking only unprotected targets or to expend larger numbers of weapons for destroying protected targets with certainty (see Brennan 1969:99; FSSS 1983; Hoffman 1986:11).[83] Because defense advocates are most optimistic about the defense of retaliatory capability (that would involve some combination of active and passive measures), they believe that an adversary can at least be induced to abandon counterforce deployments.

Crisis Stability

Advocates and opponents of defense differ in how they assess the impact of defense on crisis stability. Defense advocates exhibit a significant logical failing here.

Defense advocates insist that the protection of either military or value targets will stabilize deterrence because decreased vulnerability, of any kind, reduces an adversary's gains from an attack. A nation can deny an opponent its gains either by shielding itself from an attack or by attacking its opponent's forces, and a nation can employ an effective defense, like a strong offense, for a bargaining advantage (see Kahn 1969:76). It should not be surprising, then, that many of the advocates of warfighting are among the staunchest supporters of defense and are also wary of Soviet defensive deployments. Whereas they view the offense as the key to defensive damage limitation, they can also carry defensive logic to the

extreme and, only somewhat facetiously, offer a "silo-phase" defense—
the military implications are the same in either instance.

Adherents of assured destruction insist that the offense remains predominant, though they also maintain that the defense of value targets can
destabilize deterrence.[84] They claim that the protection of urban-industrial areas is threatening because it indicates a first-strike posture: a
country can protect its retaliatory capability out of concern for deterrence, but it will protect its cities to guard against retaliation if it plans to
get in the first blow.

A more convincing retort to defense is offered by sophisticated proponents of assured destruction. They assert that defenses can destabilize
deterrence, but only when pitted against a vulnerable offense.[85] A less-
than-perfect defense magnifies the problems of offensive force vulnerability and creates an incentive to preempt because it is likely to be more
effective against a "ragged" retaliatory attack (see Rathjens and Ruina
1986:245) than a well-coordinated first strike.[86] The vulnerable party will
preempt because its second strike is unlikely to be successful (whether
counterforce or countervalue) when the small size and limited coordination of the retaliatory strike force render it unable to penetrate or exploit
the weaknesses of the defense. Such preemption might take the form of
attacks upon defensive targets (Cimbala 1988:122).[87]

In sum, at an abstract level defense advocates are inconsistent when
they assess the primacy of defense. The strongest adherents of defense
imply that defense dominates offense, yet would probably forego defense
if it were purchased at the expense of offensive force improvements,
relegating defense to a companion or a supporting role. But even when
they promote defense, they often imply that it complements the offense
but does not replace it. Given that the most enthusiastic defense advocates are also pure warfighters, it would be premature (at the least) to
speak of their "conversion" to defense.[88]

In evaluating the relative preponderance of defense, defense advocates are not unlike advocates of assured destruction. Some assured
destruction advocates reject defense out of hand but remain troubled by
its strategic implications. They refuse to relinquish the primacy of the
offense, yet they concede that a partly effective defense (or at least one
perceived as such) will induce offensive responses and that the defense
aggravates problems of offensive force vulnerability.

At a concrete level, defense advocates fail to recognize the implications of defense for crisis stability. A nation could choose a first over a
second strike when its offense is vulnerable and it must penetrate an
enemy defense. Given that warfighters downplay even the negative ef-

fects of offense upon crisis stability, not surprisingly, they are indifferent to the less direct effects of defense. Pure warfighters are particularly prone to military solutions to strategic problems and are therefore unlikely to acknowledge the undesirable consequences that ensue.

In any case, U.S. nuclear strategy has long been predicated upon the distinction between offense and defense. Nevertheless, the strategic defense debate has openly established the interconnectedness of the two.

CONCLUSIONS

U.S. nuclear strategy can be understood and its history traced at a fairly abstract level. An abstract treatment usefully serves to highlight major policy trends and transitions, and it brings together aspects of policy that might be erroneously presumed to be disparate and unrelated. But abstraction should not be an end in itself. U.S. strategic conceptions of offense, defense, punishment, and denial are heavily influenced by a more concrete set of referents. In particular, the inconsistencies of "warfighting" doctrine reflect a failure to appreciate the abstract implications of strategy.

Furthermore, there exists a limited hierarchal relationship between U.S. nuclear strategy and operational planning, for strategy has increased the importance of certain types of targets. Still, target lists have accelerated force requirement estimates, as deployments are more easily guided by the ratio of aim points to available weapons than by overarching strategy; and technological constraints, registered in target selections, strongly affected the choice of strategy in the early postwar years. Moreover, strategy has been distorted by the geographical and temporal coincidence and the poor conceptual grounding of target sets: force targets are created out of what are ostensibly value targets, making it easier for analysts to adhere carelessly to two competing sets of ideas—deterrence by "denial" and deterrence by "punishment."

Finally, the issue of strategic defense requires special treatment. Unlike previous strategic issues, defense has not emerged within a context of concrete referents, weapons deployments, or even deeply entrenched organizational interests. The political sensitivity of the issue testifies to the power of abstract ideas in the strategic debate. Nevertheless, the current fascination with defense appears short-lived, and the justifications for defense exhibit typical abstract maladies and reinforce rather than undermine existing strategic principles.

4

STRATEGIC OBJECTIVES AND WEAPON DEPLOYMENTS

ABSTRACT ASSUMPTIONS about Soviet intentions are fundamental to the various conceptions of deterrence and are perhaps the least tractable elements of strategic thought. The reason is, of course, because these conceptions have origins in ideology and are at the very heart of why the United States needs nuclear weapons in the first place. Not surprisingly, then, assured destruction and warfighting advocates have profoundly different perspectives on Soviet objectives. The importance of these perspectives, however, says little about their soundness. Abstract thinking about Soviet intent *is riddled with inconsistencies and is deficient by neglect.*

Much of the debate over Soviet policy objectives actually centers on Soviet capability: capability assessment reinforces thoughts about Soviet objectives. The deficiency in thought about Soviet intent, then, can be pinned upon the concrete: policymakers assess Soviet capability in terms that do not allow them to reflect upon the abstract; they are preoccupied with Soviet threat assessment but not as an opportunity to reevaluate their beliefs about Soviet objectives. The concrete can even more directly shape strategy: *U.S.* strategy can be defined by *U.S.* capability. U.S. policymakers could indeed be more sensitive to new U.S. weapons technology than to the perceived Soviet threat. Perversely, then, U.S. policymakers might be that much more concerned about Soviet objectives.

This chapter first examines the nature and the deficiencies of abstract thinking about Soviet objectives. It then turns to the impact of the concrete in the form of capability concerns: it shows how Soviet force assessments can reinforce abstract thinking and yet remains disconnected from such thinking and also shows how US military technology can directly affect U.S. strategy.

ABSTRACT CONCEPTIONS OF INTENT

All contemporary strategists have one assumption in common—they assume that the Soviets place the survival of the Soviet Union above all else. What this means in practice, though, is not very clear and remains a matter of dispute, and even this fundamental assumption only gained acceptance with the U.S. turn toward a second-strike capability.

Faced with a growing Soviet nuclear threat, policymakers of the fifties focused on what the Soviets "could" do rather than on what they "might" do. Presuming that the Soviets had grandiose objectives and were willing to incur the costs of achieving them, policymakers feared that if the Soviets had the capability to attack the United States, they might simply attack (Kaplan 1983:142; Trachtenberg 1988). Eisenhower worried about a Soviet attack even though the United States could probably have retaliated with many times the destructiveness of a Soviet first strike. Few believed that a stable deterrence relationship could evolve between the U.S. and the Soviet Union.

Attitudes changed in the sixties. There are indications that McNamara believed that the emerging balance of terror was both stable and desirable (Ball 1980:198). But even in the late sixties, administration officials maintained that the United States must retain nuclear superiority (Kahan 1975:101). The United States never decided to accept parity with the Soviet Union—parity was imposed by the sheer magnitude of the Soviet nuclear buildup (Schilling 1981:56).

Assured Destruction

Assured destruction advocates seem to argue in contradictions when they assess Soviet objectives. When they promote the deterrent value of U.S. weapons, these advocates imply that the Soviets seek to overturn the status quo, and yet most assured destruction advocates are more optimistic than are warfighters about Soviet objectives. In other words, assured destruction advocates seem to confuse deterrence as a consequence of rivalry with deterrence as a direct policy objective. This is not as contradictory as it sounds. Assured destruction advocates are sanguine about Soviet motives partly because they have faith in the threat of assured destruction and the stability of deterrence: They believe that the Soviets prefer the status quo to the risk of challenging it.They might be equally hopeful about the prospect for avoiding war in Europe, because they do not believe that the Soviets will accept high risks for the more limited gains from attacks on less vital interests (see Jervis 1984:45–46). Assured destruction advocates, though, spend little time grappling with Soviet intentions or determining what the Soviets could gain from an attack, let alone resolving logical inconsistencies in beliefs about Soviet objectives. They make it hard to tell whether their optimism is warranted.

Assured destruction advocates also offer contradictory Soviet objectives when they assess the likely course of war: They typically plan with the assumption that the opening Soviet strategic shot will be an all-out "bolt from the blue"[1] while they also rely upon U.S. nuclear and conventional forces to deter lesser provocations. Admittedly, safeguarding U.S. forces against surprise attack is different from expecting one. Most assured destruction proponents believe that nuclear war is more likely to result from uncontrolled escalation[2] than from a Soviet surprise attack[3] and thereby suggest that the Soviets are conservative (risk-adverse), motivated by traditional (and thereby limited) Russian territorial objectives, and even defensively motivated (see, for instance, Garthoff 1982, 1988; Kennan 1983:131–133; Halperin 1987:98–99). Nevertheless, assured destruction advocates do not forthrightly present the political and military conditions that could spark a U.S.-Soviet nuclear confrontation and therefore leave the question of Soviet culpability unanswered.

Assured destruction advocate inattention to Soviet objectives has had important policy implications. For example, it has led some of these advocates to voice internally inconsistent arguments against strategic defense: Some advocates believe that the transition to the strategic defense of cities would be dangerous because the Soviets would respond to a fading opportunity to inflict urban-industrial damage and attack rather than wait and allow the United States to be able to strike the Soviet Union with impunity. These advocates cannot argue that the Soviets will "commit suicide for fear of death" and be true to their belief in retaliatory deterrence.

Assured destruction advocates infer Soviet objectives from Soviet capability only with caution. For two reasons, these advocates might not be all that attentive to the style of Soviet deployment:

First, some assured destruction advocates downplay U.S.-Soviet force asymmetries. They do not believe that these asymmetries give the Soviets a usable military advantage and/or they recognize that these asymmetries lie in political, cultural, and doctrinal differences between the United States and the Soviet Union. In either case, these assured destruction advocates do not assume that ostensibly offensive or defensive Soviet force deployments "speak for themselves." They do not believe that the Soviet counterforce emphasis means that the Soviet Union would willingly incur the costs of a nuclear war; that the Soviet reliance upon vulnerable land-based missiles means that the Soviets plan to strike first as aggressors; or that Soviet defensive deployments mean that the Soviet Union thinks that a nuclear war can be won (see, for instance, Garthoff 1982).

Second, some assured destruction advocates believe Soviet deployments to be a reaction to U.S. deployments (see Rathjens 1969; York 1970; McNamara 1986:62–67). As purveyors of the arms-race thesis, these advocates believe Soviet deployments to be fundamentally defensive in nature—a natural reaction, an overreaction, and, maybe even an improper reaction (e.g., the Soviet land-based missile emphasis), but nonetheless a reaction to U.S. activities (though possibly based on more deeply rooted Soviet insecurities). They view the United States and the Soviet Union to be locked in a self-sustaining cycle of competitive armament, with neither superpower its villain and both its victims.[4] U.S.-Soviet hostility, then, does not reflect a fundamental antagonism of social-political systems and interests, but it could be no less consequential. (See Russett 1983 for the role of both internal and competitive forces in the arms race.)

Pure Warfighting

Pure warfighters are generally the most articulate about Soviet goals and attend to Soviet strategic objectives and deeper Soviet policy drives and imperatives. Pure warfighters hold a stark view of the Soviet adversary: they believe the Soviet Union to be an untiring menace that by necessity is reliant upon force and coercion and is unequivocal in combat. These warfighters sometimes disagree over the actual sources of Soviet conduct, but they do agree that Soviet long-term objectives are coherent, consistent, and endure.

The contemporary warfighter does not maintain that the Soviets invite nuclear war—only that the Soviets are willing to run a higher risk of war on behalf of their objectives (on this, see Jervis 1979–80:622), but the pure warfighter certainly believes that the Soviet Union would use nuclear weapons under favorable conditions. They see the Soviet Union to be always aware of its relative capability and in search of ways to improve it. To quote one such warfighter, "Soviet strategists regard 'mutual deterrence' to be a reality of the balance of nuclear forces as presently constituted, but they mean to alter this balance in their favor and in this manner secure a monopoly on deterrence" (Pipes 1988:56). Pure warfighters insist that the Soviets have learned the lessons of a country victimized by preemption, repeatedly devastated in battle, and able to survive only through the superior application of military resources. Pure warfighters maintain that the Soviets believe that nuclear war, like any war, is winnable—that nuclear weapons, coupled with conventional forces, can defeat an opponent if employed decisively and expeditiously. They think that the Soviets are guided by a strategy that has fundamentally a military thrust. It is not a strategy of thresholds and negotiation, but one of imposition; it is, when executed, an acknowledgment that bargaining has failed. In a word, pure warfighters believe that the Soviets aspire to a "war-winning" capability.

Despite differences among them, pure warfighters depict the Soviets to be aggressive in strategy as well as in tactics. They variously describe Soviet objectives as Russian, Marxist-Leninist, or imperial, but always as expansionist; hence they variously believe the Soviets to be driven by a global mission, an insatiable quest for security, the compulsion to dominate and extend Soviet rule, resource deprivation, or the need to galvanize internal support and achieve ideological legitimacy through "forward movement" and confrontations with adversaries (see, for instance, Pipes 1977, 1980, 1984; Nitze 1984–85; Gray 1986a).[5] As a result, they picture the Soviets, not inconsistently, as "cold, calculating and in active pursuit of a master plan" and as "doomed to a never-ending search for total security" (on this, see Meyer 1984:273, 277). These images were in clear ascendance (at least early on) in the Reagan administration. Indeed, the U.S. Department of Defense (1987,1988) recently promoted both of them when it asserted that the Soviets seek "to achieve a force posture for the Soviet Union that provides for absolute security as it continues to seek world domination" and that "their national goals and objectives require that the Soviets expand their military power and political influence beyond their own borders to ensure their security and satisfy their imperialist urge."

Pure warfighters offer a conception of Soviet objectives that is nonetheless inconsistent and incomplete. First, pure warfighters leave questions unanswered when they maintain that the Soviets believe that they can prevail in a nuclear war even if such a war would have "catastophic consequences" (these assertions are found, for instance, in U.S. Department of Defense 1987). If the Soviets can prevail, why have they not used their conventional or nuclear forces against the West? The pure warfighter would respond that the Soviet Union will wait until the time is right, but in this these warfighters obscure the implication of their argument—that is, from the Soviet vantage point the time is right since the Soviets presumably base their calculations upon a *contemporary* frame of reference. Pure warfighters are confident enough of Soviet animosity and its fear of the West to argue that the Soviets can see victories in nuclear catastrophe, and yet these warfighters cannot explain why the Soviets have been reluctant to challenge the West even at the conventional force level, where the Soviets conceivably enjoy advantages. If the Soviets are indeed optimistic about the outcome of a showdown with the West, then pure warfighting assumptions about Soviet objectives seem to be in error. On the other hand, if these assumptions are correct and the Soviets do believe that they can prevail in war, then the term *prevail* must have a meaning to the Soviets that is not immediately apparent—that is, the best of least desired outcomes. If this is true, then pure warfighters should be considerably more hopeful about Soviet intentions than they currently are.

Second, while pure warfighters depict the Soviets to be relentless, uncompromising, and emphatic in the use of force, these warfighters still leave much unstated. For one thing, pure warfighters do not specify clearly whether the Soviets intend to conquer or annihilate, to vanquish or decimate, Soviet opponents.[6] This is a significant ambiguity.[7] If the Soviets seek conquests, they could be willing to bargain with the West (as political warfighters anticipate) to prevent the prize of war (e.g., economic assets that could support the Soviet economy) from being sacrificed in an all-out strategic exchange. For another thing, pure warfighters do not adequately distinguish immediate from long-term Soviet objectives. This too is significant. The Soviets might also be willing to bargain if they had no fundamental grievance with the United States; they would be less inclined to bargain if they valued the outcome of a battle or limited war only to the extent that it contributed to victory over the United States.[8]

Pure warfighters regard Soviet capability and its continued growth to be a symptom of a deeply rooted Soviet antagonism toward the West and an ominous sign for the future. They believe that Soviet long-term objectives have propelled continued Soviet force improvements, the Soviet amassing of counterforce potential, quantitative Soviet military superiority, and increases in Soviet defense spending (despite U.S. spending declines and Soviet budgetary constraints). But regardless, pure warfighters believe it wise to prepare for the worst.

Pure warfighters generally have little use for the concept of an arms race or the concept of crisis stability. Some maintain that the unwholesome implication of both concepts is that the Soviets design policy around simplistic, superficial criteria—that the Soviets merely "match" U.S. acquisitions or that the Soviets would go to war simply because their forces are vulnerable. They believe that both notions unduly emphasize the "proximate," noticeable, and even incidental sources of superpower antagonism but not the more basic and significant sources of U.S.-Soviet rivalry; they thus sanction a robust U.S. force posture to prepare for a wide range of contingencies and are hardly bothered by the potential U.S. acquisition of a first-strike capability. These pure warfighters assert that Soviet military acquisitions are shaped primarily by doctrinal, budgetary, political, and technical considerations and that the Soviets will lash out not when they are vulnerable, but rather when they believe circumstances are propitious or that war is inevitable (see, for instance, Gray 1986a:149–151, 217).

Political Warfighting

The political warfighter say generally very little about Soviet objectives. Nevertheless, whether out of conviction or for conservative planning, political warfighters can be less sanguine about the Soviets than are assured destruction advocates and suggest, if only by implication, that the Soviet Union would risk an all-out nuclear exchange on behalf of some objectives.[9] On the other hand, political warfighters are more hopeful about the Soviets than are pure warfighters and suggest that the Soviets would negotiate in war and compromise their goals. They see the Soviet Union to be cautious but potentially aggressive militarily (see Brodie 1966:44–45)—a "prudent and sober power" (see Department of Defense FY1975)—and fall back upon Soviet mysteriousness.[10] Most political warfighters do not go too far beyond this to disclose a precise reading of Soviet intent.

Political warfighters are a paradox: they are perhaps the most sophisticated and yet parochial of the strategic advocates. These warfighters present elaborate, highly refined scenarios that have the United States and the Soviet Union dancing on the precipice of nuclear conflagration and yet remain indifferent to the conditions that brought them there. They fail to recognize that the fundamental context that set the stage for war would likely determine its outcome. Political warfighters narrowly focus on the means of war rather than the purposes for and circumstances under which war would be fought. This has led one observer to exclaim:

> When I read the flood of scenarios in strategic journals about first-strike capabilities, counterforce or countervailing strategies, flexible response, escalation dominance and the rest of the postulates of nuclear theology, I ask myself in bewilderment: this war they are describing, "what is it about?" The defense of Western Europe? Access to the Gulf? The protection of Japan? If so, why is this goal not mentioned, and why is the strategy not related to the progress of the conflict in these regions? But if it is not related to this kind of specific object, what are we talking about? Has not the bulk of American thinking been exactly what Clausewitz described— something that, because it is divorced from any political context, is "pointless and devoid of sense"? (Howard 1981:9)

The point is a critical one, for political warfighters ignore a critical requirement for limited war in the contemporary world—goals that are well defined and amenable to accommodation (Osgood 1957:4), that is, goals that are "specific, concrete, and clearly stated" (Halperin 1963:8– 10). [11] "The decisive limitation upon war is the limitation of the objectives of war" (Osgood 1957:4). Political warfighters violate this assumption and inconsistently portray the Soviet adversary as at once aggressive and conciliatory—they show the Soviets to be ready to take advantage of a favorable nuclear capability balance and yet willing to defer gains through negotiation. It is hard to imagine the circumstances under which the Soviets would knowingly instigate nuclear conflict (if only through a conventional attack) and yet would make concessions in the course of nuclear combat, being the first to capitulate under duress. If the Soviets were as committed to their combat objectives as political warfighters argue that the United States needs to be to its (see chapter 5), little could be gained from negotiation. [12]

Political warfighters must recognize that even limited objectives are not enough to limit conflict. Limited objectives are a necessary but not sufficient condition for limited war: First, limited objectives must be amenable to compromise. Limited war might not be possible if the United States and the Soviets hold irreconcilable positions (Halperin 1963:8–10). Second, limited objectives must be accompanied by limited means. Limited war requires that *both* the United States and the Soviet Union view possible combat limits to be *both* achievable and desireable. These conditions have not been satisfied. The Soviets reject a limited war strategy in the belief that a "limited" nuclear war against Soviet territory would portend an unlimited one. Fearing an all-out attack and believing significant advantages to accrue from a first strike (e.g., C^3I attacks), the Soviets would likely commit all of their nuclear forces.

Political warfighters must also recognize that objectives could change with the course of battle and cease to be limited. First, political and territorial objectives could grow with success (Halperin 1963:8–10). For this very reason, the distinction between "deterrence" and "compellence" is important:[13] The Soviets might more readily forego gains (deterrence) than concede them (compellence).[14] In other words, the Soviets might revise their objectives around a new status quo, particularly one that must be maintained for reasons of credibility and prestige. "Usually the party who already possesses something will value it higher than another who covets it" (Snyder and Diesing 1977:25). Second, objectives could grow more open-ended when political stakes increase with failure or when goals change with sunken costs or with the intensity and scope of the conflict (Smoke 1977:14, 24). It should be remembered that "peace with honor" in Vietnam became a U.S. objective only after U.S. forces were mired in combat.

Like pure warfighters, political warfighters read Soviet motives into Soviet deployments.[15] They might believe that assessments of an adversary's intentions are "more subjective, tenuous, and faulty than our conceptions about the size and quality of his military forces," yet "the opponent's military capabilities are the best clue we have to his intentions" (see Brodie 1966:86). Unlike pure warfighters, political warfighters (cognizant of the symbolic utility of weapons and their many uses) recognize that Soviet weapons can serve a variety of objectives, and unlike assured destruction advocates, they are predisposed to reject the arms-race thesis for its emphasis upon misperception and Soviet defensive motives. Nevertheless, political warfighters are unable to define the Soviet threat with the clarity necessary to guide weapons acquisition.

THE ROLE OF THE CONCRETE: THE EFFECTS OF CAPABILITY UPON INTENTIONS

Warfighters often build a case for U.S. deployment upon Soviet acquisitions. They are thereby open to the assured destructionist charge that they read too much into Soviet capability, that they confuse Soviet capability with Soviet objectives. Because warfighters work with ambiguous, inconsistent, evidence, they can impose upon it their judgments about Soviet intent. They are not alone in this. Assured destruction advocates must also deal with less than definite evidence when they support the arms-race thesis. They too overinterpret evidence when they claim Soviet deployment to be a reaction to U.S. deployment. Capability is a fragile basis upon which to judge intent. [16]

Warfighter unclarity about Soviet objectives has left them susceptible to concrete, nonstrategic influences. Warfighters are open to the charge that they have indiscriminately embraced weapon systems that emerge from the military research and development process, that they base their strategy not on the actual Soviet threat but upon the weapons technology of which the United States can avail itself.

Assessing Soviet Weapons Deployments

This section examines the problems entailed in capability interpretation by, first, examining the problems in applying the arms-race model and the rival "capability-as-intentions" model, [17] and, second, examining the manner in which the intelligence community has actually dealt with assumptions about Soviet intent in Soviet threat estimates. This section thus reveals the highly concrete terms in which the policy community addresses intent.

This section testifies to the role of the abstract *and* the concrete. This section demonstrates how abstract assumptions about Soviet intent have colored estimates of future Soviet weapons deployment. It does not argue that proponents deliberately falsify or distort the evidence, but that their assumptions determine how they interpret evidence. This section also reveals the limited (concrete) manner in which policymakers address the issue of Soviet intent and thus how policymakers are bound to their existing conceptions by the concrete.

The Arms-Race Model

Application of the arms-race model requires assumptions or "rules" to guide the selection of evidence. The rules that are actually used are not always explicit and, unfortunately, are even devised after the fact.

Rules are necessary to distinguish the primary from the incidental or irrelevant features of the U.S. and Soviet military forces (even if these rules do not guarantee that the correct features will be analyzed). An incorrect selection could bias conclusions. For instance, reductions in U.S. equivalent megatonnage and self-imposed launcher ceilings appear to invalidate the arms-race thesis, but these reductions were inspired by qualitative U.S. weapons improvements that actually increased U.S. target-coverage capability.

The problems of distinguishing important from unimportant behavior are multiplied by the use of highly aggregate data. Aggregation simplifies analysis by reducing the number of force characteristics. Nevertheless, because aggregation can be conducted in a number of different ways (weapons can be grouped, for example, by their explosive yield, specified mission, and constituent technology), it is by no means a substitute for judgments about what it is that is "racing."

Military expenditure data exemplify the problems of aggregate data:[18] First, aggregate data must be expressed in the proper units. Dollar cost is an inadequate measure of a weapon's military contribution. For instance, strategic bombers cost more to maintain than do land-based missiles, belying the actual strategic significance of these weapons. Second, aggregate data might need to be disaggregated. Some parts of the defense budget are more sensitive to parts of an adversary's defense budget than are others, e.g., "defensive" expenditures might be a response to adversary "offensive" spending. Third, aggregate data must be expressed in the correct form. Relative (and not absolute) spending might be the actual basis of an arms race. Relative spending measures, however, exist in a variety of forms, and each has distinct implications: Changes in the burden that military expenditures place on the national economy (military expenditures/GDP) could be important; if the Soviets are spending "till it hurts" and are foregoing necessary capital improvements and other expenditures, the military burden could be a sign of the severity of the Soviet military buildup. (Even here, caution is in order, for the Soviets must expend proportionately higher shares on the military to counter absolute U.S. economic advantages and, as some argue, compensate for an inefficient economy.) Departures from a "norm" or "baseline" could be appropriate when conflict processes are studied (Goertz and Diehl 1986), and expenditure growth rates could be significant when adversaries react not to the status quo but to changes in it.

Rules are also necessary to define arms-race patterns. An arms race is commonly conceived to be an imitative pattern—a pattern of reciprocal and symmetric action—but any number of other arms-race patterns can be conceived.[19] For example, a U.S. led arms race could arguably exist even if subsequent Soviet actions do not match U.S. actions in kind or degree, if Soviet and U.S. actions are not proximate in time, if Soviet actions follow U.S. actions only at irregular intervals, and if the Soviets at times fail to act. Put somewhat differently, "the action-reaction hypothesis' emphasis on tightly-coupled, specific, offsetting reactions to particular weapons seems less important, even in logic, than a loosely-coupled, general competition in which each nation pursues broad strategic objectives that may be readjusted periodically, to some extent in light of forces assembled by the enemy" (Allison 1974:39). The complexity of the arms race is found in the relationship between current U.S. interest in missile defense and Soviet advantages in ICBM throw-weight and numbers of warheads: a Soviet quantitative advantage inspired an offsetting U.S. qualitative defensive response—a response that requires considerable lead time and might not even lead to deployment until well after the Soviet threat had materialized (and had possibly receded). The complexity of the arms race is also apparent when a single action inspires multiple responses or when multiple actions lead to a single response. U.S. Polaris missile deployments induced offsetting Soviet investment in antisubmarine warfare and eventually an enlarged submarine-launched ballistic missile force, yet Soviet sea-based ballistic force expansion was also spurred by the Soviet failure to devise a reliable land-mobile ICBM to offset Soviet land-force vulnerability (Berman and Baker 1982:56–63). The arms race is made even more complicated by anticipatory actions. The United States and the Soviet Union spend heavily to determine the range of likely future technological threats and the deployments that result could actually precede the threats that they are designed to meet. It has been noted, for instance, that Soviet attempts to develop an ABM system preceded U.S. ICBM deployment, that Soviet missiles introduced during the U.S. missile buildup of the sixties were developed in the fifties (Meyer 1984:258), and that Soviet weapons require on average seven to ten years to advance from the design to the prototype stage (Berman and Baker 1982:2–3).

Assumptions about arms races must reference the conditions, comparative advantages, traditions, and strategies of the adversaries involved. These factors determine the adversaries' relative sensitivity to each other's force improvements and thus the character of the arms race that could result. For instance, geographical factors can dictate the nature and velocity of an arms race. Because of geographically determined range requirements (and Soviet technological deficiencies), the Soviets spurned bomber production (in favor of ICBM deployment) despite the large size of the U.S. bomber force; and because of their geographical proximity to the European theater, the Soviets are bound to be more sensitive to nuclear weapons in Europe than is the United States.[20] Doctrinal and resource asymmetries also impact on an arms race.[21] Because of these asymmetries, the United States in the sixties looked to a secure deterrent force for freedom from the need to respond to Soviet short-term quantitative force improvements.

In the final analysis, all applications of the arms-race model suffer one critical deficiency—they cannot definitively establish causality. Coincident armament cannot be absolutely distinguished from competitive armament, and neither can be absolutely distinguished from provocative action. What some see to be a first move can be seen by others to be a second and by still others to be not a move at all. A situation in which adversaries seek superiority is, in an absolute sense, indistinguishable from one in which the parties desire to preserve or establish an equilibrium. The Soviet seizure of an "advantage" across a number of strategic force indicators in the seventies is no more conclusive of Soviet aspirations for supremacy than the accelerated pace at which the Soviets deployed missiles in the sixties. Force improvements can always be justified in the name of conservative force planning and damage limitation.

The "Capability-as-Intentions" Model

The "capability-as-intentions" model is predicated upon the assumption that weapons systems betray their purposes. As such, the model exhibits the same limitations as does the arms-race model—the appropriate methods for measuring Soviet capability and the intended purposes of this capability are not immediately apparent. But this model goes beyond the arms-race model and finds meaning in the quantity and quality of Soviet deployment itself.

Some assured destruction advocates are inclined toward the arms-race thesis and thus argue against U.S. deployments that they believe will destabilize deterrence and that the Soviets will misread as a hostile act. They might therefore believe missile defense, invulnerable forces, bombers, long-range cruise missiles, and submarines to be good and believe area defense, MIRVs, accurate warheads, strategic antisubmarine warfare, hardened command and control, and land-based missile dependence to be bad. These assured destruction advocates often emphasize the danger of a false reading of deployment, e.g., an attempt to achieve a first-strike capability, over the significance of the deployment itself.[22] Warfighters, in contrast, find force level and composition, in and of themselves, to be meaningful.[23]

Warfighters are more inclined to embrace the capability-as-intentions model. In doing so, many warfighters overstate the distinction between offensive and defensive weapons. In the eighties, they view defensive weapons as just that—a force of stability, peace, and independence; they see offensive weapons, in turn, to be instruments of change, empire building, and even aggression. These warfighters are by no means consistent in this distinction, though,[24] and they tend to judge Soviet weapons differently than those of the United States. They often treat certain weapon systems as if they are "inherently" dangerous only when in Soviet hands. Reagan administration officials thus extolled the purely "defensive" nature of U.S. strategic defense in the claim that it will provide a "better and more stable basis for deterrence" but interestingly also claimed that Soviet defensive deployments, if left unanswered, will lead to the "collapse of deterrence" and leave the United States "no choices between surrender and suicide" (see U.S. Department of Defense 1985b).[25] Elsewhere they note that "if the USSR in the future were unilaterally to add an effective advanced defense against ballistic missiles to its offensive and other defensive forces, it would pose a very serious new threat to U.S. and allied security" and yet also profess a desire for a greater U.S. reliance upon defenses "that threaten no one."[26] The contradiction in this logic is symptomatic of the larger problem of inferring intent from capability—the "facts" are only suggestive and leave much room for interpretation and thus judgments and biases of the analyst.

Warfighters also tend to overstate the distinction between Soviet countervalue and counterforce weaponry and treat the latter as if they are first-strike or preemptive weapons.[27] This distinction is even less firmly grounded than the previous one. What are ostensibly "counterforce" or "countervalue" weapons could be assigned any of a variety of tasks because of redundant targeting requirements, because technology has not yielded weapons designed optimally for a single task, and because inherent within supposed countervalue missions are counterforce tasks and vice versa. With respect to the latter point, "counterforce" weapons could be employed to suppress air defenses and open corridors for countervalue bomber attacks and "countervalue" weapons could be used against cities to militarily defeat the enemy. The distinction between counterforce and countervalue weapons is no more supportable than the distinction between the "force" and "value" targets to which they are supposedly directed—and, as chapter 3 demonstrates, the latter distinction is tenuous at best. Warfighters appreciate this when they recognize the counterforce potentials of virtually all Soviet weaponry.

The capability-as-intentions thesis invites the application problems of the arms-race model as it requires a "reading" of capability. Pure warfighters are more likely than political warfighters or assured destruction advocates to read intentions into behavior. Pure warfighters generally believe that the Soviets, in war, will employ their forces to the fullest extent warranted by calculations of advantage; they are thus most concerned about the possibility of a disarming Soviet first strike and they, more than political warfighters, anticipate Soviet efforts to incapacitate U.S. strategic command and control. Political warfighters, in contrast, assume that the Soviet Union might terminate a conflict short of its immediate objectives; they are less convinced that the level and composition of Soviet forces necessarily betrays a Soviet willingness to use those forces.

In any case, the capability-as-intentions thesis emphasizes what the Soviets have done rather than what they have not done. As Meyer (1984:261) notes, it fails to pose critical questions: "Are the Soviets really doing their best to build up their military power? Couldn't they spend more and buy more? . . . Could not the Soviets have invested more wisely to maximize military power?"[28] Pure warfighters are not likely to ask these questions, for to answer them they must acknowledge factors such as interest group competition, organizational inertia, military tradition, competing domestic priorities, and variable leadership preferences that affect Soviet deployment and therefore detract from a view of the Soviet Union as an unrelenting menace. For instance, pure warfighters see the Soviet preference for land-based missiles as the most compelling indicator of a Soviet strategy of preemption, but the Soviet ICBM preference partly reflects a historic Soviet appreciation of the value of the artillery for blunting conventional land attack.[29] In sum, Soviet policy does not appear optimally suited to expansionist objectives when the limits of Soviet deployment and the complex of factors that influence it are recognized.

The bottom line is this: warfighters focus on the "what" and "how" issues of Soviet capability at the expense of the "why" issues of Soviet objectives. As the next section shows, policymakers consistently seek to validate their assumptions about Soviet objectives in the concrete world; yet they employ only indirect tests that cannot effectively challenge those assumptions.

Intelligence Estimates

Intelligence controversies from the fifties through to the eighties reveal more than just heroes and villains within the U.S. intelligence establishment—who was right and who was wrong. The debates demonstrate that even in the intelligence business, evidence cannot be divorced from the abstract assumptions that analysts hold about enemy intentions. Assumptions about Soviet motivation determine not only how the evidence is interpreted but what is selected as evidence; the difference between an accurate and inaccurate forecast is not necessarily in the rigorousness and exhaustiveness of the process by which evidence is collected, screened, and evaluated. Nonetheless, the intelligence controversies also demonstrate the limits of evidence. Concrete evidence is disconnected from the abstract and cannot occasion a necessary reevaluation of beliefs about Soviet objectives.

Intelligence controversies are a study in bureaucratic politics. The Air Force and later the Defense Intelligence Agency (DIA) adhered to a particularly pessimistic abstract view of the Soviet adversary; they believed the Soviets to be driving toward military preponderance. Despite the bureaucratic role of these abstract conceptions of Soviet objectives, the concrete remained at the center of controversy.

The question of whether U.S. intelligence organizations have held a generally optimistic or a pessimistic view of the Soviet adversary is in itself a matter of controversy. Wohlstetter (1974) generated a maelstrom of controversy when he offered evidence of a consistent U.S. underestimation of Soviet strategic deployments and particularly Soviet ICBM deployments throughout the sixties. U.S. intelligence organizations were repeatedly surprised by the intensity of the Soviet nuclear buildup, and these organizations latter overcompensated for these earlier misestimates. Virtually all U.S. intelligence organizations underestimated total levels of Soviet missile deployments—actual deployments consistently exceeded even the highest, longer-range (four-to five-year) national intelligence estimates that were offered in the mid- to late sixties (Berkowitz 1985a).[30] Only in the early sixties did even the highest near- or long-term forecasts in the annual posture statement of the Secretary of Defense exceed the actual level of Soviet deployment (Wohlstetter 1974). The Wohlstetter position was argued strenuously by those concerned about U.S. complacency in the face of an apparent massive Soviet military buildup. Nevertheless, more recent estimates show intelligence organizations to have presented far from a sanguine view of Soviet military efforts.

Simplistic numerical presentations do not do justice to the predictive track record of the intelligence agencies. They highlight predictions that were wrong rather than those that were right by putting too much emphasis on aggregate counts. Intelligence agencies misestimated total deployments because of the unexpected Soviet decision not to dismantle aging SS-7 and SS-8 missiles (Prados 1982:198). Further, they more accurately predicted SS-9 deployments even if they underestimated SS-11 deployments; the unexpectedly high deployment of SS-11 missiles most contributed to the inflated Soviet weapons total. This is important because the SS-9 was a more sophisticated missile than the SS-11. The SS-9 could carry a larger payload more accurately over a greater distance and was expected to be the launcher for the Soviet MIRV, which was then under development, and only the SS-9 possessed the combination of yield and accuracy to serve in a counterforce role. The Soviets could have deployed the SS-11 merely as a quick fix to their quantitative inferiority in land-based missiles and might even have believed the SS-11 to be a stabilizing force given that the SS-11 was best suited for a countervalue (and hence retaliatory) mission (Freedman 1977:115).[31]

In other instances, optimistic assessments were on target. In the sixties, the intended scale of the Moscow ABM system under construction and the intended purposes and capabilities of a set of defensive complexes that were dubbed the Tallinn line were subjects of great controversy. The CIA correctly predicted that Tallinn could only defend against bomber attacks and that the Moscow ABM system was unlikely to be geographically extended. In the early seventies, the CIA maintained that the SS-9 had not yet achieved MIRV potential and, on this score, battled the DIA, the Air Force, and the White House. This assessment was validated by the first appearance of a Soviet MIRV in 1974 on a very different launcher (the SS-19).

The intelligence debates of the sixties centered on interpretation rather than on information—even to the extent that principals shown to be wrong sought to keep issues alive by redefining them. Rivalry among the intelligence organizations was redirected to the issue of SS-9 MIRV potential once a slowdown (albeit temporary) occurred in SS-9 deployment, and the Tallinn issue became one not of current system capability but of whether the system could be upgraded into an ABM network (Freedman 1977:93).

The evidence was ambiguous and left considerable room for judgment.[32] CIA predictions were therefore shaped by assessments of Soviet intent. Intelligence analysts could argue that the Soviets sought only a minimum deterrent (given overwhelming U.S. strategic preponderance) and would later accommodate increased Soviet deployments by asserting that the Soviets sought only parity and then, later, simply a small numerical advantage (Prados 1982:192). The defense intelligence agencies were no more dependent on the physical evidence in Soviet deployment predictions. Thus all of the intelligence organizations maintained fairly consistent positions throughout the sixties—the Air Force, for instance, continuously submitted the highest estimates of future Soviet missile deployments (Berkowitz 1985:586). Air Force estimates were closest to actual Soviet deployment levels, but the Air Force position most certainly reflected a greater pessimism about Soviet intentions and capabilities and not a better reading of the facts.

Assumptions about Soviet intentions were particularly important to the "missile gap" predictions of the late fifties (in which estimates were unduly pessimistic) and, accordingly, the evidence was freely interpreted. Working assumptions were always immediately at issue, but the underlying issue was consistently Soviet intent. The CIA attributed a lull in Soviet missile testing to poor weapons performance; the Air Force believed the slowdown indicated that the Soviets were ready to commence production. The Army and Navy treated the absence of the SS-6 (the first Soviet ICBM) from U-2 photographs as evidence that the missile had not been deployed, while the Air Force assumed the opposite. The Army and Navy claimed that the size and range of the SS-6 restricted the places where it could be deployed (i.e., proximate to railways and within only certain geographical regions), while the Air Force asserted that the SS-6 could have an effective range beyond that revealed on the test range. The Army, Navy, and CIA assumed that launch sites have clearly recognizable features; the Air Force disagreed. But the Air Force could not directly support its claims of an imminent missile gap. It based its predictions upon assessments of the Soviet ability and *willingness* to channel resources for this purpose (Freedman 1977:70–80).

The role of presumptions about intent are obvious from the diametrically opposed conclusions that were drawn from the same evidence. The Air Force, Army, and DIA challenged the CIA assessment that the Tallinn system had only a modest capability. The CIA believed that the limits of the Tallinn missile, the Griffon, were confessed by the Soviet introduction of a technologically more advanced missile, the Galosh, into the Moscow system. But CIA critics argued that the Galosh signaled an even greater Soviet commitment to ABM (Freedman 1977:92).[33] Shortly thereafter, the CIA battled critics over whether the observed Soviet flexibility in targeting multiple warheads, as displayed by the weapon's variable "footprint," constituted a MIRV capability. Optimists could point to the limits to Soviet targeting flexibility while pessimists could point to the gains.

The intelligence estimates of the sixties are particularly controversial because the sixties saw the superpower arsenals assume their present form and because of the rapidity of the Soviet buildup. But controversy over CIA assessments was not a relic of the sixties, and in the seventies

concerns over SALT "giveaways" and revelations about CIA underestimates galvanized concerns that the CIA had maintained too charitable a
view of Soviet motives and capabilities and had failed to duly weight
evidence that contradicted this view (see, for example, Sullivan 1980).
The controversy often centered on highly technical issues, such as the
techniques by which the CIA calculates Soviet military expenditures,
and the CIA accommodated these criticisms by altering its methods and
thereby boosting its estimates of Soviet military expenditures in dollars,
the growth rate in Soviet military expenditures, and the Soviet defense
burden (Lee 1977; Kaufman 1985). However, the vitriolic tenor of the
debate and the predictable manner in which the participants chose sides
suggests that the controversy involved more fundamental issues than
methodology.

The military expenditure debate continued. The immediate points at
issue changed, but the overall arguments did not. Protagonists selected
indicators and accordingly aggregated and disaggregated data for their
consistency with assumptions about Soviet conduct.

In the early eighties, the CIA estimated the growth rate in Soviet
military spending for 1976–1981 to be around 2 percent a year, determined that the Soviet military burden had not increased in the 1970–
1981 period as originally thought (remaining at 13 to 14 percent), and
determined that the Soviets had reallocated their expenditures in favor
of research and development over weapons procurement (Kaufman
1985:179).[34] Others, though, were more impressed with the relentless-
ness of the Soviet military buildup. Reagan administration officials resisted evidence of a spending slowdown, and the DIA was slow to accept
these downward trends (Gordon 1986). By the mideighties, the CIA and
DIA had narrowed their differences, but they again diverged significantly
when the DIA insisted that Soviet procurement costs were rising while
the CIA maintained that these costs had flattened out.[35] Nevertheless,
Department of Defense publications[36] placed emphasis on the high absolute and relative levels of Soviet military spending, amounting to a
Soviet military burden of 15 to 17 percent by the mideighties, and a rate
of Soviet military spending in excess of the now slow rate of Soviet
economic growth.[37] While not denying the downward spending trends,
these publications obscured them. These publications stressed the phenomenal growth in Soviet military investment, an aggregate budgetary
category that includes military construction, procurement, and research
and development, trumpeted the growth in Soviet research and development expenditures as heralding future procurement increases, and
pointed to increases in the procurement of specific weapons; and just as

these publications had "erased" trends through category aggregation and disaggregation, they could "create" them through the manipulation of time frames by treating the previous decade as a whole. Spending gaps that had been closed were attributed to compensatory increases in U.S. military spending.

Controversy also engulfed strategic nuclear forces, and it showed once again the impact of abstract assumptions upon interpretations of evidence. The Reagan administration allegations that the Soviets had failed to comply with treaties that restricted the testing and deployment of strategic weapons were rebutted by administration critics who were generally more impressed with the Soviet record of treaty compliance (a record that included weapons deactivation and dismantlement).

The Reagan administration was particularly troubled by the Soviet deployment of the SS-25 missile, which the administration claimed was a "new type" missile and was thus impermissable under SALT.[38] The administration maintained that the large dimensions of the SS-25, particularly in throw-weight, meant that, contrary to Soviet claims, the missile could not be a modernized version of the SS-13 and, furthermore, that the SS-25 reentry vehicle did not account for the required 50 percent of missile throw-weight.[39] Others believed that the case against the Soviets was not clear-cut and faulted ambiguities in the definition of throw-weight within the SALT treaty.

The Reagan administration also accused the Soviets of "impeding" verification of the SALT treaty by encrypting "telemetry"—the radio signals monitored in missile tests—thereby preventing the United States from gauging the actual capabilities of Soviet missiles. No one doubted that encryption had occurred, but administration critics questioned the illegality and the seriousness of this Soviet practice. Critics could again fault treaty ambiguities by noting that SALT prohibitions on "impeding" verification fell short of an encryption ban. Moreover, they noted that encryption had not prevented the Reagan administration from establishing the critical dimensions of the SS-25, and the administration refused to divulge its specific data requirements. (Administration defenders asserted, in response, that the United States cannot reveal its information needs without divulging U.S. intelligence strengths and weaknesses, that the United States cannot know if data are missing until it has access to encrypted telemetry, and that signal encryption might impede access to information necessary for future verification of treaty compliance.)

The Reagan administration also alleged that the Soviets had ("potentially," "probably," "likely," or "actually") violated the ABM treaty by, among other things, constructing a large phased-array radar at Krasnoyarsk,[40] acquiring mobile ABM system components, concurrently testing ABM and air defense components, acquiring modern SAM systems with an ABM capability, and developing ABM launchers with a "rapid reload" capability (see U.S. Department of State 1987). The administration asserted that these efforts suggested that the Soviets could be preparing an ABM defense of its national territory.

The evidence was interpreted differently by others: the Krasnoyarsk radar, though recognized by all parties in the U.S. debate to be in technical violation of the ABM treaty, was claimed to be a cost-efficient means for securing early-warning coverage, incorrectly placed and pointed for "battle management," and highly vulnerable to attack and susceptible to "blackout" in a nuclear environment; the ABM components were argued to be "mobile" only when measured in many months, stretching the very definition of this term; the Soviet SAM missiles that had been concurrently tested were denied to be ABM-capable; the point at which antitactical ballistic missiles become antistrategic missiles and when a test of the former becomes a test of the latter was believed ill-defined; and, while Soviet ABM systems have a reload capability, it was claimed not to be "rapid" enough to matter.[41]

The CIA remained a central participant in nuclear weapons controversies. The CIA played a role in the debate on Soviet noncompliance with the ABM treaty as well as the 1974 Threshold Test Ban treaty when it contradicted the administration's assertions on Krasnoyarsk and adjusted its estimates of the regional geological bias by which the yield of Soviet weapons explosions is judged. The CIA also undercut the administration by downplaying the counter-silo capability of the Soviet SS-19 (Keller 1985), maintained lower range estimates for the Backfire bomber, claimed that the Soviets could easily deploy much greater numbers of warhead in the absence of SALT constraints, presented more modest assessments of Soviet progress in laser and particle-beam weapons, and was more sanguine about the prospects for verifying an arms control treaty that permitted long-range mobile missiles.[42] Furthermore, the CIA clashed with the DIA on crucial issues that included Soviet noncompliance with the ABM treaty (Krepon 1987) and the size of the Soviet SS-20 intermediate-range missile force. With respect to the latter, both agencies based their assessments on counts of the "garages" in the field that housed missile launchers and transporters, but the DIA (even with unexpectedly large increases in the number of such garages) offered a higher assessment of the number of SS-20s that the Soviets would produce per launcher. Soviet disclosures after the 1987 signing of the INF treaty suggest the DIA to have grossly overestimated Soviet SS-20 totals (Pincus 1987).

Once again, the intelligence controversies show that assessments of adversary intent color judgments of the evidence—the evidence is always ambiguous and leaves room for interpretation and bias. The debate has centered on technical issues (what the Soviets *could* do), but evaluation of technical assumptions is not isolated from assessments of objectives (what the Soviets *would* do). Assumptions about objectives can directly intrude upon the evidence to determine which set of technical assumptions is adopted. For instance, assessments of whether the Soviets have the factory capacity to support force modernization must reflect assessments of the strength of competition for the scarce resources employed in weapons production; assessments of resource constraints, in turn, can be biased when evidence is dismissed, discounted, distorted, or selected to support a preexisting view—evidence about the Soviet leadership's commitment to the civilian sector, the costliness and complexity of future Soviet weapons, the economic contribution of resources made available for civilian use, and so on. Even answers to the most technical questions can be influenced by the predisposition of the analyst. For example, conclusions about the range of the Backfire bomber can be controlled by estimates of such things as its flight altitude and the number of weapons it will carry (Gordon 1985).

This is not to say that the intelligence debates of the eighties were really debates about Soviet intent, that independent, "objective" analysis is impossible, or that intelligence organizations are merely self-interested or dogmatic. The signs are that strategic threat assessment within the intelligence establishment has become less polarized and politicized; with this convergence of viewpoints, the intelligence organizations certainly agree more than they disagree on the fundamentals of the Soviet threat. Both agencies agree, among other things, that the sheer size of the Soviet procurement budget is a more important threat indicator than budget changes of a few percentage points. Nonetheless, it is not unfair to say that the DIA, for instance, has been more pessimistic in its assessments of Soviet intentions and behavior than the CIA and that the relative optimism or pessimism of these organizations affects their assessments—their positions have remained too consistent for it to be otherwise.

The effects of intentions upon assessment are more obvious in the public debate since attention centers on broad policy questions (that follow from threat assessment). Reagan administration charges of treaty noncompliance were certainly open to challenge, but the administration's position became even more tenuous when it assessed the implications of the alleged violations. This was apparent, for instance, when the administration charged that the Soviets were preparing to "break out" of the ABM treaty: Most of the alleged Soviet violations were in "gray areas," were militarily insignificant, and fell far short of the massive effort required to secure a nationwide defense. The administration could be correct in its assertions, but only because its conclusive judgments dominated the inconclusive evidence.

The intelligence controversies thus testify to the major role in strategy played by conceptions of Soviet objectives, a role unique among the abstract components of strategy. This should not obscure the critical role played here by the concrete. Abstract assumptions about Soviet intent unquestionably fuelled the intelligence controversies of recent decades and were validated by the concrete, but these controversies raged in the concrete and could not then elicit a reevaluation of Soviet objectives.

The debates over the interpretation of concrete evidence did not lead the intelligence organizations to alter or refine their views of Soviet objectives. The defense intelligence organizations consistently assumed that the Soviet Union is an implacable adversary that is carefully, coherently, and deliberately marshaling resources on behalf of maximum objectives. These organizations could easily maintain their position because of the way that they managed the concrete. The military was not alone in this.

In general, the concrete issues of the period (future Soviet missile deployments, Soviet military spending, Soviet treaty noncompliance, and Soviet weapons capability) were more salient than the abstract ones (U.S.-Soviet doctrinal asymmetries and the sources of Soviet foreign policy). Abstract issues were conceived in concrete terms; the questions of the time were conveniently distant from the more fundamental issues to which they pertained. Even if protagonists were inclined to modify their views of Soviet objectives, the matters of controversy were never close enough to the basic issues to warrant it.

Technological Inducements and Constraints

U.S. strategy could indeed be shaped by weapons developments—that is, U.S. weapons at least as much as Soviet weapons. Warfighters are particularly receptive to new U.S. weapons technology: political warfighters are swayed by new technology because they have a poor sense of the Soviet "threat"; pure warfighters are susceptible to technology because they believe in a virtually unlimited Soviet threat.

This sections shows, first, that technology creates its own imperatives and, second, that it can converge with organizational and bureaucratic interests to become an even more powerful force. In either case, it can shape strategy and conceptions of the Soviet threat.

Technology Without Politics

Weapons research and development (R and D) is not necessarily subordinate to strategy, and it can serve as a significant policy inducement and constraint. This section provides two different but somewhat complementary views of the impact of technology.

The Technological Imperative. Technology can drive the weapon procurement process regardless of strategy, changes in administration, operational requirements, or domestic political considerations (Lapp 1970). To put it simply, weapons are often improved and deployed because they can be improved and deployed. This dynamic is variously termed technological *drift, creep, determinism, imperative, exuberance* (McNamara's term), and *drive.* Technological drift involves incremental change—systems are upgraded (and even "overdesigned") through the cumulation of modest and relatively inexpensive changes, many of which draw upon "civilian" technology (e.g., the guidance systems on commercial aircraft). Weapon changes occur because they appear to those immediately concerned to be undramatic, technical in nature, and consistent with current practice—it is hard to oppose weapons that offer increased speed, mobility, accuracy, and range. Nevertheless, these qualities are purchased without an appreciation of the trade-offs among them and at the expense of weapon reliability and operational effectiveness. These qualities can come together in weapon systems that promise so many things that remaining unnoticed is their inability to deliver proficiently on any one.

Decisions to upgrade technology are made by a large number of Pentagon research and development agencies and offices without high-level intervention.[43] High-level oversight could not easily be achieved, even if it were desirable, for "the lengthy process from which weapons emerge involves hundreds of important, relatively independent decisions that no one political official can possibly oversee" (Allison and Morris 1975:123). Oversight is also complicated when these decisions are in essence "nondecisions" and "do not crop up in a 'yes-no' form at all" (Gelber 1974:521). Such decisions are virtually automatic and are accepted uncritically—indeed "it is hard to imagine . . . the project engineer loath to incorporate improvements, or the military planning officer who does not want a system to work more smoothly, accurately, or faster"

(Shapley 1978c:289). For this reason, the technological imperative appears to have had particularly crucial effects on the development of the U.S. strategic command and control system (Ball 1981:8). Command and control improvements have been directed at system protection, sensors for warning and damage assessment, information processing, and greater system responsiveness—efforts that merely seem to improve information acquisition and system efficiency and thus seem inherently noncontroversial. As with other military technology, "the important question is not 'whether' to introduce technical innovations but 'how to choose' from a wide assortment of possibilities, what the costs will be, and how fast to proceed" (Greenwood 1975:14).

Examples of apparent technological drift abound. The multiple warheads that were deployed on Polaris submarines in the early sixties were an outgrowth of warhead penetration aid R and D. MIRV also had origins in existing technology:[44] the propulsion system of the MIRV warhead-carrying bus,[45] the techniques for postboost trajectory realignment, the missile inertial guidance system, and the capability to launch multiple objects from a single booster all drew from the U.S. space program (Tammen 1973:81–95). Similarly, missile accuracy improvements were made possible by solid-state electronics and computer microminiaturization, more sophisticated guidance systems, increased knowledge of the physical forces effecting missile trajectories, and the acquisition of better submarine position-fix technology and terminal-guidance systems (Shapley 1978a:1102–1104). Moreover, cruise missiles largely owe their existence to the development of small, efficient engines and weapons and terrain-contour-matching guidance systems that were designed years before for other purposes (Betts 1981:3–4).

The Technological Constraint. The impact of technology assumes a second form at higher levels of policymaking. Available technology sets the terms of the strategic debate by determining how issues are defined —the questions that are asked and how they are phrased. Whatever the immediate point of controversy, issues reduce to a simple yes-no choice and are not treated as opportunities for reevaluation or redirection of policy. These numerous illusory choices could well account for the eventual profusion of cruise missiles types and deployment modes (i.e., air, land, and sea). They could also explain the U.S. development of the H-bomb (the "super," as it was then called): fusion weapons were deployed despite resistance from those who felt the bomb would be a drain on A-bomb production and would give the United States a redundant rather than a new capability;[46] deployment became almost automatic when

Truman refused to decide on anything more than matters of immediate concern so as to leave future options open (Schilling 1961; Stein 1984).

When weapon deployment issues surface, policymakers do not regard them as opportunities to reevaluate or redirect policy.[47] Available technology carries weight *because it is available* and can be promoted as an answer to an existing strategic problem or future problems that, by nature, remain immune from careful scrutiny. It also carries weight because less is known about alternative technology and its effects. Available technology is the basis of a "satisficing" solution (a solution that is "good enough," but not the best) where the attributes rather than the purposes of the technology are at issue. Thus the strategic debate "tends to get organised around the vices and virtues of particular weapons systems rather than around particular roles or missions" (Freedman 1977:128). Or the debate centers on secondary questions—not "whether" to base, but "how" to base the MX missile. Controversy centers not on the question of deployment but the means of deployment—lesser questions of numbers and modes.

This second view of the impact of technology does not deny the existence of bureaucratic politics. Wholesale policy reevaluations and redirections are certainly precluded by bureaucratic politics: all participants in the political process have turf that they want protected, old wounds that they do not want reopened, and intragovernmental understandings that they want preserved. Nevertheless, this view of technology is indifferent to much of what is central to bureaucratic politics—the sponsorship, stewardship, and politicization of a weapons concept. This view is not concerned with why and how issues emerge, but deals with the fact of their emergence (even if belated) at the highest levels of policymaking. But as with bureaucratic politics, this view centers on decisional constraints and the limits of choice—choice that centers on an existing alternative. Available technology constrains choice because it can augment existing forces and address identified deficiencies in force capability and is more salient than nonexistent technology or nontechnological alternatives.

Departing from the first view of the technological impact, technology here is more a constraint than an inducement; it limits rather than seduces. Technology offers the narrow context in which decisions are made rather than weapons concepts that appear inherently beneficial. The impact of technology, then, is not just felt "around the edges" of existing weaponry as modest shifts in weapons technology. Technology can affect change through decisions and nondecisions at all levels of policymaking.

As with the technological imperative, however, technology itself remains at issue. Policymakers consider the attributes of weapons technology within a void; they think about what *should* be done in terms of what *can* be done. "(R)equirements are most often written with specific hardware systems in mind" (Spinney 1985:108). Technology even instills urgency, as "(t)he use of exotic technologies implies the existence of major strategic problems" (Weida and Gertcher 1987:152). Consequently, strategy again plays a subordinate role in the weapons debate (and suffers because of it): Strategy does not direct weapons acquisition and serves only to ratify previous weapons choices. For this reason, contemporary strategic doctrines that feature counterforce and a protracted nuclear warfighting capability were inspired by the prospect of improved weapons accuracy and command and control at least as much as these doctrines fueled further weapons acquisition.[48]

Conceptions of Soviet intent are particularly liable to weapon influences: U.S. policymakers presume that the Soviets will certainly employ a weapon that has been shown effective and technically feasible. It is a strange irony that U.S. weapon development and deployment could lead U.S. policymakers to worry about *Soviet* objectives.

Technology with Politics

Technology can be swept into politics when organizational and bureaucratic interests create premature closure on a weapon concept. New technology is seized upon and promoted as a coherent weapon package. Under these conditions, the impact of technology is governed by the power, purposes, and interests of its advocates.

The political view of technology emphasizes invention and decision rather than incremental change.[49] Technology merely provides opportunities for exploitation and, as such, is a necessary but not sufficient condition for weapon deployment.[50] Some ideas find their way into weapon systems while others do not, and these systems could assume any one of a variety of forms.

Defense contractors are interested in selling new weapon ideas and promote them in the form of a weapon system: funding is more likely when a concrete end product, addressing a clear military need, is envisaged, for R and D that falls short of generating products is generally regarded to be a wasteful failure (Brooks 1975:91). Once conceived, the basic specifications of a system remain intact because of the economic realities of the defense industry: contractors attempt to rapidly move from research to development and then to minimize the delays and inefficiencies in the shift from development to deployment.[51] Even if contractors desired modifications in product design or established requirements, the fractionation of the development process (i.e., components must be independently developed) precludes it; significant modifications in one weapon component could make it incompatible with others.

The prevailing weapon concept is often protected and steered through the acquisition process by a variety of political interests. These interests see any concept reevaluation as a threat to their own part of a weapons package and to the coalition upon which the survival of the package is dependent.[52] These interests value weapons for their political worth (e.g., a means to achieve more organization funding or prestige) rather than for their military contribution.

A weapon concept is often embraced by a particular military organization. Military organizations define security around a key organizational mission, e.g., control of the seas, strategic bombardment, that is linked to a particular weapon capability, e.g., a carrier-based Navy, a strategic bomber force. Air Force resistance to the development of the ICBM in the early fifties is illustrative of this. The Air Force maintained a strong commitment to the manned bomber to accomplish its valued strategic attack mission despite opposition from civilian experts, defense contractors and Air Force R and D personnel. The Air Force was indifferent to ballistic missiles except to claim them to fight the encroachments of rival services; when the Air Force could not afford indifference, it combated these missiles with overly stringent technical requirements (i.e., weight and accuracy) and optimistic assessments of bomber advantages in cost, reliability, and effectiveness (Beard 1976).[53]

The cruise missile was also overtaken by competition shaped by rival organizational missions. Cruise missiles were sought initially by civilian Defense Department personnel, with resistance from the Air Force and Navy. The Air Force and Navy regarded these missiles to be a budgetary threat to weapon systems that were more closely associated with traditional service missions. The Air Force perceived the cruise missile, with its long-range stand-off capability, to be a threat to the deployment of the defense-penetrating B-1 bomber, the carrier Navy opposed the cruise missile when it recognized the missile's potential as an antiship weapon that could increase the role of the rival surface fleet, and the submarine Navy was concerned that the cruise missile would compromise its antisubmarine warfare mission and was at best unnecessary given the SLBM.

The story of the cruise missile, then, is not just one of the allure of technology. Technology made the cruise missile possible, but did not determine eventual missile specifications or missions. Missile range and deployment mode were determined through the interplay of competing interests. The purposes of the cruise missile were thus left vague: it was not clear whether the missile was to be a strategic, theater, or tactical weapon, whether it was to remedy the deficiencies of strategic bombers or to substitute for vulnerable land-based missiles, or whether it had a military or a political purpose (e.g., to reinforce the U.S. NATO commitment, to execute limited nuclear options) (Art and Ockenden 1981).[54]

Narrow political considerations have dominated other weapons deployment decisions. ABM was championed by the Army, in the sixties, as a population defense system (despite the limited effectiveness of ABM in this mode) because the Army feared that ABM would be usurped by the Air Force if deployed for hard-target defense (Allison and Morris 1975:117). The Johnson administration decision on ABM was equally political, recording the influence of contending interests. The administration decided to deploy a thin population defense against China as a compromise between the full-scale Soviet-oriented ABM deployment that was favored by the Army, the JCS, and elements within the Department of Defense and the no-ABM deployment position of Secretary of Defense McNamara. The administration hoped to satisfy domestic political opponents who clamored for deployment so as to close an "ABM gap," to placate military critics by not restricting deployment to silo defense or foreclosing the possibility of an extensive anti-Soviet deployment, and to signal to the Soviet Union that the United States was willing to pursue unilateral options should the Soviets be less than forthcoming in arms control negotiations (Halperin 1974:297–310).[55]

Technology, then, is the essence of a narrow, concrete conception of security even when coveted and cultivated by various political (defined here to include economic) interests. These interests case their purposes in abstract terms: pessimistic assessments of the Soviet threat, the acquisition of a warfighting capability, and so on; but these interests survive in a world of concrete referents: routinized procedures, budgetary considerations, organizational missions, and favored weapon systems.

Of Strategy, Arms Races, Technology, and Politics:
Discerning Impacts on Policy

This chapter deals with a variety of influences upon policy—strategy, arms races, technology, and politics. These influences are not easily distinguished in practice.

For one thing, "military policy is overdetermined by several alternative and analytically coequal explanations" (Kurth 1971:378).[56] The deployment of the Thor and Jupiter IRBMs in the fifties appears to reflect the technological imperative. These two IRBMs were deployed even though they were to become quickly outdated with the development of solid-fuel missiles and even though these two missiles shared the same basic engine and warhead design and both relied upon an inertial guidance system. Moreover, Thor components were adopted from the Atlas (ICBM) program, and Jupiter capitalized on intensive research and actual successes in weapons design. Nevertheless, the deployment of Thor and Jupiter is more correctly linked to arms-race dynamics and strategy. The Eisenhower administration anxiously sought a quick fix to perceived strategic imbalances created by Soviet advances in the missile field (as signaled by the Soviet Sputnik success) by supporting multiple programs as insurance against adverse program developments and favoring reduced missile deployment time over technological innovation.[57]

For another thing, military policy is "underdetermined" in the sense that "no one major explanation or causal theory or even a combination of them is sufficient for confident 'a priori' prediction" (Kurth 1971:379). The consequences of any one theory are not explicated in advance of testing to make legitimate tests of a theory possible.

It is easy, then, to pick and choose evidence solely to support a preexisting viewpoint, and it is difficult to devise an exclusive and definitive test of any given thesis. For instance, the arms race can conceivably accommodate any evidence.[58] An arms race can be pictured as if it were a product of a unique set of determinants when it appears as if it "runs slow, fast and even appears to stop for periods," or else it could be viewed as "a series of often severely time-lagged, broad-fronted, almost lurching responses" (Gray 1976:102–105). Alternatively, an analyst could attribute weapons deployment to strategic utilities that would apply to just about any weapons system (e.g., a "bargaining chip" for arms control negotiations) or to the always visible bureaucracies that are involved by necessity in the weapons acquisition process.[59] Without advance indications of what evidence constitutes a disconfirmation of a theory, any evidence could be interpreted so as to confirm it. The analytical problem is worsened when the actual sources of deployment are camoflauged by a plethora of contrived *post-facto* program justifications—when decisions are made to look more rational than they actually were.

MIRV illustrates the problems of determining influences upon policy. MIRV is an interesting case because it cannot be conclusively or exclusively attributed to a single source:

MIRV had a strategic justification.[60] MIRV was promoted as a highly cost-effective means for increasing U.S. target-coverage capability: it could enhance counterforce through a multiple-shot capacity, it could outperform decoys in the penetration mode by forcing the expenditure of defensive weapons and placing more weapons on target, and it improved force survivability by increasing the number of warheads available for retaliation and thereby compensated for U.S. force size and throw-weight disadvantages (Greenwood 1975:101–102,125). MIRV seemed to be a viable strategic response given the opportunities, constraints, and threats of the period, and this was evidenced by the absence of significant bureaucratic hurdles or substantive opposition to it, the extent of McNamara's personal involvement in the program, and the centralized management of the MIRV R and D process (Greenwood 1975:14,35,48).

MIRV deployment also appears to have been a product of the arms race.[61] MIRV was promoted as a means for saturating Soviet defenses as the Soviets acquired a rudimentary defense capability and fear was generated that the Soviets would accelerate ABM R and D.[62] In fact, multiple warheads had always been developed with an eye to Soviet defense: the Polaris missile had been designed so that its nonindependently targeted warheads would achieve a separation distance to prevent their destruction by a single interceptor, and MIRVs were scaled down in size and hardened and Minuteman III throw-weight was increased (so that more warheads and penetration aids could be carried) because Soviet countermeasures were anticipated (Greenwood 1975:97–98,100).[63]

MIRV also seems to support the technological imperative thesis. Given the blinding allure of technology, "in many ways MIRV was a misfit, not the optimum saturation vehicle, not the optimum targeting vehicle," and other programs at the time offered either a more effective defense penetration or a hard-target kill capability (Tammen 1973:117). Furthermore, MIRV strategic liabilities went largely unnoticed. MIRV created problems for verification of arms control compliance and U.S. force survivability by placing more warheads in single launchers and thereby increasing the Soviet marginal return from attacks upon them (creating the ICBM vulnerability problem of the eighties). Further supporting the technological drive thesis, MIRV would eventually evolve into an accurate counterforce weapon despite the earlier assurances of MIRV proponents that it would not.

The evidence also supports the bureaucratic politics thesis: The services had their own reasons for falling into ranks behind MIRV. MIRV provided the Navy a means to offset the Air Force numerical advantage in Minuteman missiles and allowed the Air Force to bolster target-coverage and counterforce capability (given the unlikelihood of additional Minuteman procurement)[64] (Tammen 1973:88–89; Greenwood 1975:38–39).[65]

A lack of definitive evidence also bedevils attempts to discern the reasons for Soviet deployment.[66] For example, the tendency of each Soviet design bureau to produce weapons that are variants of those produced by other bureaus, along with the evolutionary character of Soviet weapon deployments, suggest that the highly institutionalized Soviet R and D process is governed by technological drift, but this same evidence could point away from technological drift. "It may be . . . that the redundancy here is more apparent than real, and that the weapons designs either started with different missions or acquired new missions during the acquisition process." Moreover, incremental change could actually be a bureaucratic political outcome where (despite the preferences of the military) innovation is stifled by a cumbersome Soviet weapons decision process in which competing interests participate. Or innovation might not be obvious as such—Soviet developers are not rewarded for "fancy designs" and "commonality in the use of subsystems and components," and the use of existing technology is encouraged. (Holloway 1986:141–147.)

This does not mean that the sources of weapon deployment are exclusive of one another. Indeed, they are somewhat complementary:

First, these forces sometimes interact. The deployment of the H-bomb was spurred by the availability of technology, but deployment was also influenced by arms-race dynamics (coming soon after the first Soviet A-bomb test), strategic concerns about the implications of Soviet sole possession of thermonuclear weapons, and bureaucratic contestation over the merits of these weapons. A similar interaction of forces is found on the Soviet side, as a number of different factors set the design characteristics of Soviet weapons. For instance, the Soviets have sacrificed strategy to the arms race. The SS-11 missile appears to have been designed for a naval mission, but the Soviets eventually selected it (because of its survivability and variable-range capability) as a land-based missile to match (or so it seems) U.S. Minuteman deployments (Berman and Baker 1982:54–55,60).

Second, these forces can work in causal succession. Uncertainty about adversary intentions and force directions could inspire the research and development process, but once set into motion, the process could assume a life of its own, producing technological spinoffs. The civilian space program that produced MIRV technology was a direct result of the Soviet *Sputnik* launch (York 1970:145), suggesting that MIRV had at least an indirect grounding in U.S. security perceptions. Moreover, the increased target-coverage capability that gave MIRV a strategic justification in turn owed its existence to enhanced U.S. satellite-reconnaissance capability in the improved capability to locate and identify Soviet military force targets. MIRV was not an anticipated by-product of reconnaissance improvement, but it can be attributed to the technology that made additional targeting possible.

In the end, understanding is encumbered when proponents narrowly attend to what a thesis can explain and ignore what it cannot. The technological imperative, for instance, appears to account for some U.S. nuclear deployment, but this imperative, in and of itself, cannot account for the number of instances where the United States failed to deploy available weapon systems—antiballistic missiles, intermediate-range ballistic missiles (in the period between the deployment of Pershing II and the withdrawal of Jupiter and Thor), cruise missiles (when they were first found technically feasible), and so on.

Admittedly, the history of science testifies to the contribution of those who doggedly adhered to an idea despite contrary evidence, widespread skepticism, and even condemnation. But this cannot excuse strained or sloppy thinking. Understanding is impaired when explanation is coupled with contrived post hoc arguments, an indiscriminate assessment of evidence and an unwillingness to consider opposing points of view.

CONCLUSIONS

Assumptions about Soviet objectives are perhaps the most salient of the abstract components of deterrence thought, this because these assumptions reflect basic beliefs about international politics and have ideological import. Nevertheless, these assumptions remain largely underdeveloped and contradictory and are not a solid basis for strategy. Moreover, these assumptions owe much to the concrete. These conceptions are consistently validated by Soviet weapon deployments and persist because concrete Soviet threat assessment effectively says little about the abstract.

Some assured destruction advocates find the notion of an arms race to support their thoughts about Soviet objectives, and warfighters are inclined to judge Soviet objectives by the style and intensity of Soviet deployment. In neither case does Soviet deployment "speak for itself," leaving assured destruction advocates and warfighters to impose their respective beliefs about Soviet intent. Policymakers address issues in the concrete, but these issues cannot be tied directly to Soviet intent.

Warfighters have other concrete inspirations. They are as easily swayed by available U.S. military technology as they are by Soviet weapons deployments (particularly if the Soviets already possess the military technology at issue). The upshot is that warfighters cannot say no to new weapons and inevitably feature them in strategic debate—they respond to the virtues and narrowly conceived purposes of these weapons rather than broad-based analyses of the consequences of deployment.

Admittedly, it is hard to trace the influences on U.S. strategy. The very factors that allow policymakers to freely interpret evidence of Soviet objectives impede evaluation of the sources of U.S. policy. Clear rules for the interpretation of evidence are not available.

5

STRATEGIC PROCESSES: RATIONALITY AND NONRATIONALITY

SOME STRATEGISTS assume that deterrence is primarily maintained and undermined by rational influences; other strategists highlight the influence of the nonrational. The first part of this chapter examines the abstract assumption that deterrence has a rational basis, while the second part assesses the argument that deterrence requires, though not exclusively, the nonrational. Both parts show abstract logic to be contradictory.

This chapter also presents the concrete solutions by which strategists cope with the critical abstract dilemmas that they identify—means such as "escalation dominance" and "escalation control" and strategic command and control and the methods of credibility enhancement. This chapter shows these solutions to be inadequate because they fail to address these abstract dilemmas, duly consider the nonrational, and adequately reconcile the rational with the nonrational.

RATIONALITY

The assumption of rationality—"a calculating, value-maximizing strategy of decision" (Schelling 1960:17)—is inherent in much of both abstract and concrete deterrence thought. Abstract logic, while faulty, suggests a critical paradox to which concrete solutions have failed to respond. These solutions are also deficient in a number of other respects, most particularly in their inattention to the nonrational and their failure to recognize the nonrational as such—where the *nonrational* refers here to misperception, miscalculation, miscommunication, uncertainty, and the loss of decisional control.[1] Importantly, rationality and nonrationality can coexist[2]—for two reasons: First, nonrationality does not necessarily preclude rationality. Nonrationality assumes a variety of forms and varies in degree.[3] Uncertainty, for instance, can be rigorously addressed in the rational calculation of "probabilities" or "risk." Second, nonrationality can be rationally manipulated to advantage. For both reasons, strategic theorists and policymakers believe that nonrationality enhances deterrence.

Rationality in the Abstract

Much of strategy at least implies that strategic decisionmakers are rational. Formal theories and common conceptions of deterrence alike suggest that decisionmakers can be dissuaded from engaging in actions that pose an unacceptable risk and/or cost. Decisionmakers are depicted as being guided by prioritized objectives, as being aware of the trade-offs among these objectives, and as recognizing the conditions that threaten and facilitate the realization of these objectives, and when action is necessary these decisionmakers are depicted as being aware of available alternatives and their respective consequences and as choosing the course that provides maximum satisfaction.

Rationality and Its Limits

Humans are not omnipotent, and thus the decision process is not an exhaustive one. Decisionmakers miscalculate, exhibit bias, act out of emotion, and are slow to process information, which must always be incomplete. This comes as no surprise to many strategic theorists and policymakers who presume that decisionmakers exhibit limited rationality.[4] "You will not feel the need for deterrence without some initial doubts or mistakes as to the enemy's intentions, plans, and capabilities" and "he will not have planned attack and yet now be deterred without having initially misjudged your intentions, plans, and capabilities" (Morgan 1977:81).[5]

Although cognizant of the inadequacies of the human thought process, theorists and policymakers have found it useful to retain the rationality assumption and depict a decisionmaker who follows the right steps even if lacking grace and completeness of motion. Nevertheless, critics charge that the notion of "partial rationality" is a veritable contradiction in terms and maintain that the assumption of rationality must either be accepted or rejected. For them, the issue is not whether the nonrational impedes a deterrence process that is otherwise rational—that is, whether the logic of deterrence is incomplete. The issue is whether the logic of deterrence is fundamentally flawed: "It is one thing to approach deterrence in terms of rational decision making and then introduce irrationality and ambiguity as elements that complicate its application and limit its effectiveness . . ." and "quite another to introduce irrationality and ambiguity to explain how deterrence often works . . . for this questions the initial simplifying assumptions of the theory" (Morgan 1977:126). This argument can be stated more strongly: "No qualification of the notion of rationality can be fitted into deterrence doctrine and leave that doctrine standing whole as an explanation of the successful avoidance of nuclear war . . . ," for "if it is diluted with any really non-rational propositions, its logical structure, at least, must begin to collapse" (Green 1966:164).

Rationality in Strategic Policy

Most policymakers do not participate in this abstract debate and show little tolerance for explicit theorizing. But they do cling to the assumption that they and their counterparts abroad are rational, at least under some conditions, and offer the policy implications that ensue. Thus assured destruction advocates believe that an ability to impose unacceptable cost is sufficient to deter the Soviet adversary and warfighters feel threatened by a Soviet limited war capability that could permit combat at less than unacceptable cost.

Warfighter concerns are captured in the long-recognized "stability-instability paradox"—"the greater the stability of the 'strategic' balance of terror, the lower the stability of the overall balance at its lower levels of violence" (Snyder 1985:226). Warfighters suggest that in the age of parity the chances of war ironically have increased. They argue that contrary to standard assured destruction logic, rationality proscribes a second rather than a first strike (on this, see Kahn 1961; Steinbruner 1976:231). In other words, they maintain that a first strike is rational because it could be launched with impunity if it were limited in scope and yet large enough to constrain retaliatory options. The sole remaining option would be an irrational one—revenge. Such a strike would, in effect, leave the defender with "more to lose," but no viable options "between suicide and surrender."

Rationality, in the form of the stability-instability paradox, is at the root of warfighter fears of limited Soviet counterforce attacks in the absence of a U.S. capability for a less than all-out response—a response that would leave the attacker worse off than it was before the initial strike. But the paradox also informs the assured destruction stance. Assured destruction advocates (and warfighters) look to the paradox in arguing for conventional force deployments to deter a conventional Soviet attack (see Bundy et al. 1982:765).[6] Although these assured destruction advocates reject the argument that the balance of terror increases the chances of limited nuclear war, strangely enough, they act from fear of a strictly conventional U.S.-Soviet confrontation.

Few would take comfort in the implication that the Soviet Union has failed to attack because it is not rational. They cannot imagine how deterrence could be maintained with a malevolent adversary that is incapable of appreciating the costs of unremitting hostility. But assured destruction advocates and political warfighters turn to the assumption of nonrationality to defend their doctrines when they attend to the "credibility" of policy. The concept of credibility (treated here as a product of A's perception of B's capability and its willingness to use it) is at the very core of a nonrational perspective on deterrence because credibility only becomes an issue when policy is without a rational basis—that is, when the costs of that policy are disproportionate to its benefits: "In a world of relatively rational decision makers, if state A's goals, capabilities, and cost/benefit calculations are such that it would be rational to carry out its threats if B attacks, then A has no credibility problem" (Morgan 1977:85). Credibility becomes an issue if prior cost/benefit assessment leads B to doubt whether A can or will deliver as promised and A is therefore forced to manipulate B's perceptions.

Strategic advocates freely mix rational and nonrational explanations for behavior. Assured destruction advocates often stress the need for a credible deterrent, but most do not greatly fear that the Soviets will miscalculate and blunder into a confrontation with the United States. They believe that the stability of deterrence largely resides in the U.S. possession of an assured destruction force and are not too concerned that the Soviets will misjudge the adequacy of U.S. capability. Paradoxically, all warfighters are concerned about the logical implications of the stability-instability paradox, yet many also fear that the Soviets will misjudge U.S. intentions. They suggest that rationality can be "fine tuned" in the form of a Soviet nuclear attack that is carefully conceived and executed and yet fear that Soviet superiority on a few simple measures of the strategic balance could induce a Soviet attack (on this, see Morgan 1977:59–60). For their part, pure warfighters believe that a Soviet decision to initiate strategic nuclear war rests on cost/benefit calculations and argue that the United States must not then allow the Soviet Union a capability advantage, yet because they fail to specify Soviet wartime objectives they leave open the possibility that Soviet means might not rationally correspond to Soviet objectives. Advocates have not recognized these inconsistencies as an opportunity for policy reevaluation.

Rationality in the Concrete

The issue of rationality in strategy has increasingly assumed center-stage in the policy debate. Warfighters justify attention to rationality by reference to its troublesome implications in the form of the stability-instability paradox. But they inject an ironic twist. They offer solutions that are designed to increase the level of rationality in the decision process. The rationality that they promote is of a "mechanical" or "technical" nature, and it resides in their proposals for "escalation dominance" and "escalation control" and their proposals for improved command and control of nuclear forces. Warfighters tend to treat the stability-instability paradox as a hardware or management problem, but their solutions fall short as long as an all-out nuclear war remains a losing proposition.

Escalation Dominance and Escalation Control

Early recognition of the dilemmas posed by the so-called balance of terror led to recommendations for a "graduated deterrence" that would restrict means "to the minimum level which still permits [the United States] to achieve [its] objectives" (see Nitze 1956:188). This reasoning resurfaced with a vengeance in the seventies in proposals for "escalation dominance" and in the altered form of arguments for "escalation control."

Both warfighting strategies require flexibility in policy. Pure warfighters stress escalation dominance, the notion that the United States must at a minimum be capable of inflicting defeat at higher levels of escalation than can the Soviets and is often assumed even to require that the United States be capable of inflicting defeat at any level at which the Soviets can initiate combat.[7] Pure warfighters conceive of nuclear weapons as military instruments and covet these weapons for the physical damage that they can inflict. Accordingly, they are attuned to the rational basis of deterrence.[8] In contrast, political warfighters stress escalation control and thereby the dissuasive capacities of violence. As they attend to perception (and thus, by implication, "misperception"), they are sensitive to the nonrational antecedents of deterrence. Notwithstanding their fundamental differences, both types of warfighters believe that decision-makers can rationally control nuclear war outcomes.

Political warfighters promote means that would establish escalation control in combat. The principle of escalation control assumes that "thresholds" serve to limit the escalation of conflict;[9] thresholds, in turn, are the points around which combatant expectations converge and are thus the basis of tacit bargaining.[10] Thresholds derive power from their prominence and visibility, and they reflect characteristics of the political, social, and physical environment that individuals find meaningful—characteristics that appear "distinctive, finite, discrete, simple, natural, and obvious." Thresholds exist by merit of "qualitative" characteristics (Schelling 1960:77) that can be found in weapons, geography, targets, and combat participants. They are the basis of the distinctions between conventional and nuclear combat, tactical, theater, and strategic weapons, and counterforce and countervalue attacks.[11] Thresholds delineate a symbolic boundary that when crossed requires a new frame of reference for permissible acts. They are not imposed, nor are they purposeful—"we don't make them or invent them, but only recognize them" (Schelling 1966:135–138)—and they require consensus as to their existence.[12] In the absence of consensus, a difference in kind to one participant might appear to be a difference in degree to another: political warfighters may define a threshold between tactical and strategic weapons use,[13] but the Soviets could regard the explosion of hundreds of NATO tactical nuclear warheads with more trepidation than the launch of a small number of U.S. strategic weapons.

The notion of a threshold suggests that combatants can better control outcomes between classes of behavior than within a class of behavior. Combatants are carried along by the inexorable force of competition until they bump up against a threshold and its perceptual opportunities for restraint. Therefore, while escalation can be influenced by both the rational and nonrational, the nonrational (in the form of perceptually based thresholds) facilitates conflict management and can propel the conflict spiral.

In contrast, the principle of escalation dominance suggests the notion of a "firebreak," an idea that fits comfortably with the pure warfighter perspective. A firebreak, unlike a threshold, connotes an obstacle to conflict intensification that has a material (rather than psychological) existence.[14] Pure warfighters strive for unilateral or imposed limits to conflict rather than limits that stem from consensus or agreement, implying that limits have a basis in "reality." These limits differ from perceptual thresholds in two important respects: First, they appear substantive, conceived as if they reside in the characteristics and physical location of weapons and targets themselves, and second, they are static, endowed with a prior status rather than one conferred by such things as the changing course of battle, the specifics of a situation, or the given origins of a conflict. This does not mean that pure warfighters ignore miscalculation or intangibles like "resolve," but it does mean that they expect combat to transpire within an established, stationary context shaped by military factors and calculations of advantage. Pure warfighters, therefore, emphasize the controllability of nuclear violence and deemphasize the inherent threat of escalation. In this, though, they are not unlike political warfighters who emphasize the characteristics of conflict participants over conflictual processes that can overtake those participants, and fail to recognize that important war limiting opportunities could reside within the peculiar context within which conflict occurs (e.g., the "rules of the game"). For all of these warfighters, escalation and deescalation simply amount to a matter of strategy—"a unilateral 'act' of specifiable individuals and institutions, an independent and conscious decision to commit a certain kind of action and the deliberate execution of that decision" (on this, see Smoke 1977:21). [15]

Pure warfighters shy away from the idea of a threshold because it implies that some weapons are not "usable" and contradicts their historic view of nuclears as "just another weapon." They judge weapons by their military rather than symbolic utility and believe that the Soviets do the same. They therefore imply that the Soviets seek cheap victories and will attempt to win at the lowest level of violence at which victory is possible. [16]

Escalation dominance, unlike escalation control, has exclusively a rational basis. Neither side will escalate a conflict that they know they cannot win. Pure warfighters cannot contradict themselves on this point without destroying the logical consistency of their argument. Such contradictions can occur once pure warfighters acknowledge that a combatant can lose a war that it initiates, that conflict can escalate to levels at which no side enjoys a meaningful military advantage, or that the weaker party will resist at the level of violence at which it is attacked. Pure warfighters might allow for these contingencies when recognizing that combatants can miscalculate, underestimating the resolve and capabilities of their opponent. Nevertheless, by doing so pure warfighters edge dangerously close to the political warfighting position that deterrence requires the manipulation of risk.

Escalation dominance and control do share one fatal deficiency, however. Neither directly confronts the central implication of the stability-instability paradox: a combatant can always escalate a conflict to constrain its adversary.

Command and Control

Warfighters assume that deterrence requires that the United States have at its disposal an apparatus that is capable of providing and assessing critical warning and attack-outcome information, is responsible to the authorized command, and permits the pursuit of the widest variety of options. In other words, warfighters have directed that the United States acquire and secure the implements for the prosecution of a protracted nuclear war. As this search has centered on the acquisition of computer software, sensors, and secure and survivable communication links, it has left its pursuers open to the charge that they "have embarked upon a . . . fruitless quest for the secret keys to nuclear crisis management," a narrow preoccupation with the "external environment" of policymaking at the expense of psychological, sociological, political, and strategic considerations (on this, see Lebow 1987:18–19).

As with the strategic defense debate, the purveyors of command and control divide between the technical optimists and those who recognize the advantages of such a system but appreciate its poor prospects for survival in a nuclear environment. Because no one believes the optimal system to be currently in hand, it is useful to: first, catalog the threats to effective command and control that could lead at one extreme to system breakdown and, at the other, to precipitous escalation and, second, to assess built-in political limitations to command and control, for the structure of even the most technologically sophisticated and integrated network reflects the limits imposed by fundamental political trade-offs and constraints.

Concern for the operational requirements of protracted nuclear conflict has led to an ever more "vertically" and "horizontally" integrated system of command and control—that is, the integration of nuclear weapons with warning and intelligence and centralized nuclear war planning (Bracken 1983:6–7). The result has not been a completely coherent and comprehensive system. This should have been expected given that an end product is usually no more rational than the process by which it is conceived or constructed. C^3I has been the orphaned or estranged child in the defense community and has suffered the traditional fate of programs deprived of budgetary control and statuatory authority. C^3I programs have had to compete with more seductive, service-coveted offensive weaponry for a share of the defense budget (Latham and Lane 1987:645–647). When identified as "national" programs, they are without powerful advocates; when controlled by the various nuclear services, they have been an adjunct to service "missions" rather than responsive to the requirements of the central command (Blair 1985:57–67). Central policy guidance has traditionally played only a minor role in shaping the overall command and control system. "The lead-times for the design, development and deployment of modern sophisticated command-and-control systems are such that the rare periods when the guidance has been clear enough have generally been too brief for any systematic overall relationship to be effected." System development has been "burdened by 'ad-hocery' " and has been shaped primarily by requirements for enhanced routine communications capability, deficiencies exposed in various crises, changing threats, and the availability of new technologies (Ball 1981:3,6).

The command and control system is a highly elaborate network of command posts; communication systems that span the radio spectrum and thereby employ diverse means such as relays (e.g., airplanes, satellites) and electromagnetic echoes between the earth's surface and the lower ionosphere (i.e., extremely low frequency waves); satellite-based sensors that aid attack assessment through the detection of such things as the flash and the electromagnetic pulse of nuclear explosions and can provide both strategic warning (through photoreconnaisance and electronic intelligence gathering) and tactical warning (in combination with ground-based and airborne radar). Nevertheless, the existing command and control system suffers from major deficiencies.

Technical and Organizational Solutions and Problems

The problems and requirements of protracted nuclear war have inspired three sets of solutions — "redundancy," "predelegation," and system "complexity." All suffer inadequacies and are either unable to deal effectively with a number of important technical and practical problems or else create new ones.

Redundancy. The key to enhanced system survival is the redundant network of links and nodes that is reliant upon a wide variety of physical principles. The system is composed of numerous command centers that include the National Command Authority, consisting of "the President and the Secretary of Defense or their duly deputized alternates or successors" (Bracken 1987:363), and can now operate from its Pentagon, underground, ground-mobile, or airborne locations (the National Emergency Airborne Command Post and the airborne military command posts of the commanders in chief).[17] The system also contains multiple launch-control centers, including the hardened underground Minuteman centers that share the capability to launch each squadron of ICBMs and airborne launch-control centers that can launch these missiles with the incapacitation of the ground-control centers. Communication is facilitated by a variety of satellites, ground-based broadcast installations, and communication relay planes for contact with strategic bombers and submarines. But critical nodes remain and vulnerabilities persist. The appropriate question is not whether the system is survivable, but for how long.

Nuclear weapons can inflict lethal effects on command and control in a number of ways, and defensive compensation for some of these effects can increase vulnerability to others. Command and control is vitally dependent on systems that are "inherently large, fixed and soft" (Ball 1981:9)—early warning radar, ground-based terminals, airborne command posts, and communication relay planes are vulnerable to blast in an initial Soviet attack; when airborne, planes can be disabled through fallout and blast-generated dust and turbulence and can function only as long as their potentially scarce fuel supply will allow;[18] satellites can be spoofed, blinded, and destroyed; antennae, electrical wiring, and power and telephone lines, among other things, make parts of the command and control system the "most efficient collectors of EMP" (Ball 1981:11); and radio communications can be jammed and are vulnerable across the radio spectrum.[19]

Predelegation. Military planners have therefore devised a system to make decapitation more difficult. The military relies upon "predelegation" to assure both the execution of a coordinated response and the minimum level of destruction required to deter a Soviet attack. The system is not heavily dependent on wartime guidance from the central political or the military leadership: it provides for multiple centers of authority and devolution of command to safeguard against the loss of any or all the major political and military command centers.[20] The system requires the expeditious predelegation of release authority, and a command system that can behave coherently even when segmented from attack and its surviving parts[21] cannot directly coordinate their actions.

Predelegation is built into the very structure of the command and control system. Various conditions and practices pass control of weapons to the strategic forces themselves, and in time of nuclear combat forces cannot, and would not, realistically be made to deviate from standing plans. Reprogramming would be proscribed by, for instance, the day-to-day isolation of submarines from the external command network; the need to keep a weapon within the overall war plan so that a weapon will complement rather than interfere with the performance of others; security precautions that prevent submarines on alert from engaging in two-way communications; the limits to the survival of a weapon in a combat environment; the inability to monitor comprehensively and in "real time" weapons launches and inflicted damage; the vulnerability of nuclear command and control and the inability to halt the launch of ICBMs in "terminal countdown" or of airborne launch control centers to monitor the status of Minuteman missiles under their control. (On the constraints on weapons control, see Ball 1981; Blair 1985; Carter 1987a.) For a number of reasons, then, strategic forces could be left (intentionally or unintentionally) to carry out prewar instructions despite the changing preferences of the military and political commands (to the extent that they even remain constituted as such).

This technical predelegation significantly inhibits flexibility and creates the conditions that could lead to the massive, uncontrolled launch of U.S. strategic weapons. Submarines are particularly culpable in this respect. A submarine can fire its missiles selectively, but to do so could prematurely betray the submarine's position or strain the endurance capacity of command and communications. Each submarine might be ordered to fire its reserve of a minimum of well over a hundred warheads, then, rather than risk the loss of its payload in an attack[22] or the loss of communication with missiles left unfired. The other legs of the strategic triad are also structured with a bias toward an all-out response. The ICBMs that contain radio transmitters for relaying the messages that could order massive attack by U.S. land, air, and sea forces are within the most vulnerable part of the triad. If these transmitters are to be employed it must be early, yet this would undermine controlled escalation (Ball 1981:23, 41). Bombers cannot be long sustained in flight and will be increasingly vulnerable on the ground. They too must be used early if they are to remain a coherent force (Carter 1987a:587). In all, deficiencies and constraints combine to create a situation in which "the ability to countermand orders or to disengage forces could be very tenuous" to the point that "it is possible to imagine an intra-war pause or armistice being nullified by such deficiencies" (Ball 1981:7).[23]

It cannot be assumed that predelegation acts solely as a lag in the system, merely activating earlier war plans. Formal predelegation could actually charge those in operational control of the weapons with the initiative for action. It is impossible to predict how those authorized (or even enabled) to use nuclear weapons would behave when deprived of communication with the strategic or theater commands. For example, to the crew of a strategic nuclear submarine isolated from worldly events all the world may look at peace. Even with knowledge of an attack on the

U.S. homeland, in the absence of direct launch orders the inclination might be to "watch" the conflict unfold. On the other hand, the bias could be toward SLBM launch. Soviet conventional antisubmarine warfare could appear to the submarine crew to be part of a larger Soviet counterforce effort and thereby indistinguishable from a Soviet attack on U.S. Minuteman silos.

Tactical nuclear weapons provide another illustration of the problems of predicting the behavior of those who have been predelegated launch authority. The United States maintains control of NATO tactical nuclear weapons under the so-called dual key arrangement by which the United States retains custody of the warheads and a host nation controls the launchers. In peacetime, warheads are stored in a few vulnerable locations, and the U.S. command will likely feel compelled to disperse these warheads and release authorization codes early on in hostilities so as to ensure the timely availability of these weapons for forward defense. Nuclear land mines, artillery shells, gravity bombs, and surface-to-surface and air-to-surface missiles could then be distributed to a myriad of commands and subcommands. The various forces that would acquire control of these weapons are conventionally oriented, are connected by a potentially fragile system of command and control,[24] differ in national composition, training, and military practices (Bracken 1983:140, 157), and would differ in encountered battlefield conditions. The dispersal of thousands of tactical warheads, rather than increasing the options of the central command, could thus have the opposite effect, amounting to a tacit surrender of control to local commanders. As with nuclear submarines, there is the ever-present possibility that those "enabled" to use nuclear weapons will assume launch "authority" (on this, see Carter 1987a:589).

Predelegation of authority is also built into the command and control organizational structure. The military has largely designed current options, and it is more than likely that they reflect parochial military viewpoints and concerns. When the military creates options: "They shape them in terms of standard operating procedures and tailor them to service capabilities and preferences. The resulting plans are likely to maximize traditional military objectives at the expense of precision, flexibility, control, or other values that political leaders will come to consider critical in crisis" (Lebow 1987:77). In the creation of options, policy development passes for implementation. This problem is aggravated when sanctioned procedures are bypassed so that the organization can perform its assigned tasks. "Such rule shortcutting is likely to be oral and informal and therefore invisible to outside observation except under the high-stress conditions of actual war or crisis" (Bracken 1983:12–13). Practices that permit optimal peacetime performance could hurt the war effort (particularly if their presence was unknown to the military command). In this regard, it should be noted that the military has emphasized peacetime over wartime performance in procurement by favoring satellite communication capacity over satellite protection (Blair 1983:205).

Political leaders have long been ignorant of the standard operating procedures that govern military operations, and it is unlikely that leaders could compensate for their knowledge deficiencies in the intense confusion of a strategic nuclear war.[25] Time compression would allow limited opportunity for inventiveness or trial and error. Political leaders would be highly reliant upon the military command for the selection of options and would probably become even more reliant as the war exacted its toll from the top of the presidential succession list.[26] The military would likely prefer to avoid political interference (given its peacetime predilection toward a "launch-on-warning" policy).

System Complexity. Political and pure warfighting both require the information necessary to obtain targets and assess damage and the capacity to direct appropriate and effective action. These requirements have led to an increasingly complex system of command and control. However, in the very complexity of the desired system lies the greatest potential for system failure.

There are at least four major sources of complexity-induced system failure. First, errors can reverberate throughout the system because it is tightly coupled. A computer malfunction, human error, and the false triggering of sensors have led, in the past, to a heightened alert status and could seriously hamper attempts to sustain a controlled nuclear engagement.[27] Breakdowns in support installations and equipment could have wide-ranging system-disabling effects (e.g., electrical outages). Second, the system is better at safeguarding against the "discrete, isolated failure" than against the compounding of unrelated failures. Compound failures produce interaction effects that defy diagnostics and are likely to create alarm because they will appear to be related. Third, complex systems generate a mix of information that could permit operational flexibility, but could also overwhelm decisionmakers under stress. Fourth, the synergism between the U.S. and Soviet command and control systems could multiply other problems (Bracken 1983:52–67). A U.S. strategic force alert or decision to disperse tactical nuclear weapons could lead to further escalation if it induces an offsetting Soviet reaction.

Political Constraints on Command and Control

The literature on command and control tends to center on technical and organizational issues at the expense of the political. But even a relatively proficient and comprehensive command and control system must operate with political constraints in the form of trade-offs and limits to its scope that will inhibit the effective execution of its tasks.

Trade-offs. A command and control system is constructed with an eye to important trade-offs — the effective performance of one mission results in a diminished capacity to perform others. One widely acknowledged trade-off exists between the twin objectives of "negative" and "positive" control — the former referring to the prevention of accidental and unauthorized launch and the latter to the actual conduct of an attack mission. Strategic forces could be made as responsive as a cocked pistol,[28] but not without an increased risk that these forces will end up "firing at shadows" or accidentally discharging. This is significant because at some point all commitments to use nuclear force are irrevocable (though this point occurs latter for bombers than for ICBMs), and the penalties for a "false start" are obviously considerable. On the other hand, strategic forces can be made absolutely safe only by compromising their ability to perform their missions with the degree of certainty required. If weapons are separated from launchers, launchers are not maintained on alert status (e.g., they require fueling or crews are not immediately available) or weapons are not fully assembled, the system is secure from unauthorized or precipitious use, but these practices will also extend the period in which the adversary can execute a knockout blow and will expand the number of targets that could be hit to accomplish this objective (i.e., attacks on an assembly factory, an arsenal, or a weapons launcher could have an equally disabling effect).

The trade-off between negative and positive control is an ever-present part of strategic command and control planning. It is reflected in the question of who should possess weapons authorization codes and whether submarines should possess the same "permissive action links" that physically prevent an unauthorized ICBM launch or bomber attack. It also frames issues of crisis management. The evacuation of the President, the sheltering of high-level political and military officials, the dispersal of bombers or a mobile-missile force, and an increase in strategic force alert status will all improve operational readiness, but could also create an expectation of war and loosen safeguards against accidental, precipitous, or premature weapons use.

Another fundamental political trade-off exists in the choice between weapons survivability and performance. Weapons systems that are most responsive and versatile (e.g., ICBMs) are unlikely to survive the first round of strategic warfare; those systems, (e.g., submarines) that are most tenuously linked to the central command and blunt in performance would have greater longevity (Steinbruner 1978:421–423). Submarines are particularly illustrative of this trade-off. They are highly survivable but do not yet possess highly accurate weapons. Moreover, they might not be available on demand. Submarines on patrol will not engage in two-way communications, operate at depths that prevent the continuous receipt of radio signals, and might avoid communication rather than risk revealing their position by trailing an antenna.[29] Submarines are also more likely to be swept into tactical engagements that could disable them or at least isolate them for prolonged periods.

This trade-off is of course viewed differently by assured destruction proponents than by warfighters. Assured destruction advocates believe the command links with submarines to be sufficient for the performance of the essential mission—retaliation against Soviet cities. The assessment of trade-offs is not a value-neutral task. Assured destruction proponents do not greatly worry about the survivability of command and control, partly because they believe that strategy ends with a strategic nuclear exchange; the task of the U.S. command is simply to give the one and only "return-fire" order.

Political trade-offs have also shaped the organizational structure of the command and control system. Decisionmakers have had to choose between "centralization" and "decentralization." Under the best of conditions, centralization permits a coherent response, and under less favorable conditions decentralization permits a graceful devolution in system operation and a gradual degradation in system performance. Decisionmakers cannot choose either centralization or decentralization, or both, without cost. In support of decentralization, the civilian leadership could direct the military to follow a specific attack plan in the event of a combat-related communications disruption; or, short of this, the President or his top civilian advisors could detail the likely U.S. plan of attack well before a force engagement. But these actions would infringe upon the wartime prerogatives of the civilian leadership. The military could become overly wedded to an anticipated plan (even to the extent that it shapes the design of other options), and might implement the plan whether or not it fits the circumstances. In support of centralization, the civilian leadership could attempt to maintain flexibility by generating options while deferring choice and the delegation of authority. But any operation that this highly centralized system directs could well be its last.

The important feature of both sets of trade-offs is the precariousness of the middle ground. As the control of tactical nuclear weapons exemplifies, the danger to negative control resides in movement to positive control: "The transition may or may not be centrally directed, orderly, or complete" (Blair 1985:282). Existing negative control procedures may be inadequate or inappropriate at higher alert statuses, though this could go unrecognized as attention shifts to positive control. But neither is the system geared for positive control, since safeguards have not been fully lifted. Similarly, a system that is neither vulnerable nor versatile, centralized nor decentralized, offers the costs of each condition. Resilience is acquired at the expense of central direction and control, and vice versa.

Uncoupled Elements. The United States has integrated all of its strategic forces into the SIOP, including those assigned to NATO, and the long-range quick reaction alert force is under the control of the Supreme Allied Commander in Europe. The hope is that this integration will improve the control of forces in time of a nuclear confrontation. The British and French, however, each retain an independent nuclear deterrent force. Though somewhat integrated into the NATO command structure, these forces could thwart U.S. efforts to achieve a consistent anti-Soviet weapons employment policy. Allied forces, with the exception of the quick reaction alert force, could be withheld or independently employed by their respective national commands.[30]

The British submarine force, when modernized, will be capable of firing the extremely accurate Trident II missile and over five hundred independently targetable warheads. The French possess a diverse force of Mirage jets, eighteen land-based missiles in underground silos, and, most important, a modernizing submarine force that will soon boast almost five hundred warheads. These are not inconsequential numbers. There has been a tendency to dismiss European strategic forces in discussions of the U.S.-Soviet force equation because of the relatively small size of these forces and a long-standing U.S. desire to prevent the Soviets from counting NATO strategic forces with U.S. totals in strategic arms control negotiations. But European forces could dictate the pace, nature, and outcome of a U.S.-Soviet nuclear exchange. Indeed, within the next decade, British and French strategic forces (which are highly survivable given their reliance upon SLBMs) could inflict levels of damage independently that would meet McNamara's "assured destruction" criteria (Prados et al. 1986:36–37).

These damage levels do more than augment U.S. capability. The French are not formally bound to NATO war plans and in public have long objected to the NATO flexible response strategy in favor of the threat of precipitous escalation (Yost 1986). Recent revelations show France, in developing its nuclear force, to have extensively collaborated with the United States and to have somewhat coordinated its nuclear targeting with NATO's (see Ullman 1989). Such cooperation might increase French restraint and lower the risk of a catalytic, preemptive Soviet attack on French forces, but it certainly does not preclude these forces from triggering a more global conflagration. For their part, the British reserve the right to reassign their NATO forces when warranted by their national security. To this end, the British maintain target lists apart from those prescribed by the NATO command and publicly argue that their nuclear forces serve primarily to deter Soviet attacks on Britain.[31] The lack of comprehensive U.S. control of strategic targeting means that a U.S. counterforce employment policy could be undermined by British or French adherence to a countervalue policy.[32]

The Soviet Union could not be certain of the national origin of an attacking force, and even if it could, it might simply presume that British or French strikes were coordinated with American strikes, rendering the matter of origin a simple technicality. British targeting flexibility and coverage will improve with fleet modernization, but it should not be presumed that this reflects a British rethinking of its countervalue strategy. The new fleet capability appears "to have been acquired without any clear sense of how or when, even, it should be employed" (Freedman 1985:96). Differences in allied policies are thus likely to remain.

Impediments to Rationality

The implication of the warfighter critique, in the form of the stability-instability paradox, is that deterrence requires "rational" solutions in the ability to deny an adversary its gains. Warfighters have believed this to require that the United States be able to compete at levels of violence short of an all-out strategic exchange; this, in turn, requires that the United States be able to determine the scope and intensity of Soviet action and to calibrate U.S. action accordingly.

It might not be easy to determine the nature of Soviet action under wartime conditions. The limits of signals pose a direct challenge to political warfighters who must read "signals" in order to judge Soviet intent. But pure warfighters must also come to grips with these limits. Tied as they are to the "rational" basis of deterrence, pure warfighters downplay the importance of signals, but they cannot escape the fact that all actions have symbolic content and do not "speak for themselves."

Political warfighting arguments for escalation control and for developing and extending command and control are often predicated upon the assumption that messages are easily communicated—that signals can emerge unaltered from the "noise" and confusion of the nuclear environment, that signals are endowed with the information content of the intended message, and that the characteristics of the recipient do not affect the way in which a message is conveyed. Nevertheless, signals are given meaning by the context in which they occur. Signals can be distinguished by whether they are "intrinsic" or "extrinsic"—that is, whether the medium of communication is itself the message or whether the signal stands for something else (Cohen 1981:39). The U.S. quarantine line during the Cuban missile crisis intrinsically communicated the U.S. unwillingness to allow the Soviets to further equip and thereby enlarge their offensive missile force in Cuba, but it only extrinsically communicated the U.S. demand that the Soviets forego deployment of missiles already in Cuba and dismantle those that had been deployed.[33] The Soviets could not have misread the first message, but they could have missed the second (in the absence of a verbal explanation). Nonetheless, the meaning of a signal is imparted by things other than the contents of the transaction itself. The same act can mean something else in a different context. Although it has been said that "verbal messages . . . can be contradicted by later verbal messages, while actions tend to be irrevocable . . ." (Schelling 1966:150), in actuality "the meaning of a nonverbal signal is what observing actors understand it to mean" (Cohen 1981:47).[34] The display of naval force off Cuban shores in 1962 could have been interpreted differently in another time and place. For instance, U.S. naval forces have been used more recently to communicate "support" to a beleagured Lebanese government, "defiance" to Libyan claims of sovereignty over the Gulf of Sidra, "resolve" in the face of Iranian threats to Western oil supplies through the Straits of Hormuz, and a "threat" to the Sandinista government in Nicaragua.[35]

The point is well taken in U.S. nuclear planning. A limited attack cannot be engineered in a vacuum, for any signal is neutral on key dimensions. An increased force commitment can as easily be read as an act of escalation as of restraint, and in the logic of the political warfighter it is both; but in a very important sense it is neither. The sender could believe its intent to be clear and the recipient could be confident of its interpretation, and yet a message may not get through as intended. A signal itself has limited content and does not fully capture the message. (This assumes that a signal will be transmitted. "Signal transmission" is likely to be disrupted by the collocation of Soviet targets, and hence collateral destruction and the similarity of incoming missile trajectories, plus the vulnerabilities and inadequacies of Soviet command and control.[36])

The problems of communication are multiplied under conditions of compellence. Schelling (1966:69–91) thoroughly identifies these problems. Deterrence threats are likely to be well defined, while compellence threats could require considerable elaboration because they "are less likely to be self-limiting, less likely to communicate in the very design of the threat just what, or how much, is demanded." The NATO defense line is a clear indication that a Soviet attack would be immediately met with a repulsive attack. The meaning is implicit and yet well defined. In contrast, compellent threats leave open the questions of what, when, where, and how much. "There is a tendency to emphasize the communication of what we shall 'do' if he misbehaves and to give too little emphasis to communicating 'what' behavior will satisfy us." In compellence, the status quo cannot serve as an easily recognized line between acceptable and unacceptable behavior. This point is particularly significant for political warfighting: intrawar bargaining would be more a process of compellence than deterrence if its purpose were to induce a Soviet withdrawal from captured territory or even to induce a lower level of Soviet hostility.

Evidence indicates that decisionmakers who invest time and effort in the planning of a communicative act fail to recognize the extent to which their own interpretation of the message results because "they know what to look for" (Jervis 1969:251). Signals suffer from errors of commission as well as omission, and the intended part does not stand above all the rest. Unintended signals disseminating from the style of presentation, the peculiarities in the way intelligence information is actually gathered, evaluated, and presented, coincident or accidental occurrences, and a fragmented and dissenting bureaucracy or alliance confound interpretation.

The problems of interpretation are aggrevated by the fact that any given event can be cut an infinite number of ways, with various of its aspects featured or suppressed. A discrepancy in U.S. and British targeting, even if recognized by the Soviets, can be given opposing interpretations; it as readily conveys British dissent from U.S. policy as it does a NATO coordination that plays upon ally comparative force advantages (i.e., U.S. possession of ICBMs and British possession of aircraft and

SLBMs). The evidence that policymakers interpret must always be inconsistent and ambiguous. To quote Schelling (1960:76), "one cannot nearly so easily commit 'some' forces and communicate a persuasive limit to the 'amount' that one intends to commit."

No matter how rich the signal, the literature on cognitive psychology hammers the point that decisionmakers fit information to their preexisting viewpoints. This is important because the political deescalation of a conflict has a critical prerequisite: "both sides must have a shared understanding of what is happening" (Kahn 1968:231). This point is well taken in devising a limited war strategy. The receipt of hostility is likely to reinforce recipient feelings of hostility and the conciliatory content (if any) of the signal ignored (making future perception of that content even less likely). Evidence of a slowdown in a Soviet offensive could as easily be interpreted in the United States as a deceptive ploy, a sign of military incapacitation, or a marshaling of resources for the next offensive as it can be interpreted as a sign of cooperation; the evidence could even be dismissed when attributed to a degeneration in the U.S. capacity for attack assessment. Events will be colored by expectations. The Soviets expect a U.S. counterforce strike to be followed by strikes against Soviet economic targets (in keeping with their own plan of attack)—a limited counterforce attack thus might appear to the Soviets to portend an all-out attack (Meyer 1985a:173).[37]

The problems of interpretation are also complicated if the United States and the Soviet Union were to seek to limit war on competing dimensions. "Even the principle of equality in nuclear reprisals could produce escalation if the contestants disagreed on what was supposed to be equal" (Read 1962:90). What is limited in some respects can be unlimited in others. If the United States limited its attacks by "means" and the Soviet Union limited its attacks by "effects" and they so judged the attacks of the other, the two combatants could be drawn into all-out war.

Ironically, both warfighters are their own worse enemies when they treat command and control centers as military targets and fail to see that a blind and deaf adversary cannot engage in rational nuclear combat. Problems of interpretation worsen as the command system is severed in combat and decisionmakers within the various surviving system fragments must predict independently the behavior of allied fragments, assess damage, and judge enemy intentions. The latter task is enormously complicated by segmentation. A partially blinded and isolated command must make inferences from the combat environment within which it finds itself even if that environment was more the creation of still other allied and enemy segments, similarly blinded and isolated. For instance, A(1) attacks B(2). B(2) retaliates against A(2), despite the latter's passivity, because B(2) assumes either that A(2) is in complicity with A(1) or is unable to determine the exact source of the initial attack. A(1) and A(2) are then forced to interpret what they perceive to be a response by "B" (presumably operating as a whole) that bears little resemblance to their respective actions. A(1) might be emboldened or conciliatory in the face of B's "passivity," and A(2) may be incensed by B's "treachery." Each segment of A may continue to act as if it were operating with B in a closed system, interpreting all evidence as if it were directed at it alone by a calculating and coherent opponent. [38]

Policy skeptics offer a similar critique. They ask whether information alone is enough to make nuclear conflict more rational, wondering whether the bigger problem for the U.S. nuclear command is not too little information but a large, overwhelming amount. Much of the information available would be superfluous and misleading, and in the compressed time frame of strategic nuclear conflict there would be little time to sift through it. Problems of interpretation will grow enormously with an increase in military activity and an accompanying decline in the capacity to monitor it. Interpretation will not be eased by direct communication links between Washington and Moscow (the so-called hot line), which, given their vulnerability, will not be available when needed most. [39]

Perception will determine conflict outcomes. No matter how sophisticated the technology of contemporary command and control, "the central feature remains human decision-making" (Arkin and Fieldhouse 1984:455).

Reconciling the Abstract and the Concrete

The command and control system that warfighters envisage is not a cure-all, and system construction requires fundamental trade-offs. Notwithstanding these inadequacies, the cost-effectiveness of a command and control system cannot be considered apart from its abstract purposes. Plans for escalation control and dominance and command and control fail to address the problems of the stability-instability paradox (or indeed the abstract omissions of pure warfighting) and indeed create new ones. In this regard it is useful to reflect upon words written decades ago: "It would be a mistake to think that conducting war in the measured cadence of limited reprisal somehow rescues the whole business of war from impetuousity and gives it rational qualities that it would otherwise lack. True, there is a sense in which anything done coolly, deliberately, on schedule, by plan, upon reflection, in accordance with rules and formulae, and pursuant to a calculus, is rational but it is in a very limited sense" (Schelling 1966:183).

Political and pure warfighters alike can be faulted for their failure to recognize the psychological impediments to "rational" command and control—this lapse is all the more glaring for political warfighters because they *are* generally sensitive to the perceptual basis for bargaining and are willing to employ nonrational instruments to enhance deterrence (see below). Moreover, warfighters of both types can be faulted for their failure to recognize impediments to rationality for what they are—they treat command and control trade-offs as technical deficiencies and fail to acknowledge that these problems undermine the very assumption of rational nuclear combat.

NONRATIONALITY

The assumption of nonrationality, like the assumption of rationality, underlies much of deterrence thought at both an abstract and a concrete level. Here as well, abstract logic is contradictory and concrete solutions do not fully address the abstract dilemmas posed. But nonrational approaches to deterrence are hampered by an additional problem—concrete nonrational solutions inconsistently combine rational and nonrational logic.

Nonrationality in the Abstract

The nonrational approach to deterrence certainly does not assume that decisionmakers are unpredictable or self-destructive. In response to the stability-instability paradox, the nonrational approach highlights the limits to human comprehension, reason, and control. The approach focuses on perception and manipulative techniques that draw from the concept of credibility. Nevertheless, in attempting a response to the stability-instability paradox, the purveyors of nonrationality create a paradox of their own.

Nonrationality in Strategic Policy

Pure warfighters have little appreciation of perception and put little faith in persuasion. What counts most is the cards that the players are dealt, not how they play them or even less their willingness to bluff. "Credibility" is at best a direct function of capability and adds little to the explanation for why nations are deterred. Pure warfighters would agree with the propositions that "credible commitments are defensible commitments" (Lebow 1981:88), that "(o)ne cannot build a credible deterrent on an incredible action" (McNamara 1983:73), and that "a threat's efficacy flows from the plausibility of following through at acceptable cost" (on this, see Betts 1987:12). U.S. threats have been successful when the United States could marshal the forces to back them up; thus they are far less efficacious now that the size and survivability of Soviet nuclear forces have rendered nuclear weaponry less usable. Pure warfighters claim that U.S. policy has suffered from an unwholesome reliance on bluster and too little attention to the consequences of threats that fail. They regret that U.S. success in the Berlin, Taiwan Straits, Cuban missile, and 1973 Middle East crises fosters the illusion that in the crunch it was superior U.S. will, the legitimacy of the American case, or the preeminence of U.S. interests that mattered—not what the United States had but how and why it used it. These warfighters insist that the United States must not overplay its hand; the United States might be forced to retreat at considerable cost.

Most current assured destruction advocates are quite unwilling to incur the potential costs of a credibility-based policy that is heavily reliant upon risk manipulation and explicit threats. Minimum deterrence advocates, for instance, believe that deterrence results from the destructive properties of nuclear weapons themselves, and believe the magnitude of such destruction to more than outweigh, in the adversary's decision calculus, the chance that these weapons might not be used. These advocates do not ignore the matter of risk; they believe that the risk of war instills caution—nuclear weapons, by their very existence, create an awareness that they might be used. These advocates argue for a *"passive"* or "existential" deterrence that "works independently of policy or declaration and is universal in its application."[40] Deterrence, then, is more a "condition" than a "policy."

Political warfighters believe capability to be necessary for credibility. But true to their credentials as warfighters, political warfighters also believe capability to contribute to credibility. This has created a logical inconsistency. To say both that capability is necessary for credibility and that capability induces credibility is to say that capability is the "one and only" source of credibility. Political warfighters may take exception to this inference that they are thus in essence pure warfighters—the fault, however, lies not with the conclusions but with the political warfighter's own initial assumptions.

Evidence of conflict in these critical assumptions can be found in the public record. To the extent that the countervailing strategy is a product of political warfighting, statements of Defense Secretary Brown are revealing—Brown argued for a capability to destroy selectively a wide range of military, political, and industrial targets so as to enhance U.S. policy credibility (a necessary condition) while he also argued that a selective-strike capability would induce credibility (a sufficient condition). (On this, see Jervis 1984:81–82.)

Political warfighters will argue that capability alone is not enough, however. The United States must also effectively communicate to the Soviets a willingness to incur the high cost of nuclear destruction on behalf of certain objectives. For this reason, they are attracted to a host of symbolic acts and deployment modes to communicate necessary resolve, though they are not indifferent to the potential provocativeness of these measures (see, for instance, Allison et al. 1985).

Warfighters are particularly attentive to credibility when they address the issue of "extended deterrence"—the extent to which U.S. strategic nuclear capability can prevent Soviet nuclear and conventional attacks on U.S. interests abroad. Here the failings of assured destruction seem most apparent. Warfighters wonder how the United States can deter Soviet attacks on U.S. interests abroad when it cannot credibly deter Soviet attacks on U.S. territory. They assert that the U.S. commitment to these external interests must be less credible because the benefits derived from their defense are lower and they are more costly to defend (see Gray 1986a:286), i.e., the requirements of compellence are greater than those for deterrence. As noted previously, some assured destruction proponents insist, in retort, that the Soviets would be willing to run only a lower risk of U.S. retaliation for an attack on Europe than one on the United States. U.S. commitments abroad require less credibility because they offer the Soviets a smaller prize than would the defeat of the United States. However, neither assured destruction nor warfighting proponents have indicated exactly what Soviet objectives are (see chapter 4), and it is therefore hard to judge the merit of these assertions.

It is difficult to determine the extent to which credibility concerns have motivated U.S. policy. The concept of credibility, more so than any other, captures the contribution of the renowned strategic thinkers. Accordingly, postwar history can be told in terms of leaders haunted by the memory of the Munich appeasement and the fear of nations fallings in succession to communism like dominoes, induced to hold their ground or undertake bold initiatives so as not to appear irresolute or on the defensive, seeing in every crisis a fundamental threat to the global order and in every conflict the high symbolic stakes of the Cold War. But though policies have been sold to the American public in these grandiose terms and the historical record can be selectively presented to show leaders to be high-stakes gamblers, crises are, by definition, exceptional periods, and even in these periods leaders were quite conscious of the limits of brinkmanship, the dangers of recklessness, and the untoward consequences of a called bluff. "Threats were never as blatant as a direct ultimatum and were usually hesitant and elliptical . . . and were less often a bludgeon than a crutch." Moreover, the behavior of any of the major political players hardly conformed to a single game strategy. "Politicians exhibited more flexibility and less coherence in practice than theorists do in principle" (Betts 1987:8, 13).

Risk manipulation is a heralded aspect of international influence because it is associated with brinkmanship and hence high risk confrontation. But evidence does not show U.S. policymakers to be risk lovers and, if anything, they appear to be risk adverse. Policymakers more often attempt to enhance U.S. nuclear-use credibility through the manipulation of U.S. interests and capabilities, appearing (but only appearing) to give credibility a rational basis.

The Lessons of the Cuban Missile Crisis

The Cuban missile crisis seems to embody U.S. nuclear diplomacy. But the lessons of the crisis are not clear-cut. The crisis actually suggests competing perspectives on the value of risk manipulation and nuclear capability in U.S.-Soviet deterrence.

The Cuban missile crisis brought U.S. strategic forces to their highest alert status in history, and it is only one of two occasions when U.S. nuclear forces were intentionally placed on global alert. The crisis can be remembered as a time in which the United States stood up to the Russians in an "eyeball-to-eyeball" confrontation and forced the Soviets to "blink first"—as a time in which the United States risked engaging Soviet forces and, in so doing, willingly accepted a high probability of nuclear war.[41]

In contrast, the Cuban crisis can also be remembered as a period of prudent U.S. decisionmaking—as a period in which numerous options were repeatedly scrutinized and verbal and nonverbal messages were communicated to the Soviets in ways that minimized their conflictual content and left considerable room for maneuver and compromise. In this view, U.S. demands were kept to the necessary minimum, required violence was to be initiated low on the escalation ladder (e.g., shoot to disarm rather than to kill), and the burden of first use of force was shifted to the Soviets (Snyder 1976:706–709). Even the U.S. decision to announce the Cuban quarantine without prior announcement of the Soviet missile discovery is seen promoting a peaceful resolution of the conflict: the Soviets were not given an opportunity to publicly commit to a position from which they could not then back down. U.S. decisionmakers acted out of fear that any little miscalculation, accident, or incident could force escalation beyond control.

For our purposes, the question is whether U.S. policymakers chose deliberately to manipulate risk or to adopt a position consistent with U.S. capability. For instance, it can be asked whether members of Kennedy's Executive Committee (ExCom) chose a firm stance not as a maneuver but because they believed the United States to enjoy a usable nuclear advantage. U.S. nuclear superiority could indeed account for the consistent resolution of Cold War crises on terms favorable to the United States, despite the differences in the issues and the U.S.-Soviet conventional balance within the region of conflict (on this, see Betts 1987). However, ExCom members gave virtually no thought to the military advantages of nuclear superiority or the discriminate use of nuclear force, even though the United States then officially subscribed to a damage limitation policy (Trachtenberg 1985; 148). Indeed, ExCom participants have asserted that U.S. and Soviet strategic forces "cancelled each other out" or that these forces "serve no military purpose whatsoever" (Trachtenberg 1985:138–139).

More generally, it can be asked whether the United States eventually chose a course that was consistent with its capability—in other words, whether the United States adopted a defensible stance rather than one reliant upon the threat of escalation. The evidence is that the participants viewed nuclear weapons neither as militarily usable nor as political instruments and that accordingly the Kennedy administration chose to flex its conventional rather than nuclear muscle. ExCom members can be said to have acted with prudence by taking advantage of U.S. conventional naval superiority in the Caribbean and by not engaging in nuclear coercion.[42] Some ExCom members believed that the Soviets would also calculate military advantages. Those who favored military action against the Soviet bases in Cuba did so with the belief that the Soviets would not retaliate and appear to have shared one proattack member's disconcern for "the risks of accident, inadvertence, miscalculation, desperation or the breakdown of command and control procedures" (Blight et al. 1987:174–175).

Nevertheless, it cannot be forgotten that the eventual U.S. act of quarantine was a symbolic one—one that implicitly invoked the threat of nuclear war. Short of a nuclear threat, the quarantine certainly symbolized the U.S. willingness to resort to force and to impose a military solution to the missile problem in the form of an air strike or invasion.

It is by no means clear, then, whether U.S. policymakers have been more reliant upon calculation or bluster in times of U.S.-Soviet confrontation. The evidence can be interpreted to support either contention. Crises are often depicted as periods ruled by irrational forces—where emotions are engaged and perception triumphs over reality. But warfighters can note that in Cuba the United States chose a "rational" course of action—one that did not invoke the explicit threat of nuclear war and that involved a level of violence at which the United States enjoyed an advantage (i.e., a conventional confrontation in the Western Hemisphere).

The Credibility Paradox

The implication of the stability-instability paradox has led many to seek salvation in the credibility concept. But even these strategists disagree. Some regard credibility as the virtual currency of international politics, while others argue that policy must not be overly reliant upon credibility, responding with what can be pronounced the "credibility paradox": specifically, "how is it possible to advance or protect one's interests by coercive threats and maneuvers, which necessarily require posing the prospect for war, without actually raising the risk of war to an intolerable level?" (Snyder 1976:705.) Almost all policymakers will concede that policy requires prudence, but they differ in whether they emphasize resolve or restraint. Many policymakers believe that it is not enough to strike a balance between the two.

To some, nuclear war is an onerous proposition and the very existence of nuclear weapons is a sufficient deterrent—to raise the risk of war is not only unnecessary but has grave consequences—but to others, restraint is less an intent than a consequence: restraint is possible only when the opponent's options have been constrained by the risk of further escalation. The latter stress the importance of limiting rather than preserving the opponent's options. Kissinger (1979a:622) thus reflects on his White House experience and notes that "what seems 'balanced' and 'safe' in a crisis is often the most risky." The "obligation is to end the confrontation rapidly," and this requires that the leader "convey implacability" and "be prepared to escalate rapidly and brutally to a point where the opponent can no longer afford to experiment." Proponents of the Kissinger stance might feel uncomfortable with the very description of a credibility paradox. For them, the risk of war dangerously increases only when policy is not decisive. If there is a credibility paradox, it is the antithesis of the one stated above: "How is it possible to decrease the risk of war by avoiding provocation without calling into question one's willingness to fight?" This is only a rhetorical question, one that these proponents answer simply—"it is not."

The credibility paradox, however conceived, is robust in its applications. It sets the parameters of the debate over weapons acquisitions and use and appropriate crisis tactics. It manifests itself in whether or not conventional defense diminishes the credibility of the U.S. pledge to use nuclear weapons, whether intermediate-range nuclear weapon deployments decouple the United States from the European nuclear deterrent, and whether a counterforce posture weakens or strengthens the credibility of the U.S. commitment to engage all of its strategic forces against the full set of Soviet targets if necessary.

Credibility is more likely to be coveted by warfighters than by assured destruction advocates. Pure warfighters shun the concept of credibility because it implies that "it is not what you have but what you do with it," but even so, warfighters tend to more readily accept a strident stance. Nonetheless, the means that warfighters propose are not inherently more credible than those proposed by their intellectual adversaries. Any policy or act, no matter how provocative, is open to the charge that it undermines credibility. For instance, a counterforce posture could communicate timidity (i.e., an unwillingness to engage in an all-out nuclear exchange) just as a purely conventional buildup could be perceived as a reckless provocation, a substitution of bluster for a viable and sustainable policy. Indeed, even assured destruction advocates can confess a concern with the credibility of policy by challenging the wisdom of counterforce deployments. When arguing that preparations for limited engagements make nuclear war more likely, they suggest that these preparations decrease the credibility of U.S. strategic force use.

In sum, the credibility paradox draws attention to the profound tension between those who seek to manipulate conflict and those who seek to manage or prevent conflict. Some policymakers believe that war is avoided by a willingness to fight them; others emphasize the grave risks of conflict escalation to show that no one gains from a military confrontation. The differences between policymakers are not just in choice of means—these differences reflect a fundamental conflict in world views. Those who stress the importance of resolve are likely to see cooperation as an aberration, a confession of weakness, or at best a temporary departure in a continuing struggle among nations; those who emphasize the necessity of restraint probably believe that nations share more than they differ, that differences are reconcilable, and that common interests must be recognized in the nuclear age where the stakes are no less than human survival.

Policymakers who emphasize the importance of the nonrational[43] are also reliant upon the rational. This is even true of policymakers who note the coercive utility of appearing irrational (see Kahn 1968:58). Former president Nixon (1980:255) stresses the need to keep an opponent off-guard—to " 'never let the enemy know what you will not do.' " "If the adversary feels that you are unpredictable, even rash, he will be deterred from pressing you too far." Nevertheless, policymakers who push credibility depend upon the adversary's rationality to prevent or to end a confrontation. A strategy of nonrationality will certainly fail if both parties pursue it simultaneously.

Appreciating the tension in this, Deutsch (1966:70) remarks that deterrence theory "first proposes that we should frustrate our opponents by frightening them very badly and that we should then rely on their cool-headed rationality for survival." Those who most strenuously argue the case for risk manipulation are most reliant upon adversary rationality to extricate both parties from nuclear confrontation. Kissinger (1957:144–145) can thus argue that "the purpose of limited war is to inflict losses or to pose risks for the enemy out of proportion to the objectives under dispute" while also asserting that "the psychological advantage will always be on the side of the power which can shift to its opponent the decision to initiate all-out war."[44] The rational opponent presumably would make a negative decision.

Those who coach restraint might also find hope in rationality, but their rationality is that of Morgan's (1977) "sensible" decisionmaker—a decisionmaker that is rational enough to avoid situations where he/she is likely to be nonrational. Sensible decisionmakers recognize the untoward ramifications of threat and heightened tension: these factors induce stress and result in, among other things, stereotyping, oversimplification, hostility, loss of creative and analytical thinking, and misperception, they create political opportunities for internal adversaries (or for foreign allies) who would place their own interests first, they undermine and replace attitudes, beliefs, and routines that support the status quo, they engage emotions and create an expectation of war, and they must be handled by decisionmakers that are never fully rational and are therefore unable to recognize trade-offs, adequately process inconsistent information, evaluate contingencies in probabilistic terms, or recognize the values, perceptions, and constraints that shape their opponent's behavior.[45] These factors can mean in effect that, among other things, threat initiators are overconfident and recipients are fatalistic, initiators overestimate the extent to which they are in control and recipients underestimate their own freedom of action, and initiators are convinced of the merits of their case, while recipients fix upon the unreasonableness and provocativeness of opponent actions.

Sensible decisionmakers would argue that despite initiator judgments to the contrary, threats are propitious under rather restricted conditions. Threats often reinforce the negative attitudes and expectations of the recipient and, when executed, simply carry out that which the recipient has already chosen or been conditioned to accept (see Fisher 1969). Threats might also contain demands that the target cannot accept. As a conflict intensifies, the number of such demands could grow while concession could be made more difficult,[46] effectively diminishing both parties' options. As the parties stake their claims and voice their commitments, opportunities for conciliation could dissipate.

The sensible decisionmaker skirts confrontation as a "dialogue of the deaf" and recognizes that "there is no obvious way for governments to appear appropriately irrational for making threats without at the same time appearing too irrational to be deterred" (Morgan 1977:121). They would agree with Kahn (1968:12) that the analogy of the game of "chicken"[47] hardly does justice to the reality of an international confrontation: " 'Chicken' would be a better analogy to escalation if it were played with two cars starting an unknown distance apart, traveling toward each other at unknown speeds, and on roads with several forks so that the opposing sides are not certain that they are even on the same road. Both drivers should be giving and receiving threats and promises while they approach each other, and tearful mothers and stern fathers should be lining the sides of the roads urging, respectively, caution and manliness." Sensible decisionmakers thus believe confrontation to be counterproductive and dismiss the idea of "controlled risk" as a contradiction in terms.

Sensible decisionmakers draw their own inferences from the Cuban missile crisis. These decisionmakers might be heartened by recent revelations on the Cuban missile crisis that challenge the naive portrait of crisis decisionmakers as unflinchingly resolute. It is now apparent that U.S. crisis decisionmakers were willing to compromise on matters that they had claimed were nonnegotiable (e.g., an explicit linkage between the dismantlement of Cuban- and Turkish-based missiles). Sensible decisionmakers might be sobered by other revelations. Indeed, the best administration efforts to control the crisis outcome could have been undermined by various developments that surprised or were unknown to decisionmakers at the time—Navy antisubmarine warfare operations,

reconnaissance ship and aircraft activities in hostile territory, a host of
novel, intense, combat-readiness measures, ill-timed but coincident political actions (e.g., the U.S. turnover of Jupiter missiles to Turkey), ill-
conceived public statements (e.g., the President's call for a free Cuba),
U.S. sponsored operations in Cuba, and even tension between Cuban
and Soviet military forces (on the crisis, see Garthoff 1987). Sensible
decisionmakers recognize that they have only a limited capacity to control events and that this is often lost on their foreign counterparts. No
matter what their intentions, these counterparts could act to escalate a
conflict even as they struggle to "make sense" of it.

The credibility paradox serves to highlight the inconsistencies of abstract strategic thought on the question of whether deterrence is best
served by rational or by nonrational forces. Most policymakers find it
difficult to strike a balance between resolve and restraint[48]—the reliance
on threat and the desire to preserve the rational inhibitions to escalation.
As will become apparent, the dilemma is no less severe at a concrete
level.

Nonrationality in the Concrete

The strategic debate often centers on the tactics of credibility enhancement in addressing (if only implicitly) the dilemmas of the stability-
instability and credibility paradoxes. Issues of weapons development,
deployment, or employment are constantly framed in terms of implications for credibility. Even ostensibly nonnuclear issues, such as the
appropriate U.S. response to Soviet third-world intervention, communist
insurgency, and global terrorism have been debated for their effects on
the credibility of the U.S. commitment to use nuclear weapons on behalf
of certain objectives.

Strategists present the concrete methods of credibility enhancement
with little regard for the abstract implications of the credibility paradox.
They also fail to deal adequately with *still other abstract implications*,
which again points to their inability to juggle the rational and nonrational.

Credibility Enhancement

The means of credibility enhancement assume three distinct forms—
signaling, "rationalizing" conflict, and "automaticity." These are not exclusive types of actions—policies that serve one function are likely to

serve another. In presenting these types, theorists have had their greatest impact upon policy.

Signaling. The most common means of credibility enhancement is the use of signals. When these signals are verbal, they assume the form of declarations of support, warnings against Soviet trespasses, and declarations of vital interests; when nonverbal, they assume the form of diplomatic visits, protocol, port visits, military consultation and assistance, and, in their most severe form, weapons tests, global nuclear alerts (on this, see Sagan 1985), nuclear warning shots, and nuclear-war-limiting tactics.[49] Signals exist in both the routine and the sensational,[50] and, as subjects of policy controversy, give substance to the credibility paradox.

Political warfighters have built a strategy around signals. But these warfighters insist that nuclear weapons must be more than a "shot across the bow." NATO defense ministers have long proposed that nuclear weapons be used first as a demonstration or "warning shot" (Halperin 1987:94), but warfighters often argue that opportunities for conciliation must appear to the Soviets to be almost incidental to combat and not intended. Effective signals must not seem to be signals; the involved actions must appear to serve directly foreign policy objectives. A signal that falls short of affirmative action in an age of nuclear parity could actually be read as a sign of weakness and limited commitment. For this reason, it seems, Schelling (1966:194) suggests that threatening enemy cities symbolically "in a counterforce campaign that caused a measure of civilian damage might be better than doing it in a cold-blooded demonstration attack on a few population centers." Credibility requires more than threats or "showing the flag."

It should be obvious by now that signals can be misread despite the confidence of policymakers to the contrary. Messages are often lost to the style with which, and the context within which, they are transmitted —a style and context that might indeed convey unintended messages. A message of conciliation can be read as one of provocation. Even if the intended message gets through, a resistant adversary could discount it easily. Nevertheless, strategic theories ironically value bargaining strategies for their subtlety even under circumstances in which direct messages are not conveyed. Such subtlety would be the undoing of ploys such as the "incidental signal"—the signal that is designed not to appear to be one. Theorists are not the only culprits here. Statesmen have also been partial to nuance and "frequently adopt complex and finely calibrated strategies of coercion that make quite unrealistic demands on their adversaries' interpretative abilities" (Lebow 1985:205).

Furthermore, even a clearly communicated message might not be a sufficient deterrent. In this regard, some theorists note that a nation's credibility is related to its interests. Snyder and Diesing (1977:190), for instance, stress the contribution of "inherent resolve" to a strong bargaining stance—the benefits of an action must be proportionate to the costs. Accordingly, U.S. policy has been criticized then for its wholesale reliance upon "technique"—misguided attempts to achieve credibility by substituting signals for interests. Critics charge that this overreliance upon signals leads to a policy without necessary limits, a policy that requires excessive vigilance because it mistakenly assumes that all political commitments are interconnected (on this, see Morgan 1985:130). They argue that the key to deterrence is not commitments and reputation, but rather the intrinisic merits of commitments. These critics assert that "the task of achieving credibility is secondary to 'and dependent upon' the more fundamental questions regarding the nature and valuation of interests" (see George and Smoke 1974:559). They conclude that a U.S. history of use of its military forces in diverse parts of the world—Grenada, the Persian Gulf, Vietnam, or Lebanon—might not communicate that the United States is willing to use nuclear forces to meet its objectives and might communicate just the opposite: "a state confident in its readiness to use nuclear weapons may well take a more relaxed attitude toward lesser challenges" (Morgan 1985:135).

Stakes, like signals and capability, can be manipulated. The manipulation of stakes—termed here the *rationalization* of conflict—has greatly inspired policy.

"Rationalizing" Conflict. Conflict can arguably be "rationalized"[51] to enhance credibility in two different ways—from shifts in the "balance of intentions" or "interests" and in the "balance of capability" or "forces" (Snyder 1961; Snyder and Diesing 1977:185). The balance of intentions suggests that the United States can manipulate its interests to advantage by increasing stakes in a conflict; the balance of capability assumes that the United States can manipulate situations to advantage by altering relative nuclear capability.

U.S. policymakers use the balance of intentions to respond to the illogic of using nuclear weapons to support less vital interests. The United States can adjust the balance of intentions in four ways. The United States could make its commitment to defend certain interests more believable if it: first, were able to convince the Soviets that an attack on these other interests would be equivalent to an attack on the United States; second, could raise the symbolic stakes to the point that a Soviet threat or erosion of U.S. support for these interests would appear to jeopardize more vital interests; third, sought objectives that were valuable in themselves; or fourth, could raise the practical stakes so that a failure to respond to a Soviet attack on these interests would "weaken" the future U.S. military position.[52]

The first and second of these devices suggest the easiest way for the United States to increase its stakes in a conflict—through declaration. Verbal pronouncements are not only "informative," but have the effect of engaging a nation's reputation and prestige. Nevertheless, these pronouncements can be ambiguous and, thus, freely interpreted. But they are not unlike deeds in this respect—actions do not necessarily "speak louder than words."

The first, second, and fourth means for altering the balance of intentions suggest a more controversial means by which the United States can upgrade its interests in a contested area—through a military presence in the form of troop or weapons deployments. Such deployments establish a U.S. commitment by making the United States vulnerable to material loss. If the United States is vulnerable to loss, the Soviets might believe that the United States will act rather than risk a further erosion of its military or political position. For just this reason, policymakers preferred U.S. intermediate-range nuclear missile deployments in Europe to NATO-controlled SLBMs—a land presence is a more effective guarantee than missiles that are only proximate to the European land mass.

U.S. policymakers also look to the balance of capability to rationalize conflict. In other words, they seek to lower the costs of defending interests. As a nuclear policy device, the balance of capability is beholden to Kahn's (1961) argument that more capability is required to extend deterrence[53] because less benefit accrues to the U.S. from interests outside than interests within the United States. This argument has been used to support a secure counterforce capability (see Luttwak 1981), strategic defense (see Yost 1982),[54] and weapons for the conduct of limited nuclear war (e.g., neutron bombs).

The balance of capability suggests a damage limitation posture.[55] Indeed, McNamara's faith in damage limitation was the source of his reservations about the viability of the "multilateral nuclear force" and U.S. reliance upon tactical nuclear weapons in Europe. He believed that these forces would not only complicate command and control, but were at best irrelevant and redundant; he believed that the strength of the U.S. commitment to Europe was not in symbols but in U.S. strategic nuclear and conventional military strength (Schwartz 1983:94, 161). Advocates of the balance of capability argument seem to be inclined toward the pure warfighting posture, but they fall short when they recognize the effective limits to nuclear capability (e.g., the limits of counterforce), if only through implication, when they attend to policy credibility.

Even if U.S. policymakers are able to convince the Soviets that the United States will regard an attack on its overseas interests as an attack on the United States itself, basic questions remain: is it any more rational to strike second than it is to strike first? Are there any interests that the Soviets can believe that the United States will defend at any price? Is defense of interests possible when war will result in the destruction of the interest under contention?

These questions are difficult to answer because, to put it simply, to "rationalize" nuclear conflict is not to make it "rational." If nuclear conflict were rational, the United States would not need to worry about policy credibility. The fact of the matter is that " 'there are no intrinsic interests of sufficient value to make that commitment [to use nuclear weapons] inherently credible' " (Morgan 1985:131). Ironically, U.S. attention to policy credibility implicitly confesses the nonrationality of strategic retaliation. Therefore, while the rationalization of conflict has clear implications for the credibility paradox—the manipulation of interests and capabilities is certainly not without provocative content—it suggests another abstract dilemma in the form of a question of whether rationalized conflict differs from rational conflict in form *or* in degree.

"Automaticity". The third approach to credibility enhancement, "automaticity," plays upon the manipulative opportunities that are available to rational decisionmakers when they choose to be nonrational with a rational adversary. Significantly, automaticity contrasts with the logic of signaling and rationalization when the latter require a credible limited war capability—this though policymakers have sought a limited nuclear war capability while creating simultaneously through automaticity the conditions for a war without limits. Moreover, automaticity shares with rationalization, in contrast to signaling, an emphasis upon what has been called inherent deterrence—that is, deterrence that stems from the nature of a situation rather than from explicit threats (Nye 1986:11–12). Unlike the "existential" deterrent, however, automaticity requires deliberate manipulation. As such, automaticity is tied to the "credibility paradox," but finds policymakers, in another important way, unable to reconcile the rational and nonrational (as addressed in the next section).

Under automaticity, rational decisionmakers can opt profitably for a strategy of "irrevocable commitment" (Schelling 1960:22–43), in which a large-scale nuclear response is made automatic: these decisionmakers can rely upon the rationality of the adversary for extrication from the potentially negative consequences of this strategy. Automaticity takes guidance from classic metaphors—Dr. Strangelove's "doomsday device" and strategies for winning at chicken that include playing the game blind, drunk, or without a steering wheel (Kahn 1968:11), tactics that, in essence, suspend the initiator's rationality.

The doomsday device arguably exists in the strategic launch-on-warning option. This option does not allow choice given the limited time frame within which retaliatory launch decisions must be made.[56] The device also exists metaphorically when war is planned around only a single option so that war mobilization activates complex and interrelated routines that proscribe future flexibility. It is also inherent in the predelegation of authority for nuclear weapons use when weapons use becomes more a matter of "implementation" than of "choice" (i.e., a matter of determining the appropriate time, place, and contingencies for use rather than whether they will be used). Automaticity is even implicit in attempts to bolster credibility through a history of forceful action: decision-makers attempt to convince their opponents that their undesirable actions will be met almost unthinkingly with a forceful response.

Automaticity has been the "nonrational" basis for theater nuclear and conventional force deployments in Europe. NATO theater nuclear forces of the early sixties would have to have been used preemptively due to their vulnerability and military criticality (Cordesman 1982:8), while some theater weapons of the eighties had to be used early in hostilities to avoid capture or destruction because of their proximity to the front (e.g., Pershing II missiles in West Germany) and exposed position (e.g., the so-called quick reaction alert force composed of aircraft and ballistic and nonballistic missiles).[57] Even with the INF treaty, some theater nuclear weapons remain biased toward automatic response. But even if NATO were not the first to use nuclear weapons, NATO theater forces present lucrative targets for preemption—the Pershing II, for instance, threatened Soviet command and control, ICBMS, and SS-20s—and, as such, could trigger a wider nuclear engagement.[58]

Conventional forces might seem to proscribe precipitous nuclear weapons use. These forces present opportunities for conflict deescalation short of a nuclear exchange; an adequate conventional response to a Soviet conventional attack would effectively create a "pause" in which the Soviets could reevaluate their stance with forceful evidence that the United States stands by its European defense commitment. However, a large conventional force could serve as a "plate-glass window" to activate U.S. nuclear retaliation. Forces would only have to be "large enough to assure the enemy that any attack powerful enough to break through 'would' bring about nuclear retaliation" (Snyder 1961:129).[59] In this regard, it should be noted that the effect of McNamara-era NATO conventional- and nuclear-force improvements was to "create a situation where any initial Soviet attack would have to be so large that it ran a severe risk of triggering the SIOP" (Cordesman 1982:10). Even a small conventional force could serve as a trigger or, more specifically, as a "trip wire" (as NATO forces did in the fifties), requiring that the Soviets risk nuclear war to gain territory. Nevertheless, a small force might not be an effective deterrent. The Soviets might be deterred more from launching a full-scale than a small-scale attack. The Soviets might be tempted by the prospect of incremental territorial gains if they believe that the United States will not employ nuclear weapons in response to a small-scale attack on a trip-wire force—that is, an attack that poses only a small and indirect challenge to U.S. security. Accordingly, the Soviets might believe that the shock and fear that would follow a full-scale attack would inspire the U.S. to accept a high cost for defense.

The size of the defending conventional force must nonetheless have an upward limit. Snyder (1961:149) recognizes that the conventional "shield must be larger but not large enough to defeat a full-scale conventional ground attack by the Soviets, for this latter move is one which [the United States] would presumably consider serious enough to justify massive retaliation; therefore it would be deterred." An excessively large conventional shield would effectively decouple the conventional engagement from a nuclear response.[60] Thus "the NATO ground force shield . . . tends to narrow the gap between the 'independent' deterrent effect of the shield's capacity to defend territory and the independent deterrent utility of the strategic nuclear forces" (Snyder 1961:134).

The issue of optimal force size also plagues nuclear force deployment. It too can be thought to involve a tension between a high and a low threshold by which U.S. nuclear forces can be decoupled from NATO. "If they fall below a certain point in strength, American nuclear forces in Europe would be 'inadequate' both as a symbol of American power and as immediately available reservoir of firepower," "if they rise above a certain point, American nuclear forces in Europe would be 'excessive', insofar as they might constitute an excuse for the U.S. to hold back on the use of its ultimate weapons, ICBMs and SLBMs" (Talbott 1985:23). The argument is a familiar one, though it can be argued that automaticity also plays a key role in determining the deployment floor: nuclear forces must be of adequate size to ensure that a Soviet counterforce attack on Europe would trigger a U.S. response.

The tension between these two amorphous thresholds fuels European insecurity about U.S. intentions and Soviet beliefs about them and has left the Europeans perceptually wedded to the status quo. European opposition to the "zero-zero" option (by which the United States would cancel its deployments in exchange for Soviet SS-20 dismantlement) grew in response to U.S. INF deployment—once the United States had deployed intermediate-range nuclear missiles, the missiles became the standard by which the strength of the U.S. commitment to Europe would be judged. This is an old pattern. Europeans were wary both of the Kennedy administration's conventional flexible response proposals and the alternative in tactical nuclear defense. [61]

The tone of these remarks suggests that automaticity rests on a mechanical solution to the credibility problem. But this is not really the case. Automaticity simply requires means by which a set of decisionmakers can suspend its rationality given joint cognizance of the ways in which things are likely to get out of control. Such a means is available in the "threat that leaves something to chance" (Schelling 1960:188), when chance signifies the complex interplay of forces that induce uncertainty, emotional response, decisional lapses, bureaucratic snafus, political infighting, and miscalculation and thus wrest the conflictual outcome from rational control. The threat of losing control is the essence of "brinkmanship"—a threat that "involves getting onto the slope where one may fall in spite of his own best efforts to save himself, dragging his adversary with him" (Schelling 1960:200). The threat can be used to the manipulative advantage of the instigating party: the party that moves first places the burden of controlling the outcome on its opponent, and its opponent has no option but to back down; the opponent is in effect given the "last clear chance" to save itself with any measure of certainty.

Reconciling Deployment Assumptions

U.S. conventional and nuclear deployments abroad can be justified with any number of different logics. Policymakers have simultaneously invoked all of them to justify a single policy even when the justifications have had contradictory rational and nonrational underpinnings. [62]

This creates problems, for instance, for conventional European defense. Policymakers invoke the nonrational when they assert that a conventional response to a Soviet conventional attack could credibly force "automatic" U.S. nuclear retaliation if NATO conventional forces were to be overpowered, it could credibly signal a U.S. willingness to support Europe even at the price of a strategic nuclear exchange, it could credibly bring costs into line with benefits, and it could implicitly suggest a credible risk of escalation to nuclear conflict. Policymakers invoke the rational when they assert that conventional defense can increase the number of rungs on the escalation ladder, and they therefore propose escalation dominance with the argument that the cost-benefit calculus at each level of escalation determines the value of a deterrent force and not the threat of escalation per se. In this spirit, policymakers offer a conventional defense (like tactical nuclear weapons and counterforce) as a way of fighting conflict on Soviet terms and thereby to avoid the implicit and explicit threat of escalation,[63] preventing Soviet territorial gains and leaving the Soviets with no rational options to further their designs (Schwartz 1983:177). Echoing this logic, McNamara (1983:64) asserts that the U.S. reliance on conventional forces presupposed that NATO's nuclear capability "did not translate into usable military power." The contradiction in rational and nonrational conventional force justifications means that proponents can argue for maximum flexibility in force usage while they also promote conventional deployments as a U.S. option constraint. This contradiction also means that McNamara can stress the disutility of nuclear weapons while condemning weapons acquisitions, deployments, and potential employments for increasing the risk of an all-out nuclear war (on this, see Freedman 1988:188).

The contradiction in the rationality and nonrationality logic is also apparent at the higher end of the escalation ladder. This contradiction accounts for the antagonism within the Reagan administration over the INF issue.[64] The "zero-zero" option was opposed by those who saw U.S. INF deployments not as a means of achieving an intermediate-range force balance with the Soviet Union, but as an extension of the U.S. nuclear umbrella—a trigger that when used or attacked would precipitate U.S. strategic weapons launch (Talbott 1985:39, 71, 187). The latter argument is "logically distinct from any concern about the Soviet SS-20s" (Bundy et al. 1982:755) and was initially used to justify U.S. deployments as the United States sought to reassure its NATO allies that the U.S. strategic force commitment is viable given the SS-20 " 'political'-military threat" (Garthoff 1985:879). This trigger argument has been made periodically by the German government on behalf of tactical and theater nuclear weapons deployment and explains why NATO plans tactical nuclear weapons use despite a widespread questioning of their utility—"they have become steeped in political symbolism" (Freedman 1981–82:66). But this argument is in sharp contrast to the one that theater nuclear weapons serve as a firebreak between tactical and strategic weapons use

—suggested by Kissinger (1979b), with ensuing controversy, when he recommended that U.S.-Soviet tactical and theater nuclear force imbalances be corrected because U.S. strategic forces were no longer usable.[65] It is in even sharper contrast to the pure warfighter regard for extended deterrence as a "free gift" of a once favorable strategic imbalance that, in its demise, requires "ways in which NATO-Europe can diminish its politically debilitating client status vis-à-vis U.S. strategic forces" (see Gray 1986a:289).[66]

The tension between rational and nonrational force justifications finds its way into policy. In NATO nuclear planning, "flexible response" is supported both as a means to "respond appropriately to any level of potential attack and . . . pose the risk of escalation to higher levels of conflict."[67] This internally inconsistent posture is based on the necessity of "defeating the enemy 'on the level at which he chooses to fight' " and yet, if this fails, a strategy of "deliberate escalation" and then a "general nuclear response" (Arkin and Fieldhouse 1985:96). This posture, despite its contradictions, has been boldly pronounced in high-level U.S. policy documents.[68]

Warfighters, as the architects of current strategic policy, are hobbled by the issue of escalation control (in its more general sense). They would like to avoid escalation of conflict and seek means to limit the scope of conflict, but they have not clearly determined whether escalation control is a means or an end—whether it is achieved militarily or it is a by-product of risk manipulation and the explicit or implicit threat of escalation. This is apparent, for instance, in their failure to distinguish the requisites of a combat from a trigger force.

Assured destruction advocates, as a policy outgroup, are not saddled with an identification with recent policy or the onus of defending it. They therefore hold what appears to be a more consistent position and can afford to maintain it (see Bundy et al. 1982). Nevertheless, the policies of the sixties[69] show that assured destruction advocates are not immune from the intellectual tensions of current policy. Moreover, while these advocates carefully distinguish between conventional and nuclear weapons, at least implicit within their prescriptions is the ever-present threat of nuclear weapons use.[70] Illustrative are the words of Warnke (1984:86):

It is . . . highly conjectural that whatever oblique and nebulous form of "extended deterrence" nuclear weapons may be deemed to provide, anything can be gained from the development and deployment of categories beyond the existing strategic systems. The fact that a major conventional conflict can readily escalate to a nuclear exchange inescapably must induce caution on the part of the nuclear superpowers.

Assured destruction advocates make nuclear weapons distinctive by reinforcing the conventional/nuclear firebreak. This had led them to promote such things as "no-first-use" of nuclear weapons, the separation of the nuclear and conventional command structure, the development of procedures by which conventional forces can be alerted apart from nuclear ones, the elimination of dual-capable weapon systems, and the deployment of weapons in more-survivable modes so that the nuclear command is not in the position of having to "use them or lose them" (see Halperin 1987). Assured destruction advocates nonetheless recognize that there are no absolute inhibitions to nuclear weapon employment, but they would probably not be relieved if there were.

Therefore, the issue of force structure and size has significant policy implications. A conventional force deployed as a trigger would look different from one designed to fight and to win a conventional (or conventional/nuclear) conflict, and intermediate nuclear forces designed to fight a limited nuclear war rather than to trigger a broader one should not have been placed in vulnerable or front-line positions. When the dilemmas of escalation control remain implicit rather than explicit, forces will be at variance with their objectives; devised tactics, weaponry, and strategy could be inappropriate, counterproductive, and even self-defeating.

CONCLUSIONS

Abstract policy thinking about deterrence as rational has spawned the "stability-instability" paradox. The paradox draws attention to the manner in which assured destruction advocates promote their doctrine for its rational underpinnings and yet are profoundly beholden to the nonrationality inherent in the suicidal threat of all-out nuclear retaliation. Warfighters attempt to salvage rationality at a concrete level by proposing means for escalation control and dominance and for strategic command and control. But these solutions fail to address the key dilemma of deterrence in the nonrationality of a full-scale nuclear exchange. Moreover, warfighters fail to appreciate fully the limits to rationality for what they are.

Policymakers seek abstract remedies in the nonrational concept of credibility—remedies that translate into concrete proposals for credibility enhancement and variously involve demonstrations, foreign deployments, and improved counterforce capability. Nevertheless, those who emphasize credibility in policy create another logical paradox: they assume that a "nonrational" U.S. policy stance will be met with a rational Soviet response. When policymakers do recognize that U.S. nonrationality can undermine Soviet rationality, they are led to policies that balance resolve and restraint, but do not establish the proper mix between the two. They are no more successful in maintaining logical consistency in their concrete proposals. They propose means designed to communicate resolve and are not clear on the requirements for restraint; they propose means to limit the costs of a nuclear exchange (and thus enhance credibility) that can only be meaningful if nuclear force use is thereby rendered a rational choice (and credibility was no longer at issue), and most important, they devise means around a cost/benefit calculus yet value them for the risk posed of total destruction. Therefore, policies may rest on self-defeating logic and have undesirable consequences.

6

CONCLUDING THOUGHTS
ON ACHIEVING
NUCLEAR CONSENSUS

IDEAS THAT appear complex might actually be very simple. So it is with strategic thought. Nuclear strategy offers an expressive and arcane vocabulary and an intricate, if often convoluted, set of arguments. Yet strategy has a recurrent feature—the dominance of the concrete over the abstract at the expense of strategic clarity, consistency, and coherence.

The concrete is primary to three different schools of strategic thought —assured destruction, pure warfighting, and political warfighting—and thus all of these strategies falter under scrutiny. Each school exhibits debilitating intellectual tensions.

THREE HYPOTHESES REVISITED

This study is guided by three hypotheses suggested by the cognitive psychology and foreign policy belief system literature.

H1: Goal components are primarily conceived in concrete rather than in abstract terms.

This hypothesis is valid for all three nuclear strategies:

Assured Destruction

Assured destruction offers weak conceptions of three components of deterrence—"capability," adversary "objectives," and the "processes" by which deterrence is maintained. As with the other schools of thought, these deficiencies stem from concrete thinking.

Assured destruction advocates believe that deterrence requires the capability to inflict unacceptable costs upon the Soviet Union under all attack scenarios, but they lack abstract criteria for capability assessment. Assured destruction advocates have not agonized over the requirements of assured destruction—what it "really" takes to deter the Soviets; accordingly, they devise requirements apart from an understanding of the Soviet system or mentality and even apart from the political circumstances under which strategic nuclear weapons are likely to be used. As a result, assured destruction has not served as an independent standard in the policy debate and, since the sixties, it has been used to justify the status quo. Moreover, assured destruction advocates employ ad hoc capability measures. Assured destruction advocates may recognize, in the abstract, that retaliatory capability is what counts and not pre-attack capability—yet they start with the assumption that a large portion of the U.S. arsenal can survive a Soviet first strike and then fall back on pre-attack measures of convenience. They thus spend little time exploring the physical intricacies and complexities of nuclear combat.

Most assured destruction advocates do not assess in any great depth the objectives for which the Soviet Union would go to war. Their indifference to Soviet motives stems partly from their confidence in deterrence, but also from their more sanguine view of Soviet intent and their appreciation of Soviet doctrine. Some assured destruction advocates explain Soviet behavior in the universal terms of the "security dilemma": they believe that the Soviet Union, like the United States, is forever on the defensive, wary of its adversary's intent. However, this explanation for Soviet behavior amounts to a "self-verifying" theory: these assured destruction advocates look to the concrete world in the form of Soviet weapon deployments and find ever-present validation for the arms-race model upon which they can pin their assessment of Soviet intent. But the arms-race model is defined loosely, and thus any occurrence can be claimed to be consistent with it. The model can therefore only confirm prior assumptions about Soviet intent: the Soviets can always be seen to be responding to a U.S. initiative.

Assured destruction advocates also have problems assessing the processes by which deterrence is maintained—whether deterrence is rational or nonrational in essence. They recognize that retaliation could be no more rational than preemption, and they thus seek comfort in a credible policy—one that assures that the United States would do the nonrational and invoke the full U.S. arsenal to support its interests.

Nevertheless, they are somewhat ambivalent when they deal with concrete policy. They are not sure whether U.S. conventional forces are, or should be, coupled to U.S. strategic nuclear forces, invoking the threat of a nonrational response, or are, or should instead serve as, a firebreak that inhibits strategic force use, presenting a rational obstacle to strategic force employment.

Pure Warfighting

The pure warfighting strategy can be criticized for being impractical and invalid at least as much as for being logically deficient and inconsistent. It therefore invites controversy when it argues that the United States can achieve a meaningful force advantage over the Soviet Union, that the effects of nuclear war can be limited, that firebreaks can exist at various levels of nuclear combat, and that cost/benefit assessment will determine the level at which a nuclear war would be fought. Nevertheless, the pure warfighting strategy has serious internal flaws—most particularly when it addresses U.S. "strategy" and Soviet "objectives."

Pure warfighters are inconsistent (or at best ambiguous) when they renounce a first-strike capability and yet support a second-strike capability that can deny the Soviets their objectives and thereby allows the United States to "win" wars or achieve "victory." Pure warfighters might believe that a U.S. preemptive capability is politically unacceptable and practically unachievable given offsetting Soviet deployment. Nonetheless, they fail to provide a standard apart from a first-strike capability by which to judge the adequacy of the U.S. retaliant. They could very well desire in a second-strike capability what they are inhibited from seeking in a first-strike capability. Furthermore, pure warfighters contradict themselves when they claim that the purpose of either strike is to "deny" an adversary its objectives and yet identify "value" targets to be hit to inflict cost and thereby "punishment" or fear that nuclear war could escalate to involve punishment.

Pure warfighters offer the clearest statement of Soviet objectives—and, in fact, present Soviet objectives in stark terms. They generally assume the Soviets to be purposeful and unrelenting; nevertheless, they are at a loss to explain the Soviet failure to capitalize on supposed U.S. strategic deficiencies and to marshal military resources more efficiently. Warfighters offer concrete evidence to support their claim that the character of Soviet deployment reveals aggressive intent. However, the evidence that they offer is not a true test of the abstract—all Soviet deployment can be found consistent with a pessimistic view of Soviet motives.

Nonetheless, fearing the worst of the Soviet Union, pure warfighters tend to promote U.S. deployments without adequately considering weapon trade-offs or strategic utilities.

Political Warfighting

Political warfighters offer the most inconsistent view of deterrence and provoke more questions than they answer. They are deficient in every area of deterrence thought.

Political warfighters have not established the abstract requirements of the nuclear balance because they have not decided whether nuclear weapons are military implements or instruments of coercion. Political warfighters thus inconsistently argue for weapon diversification and performance upgrades while they lament Soviet "symbolic" force advantages (aggregate advantages) that they confess are of limited military utility. The confusion intensifies when concrete capability measures are involved: Because political warfighters have not determined "what" should be measured, let alone "when" it should be measured, they too fall back on simple measures of convenience.

Political warfighters fare no better when general strategy is at issue. They are once again entangled in abstract contradictions. They covet nuclear weapons for their military effectiveness and yet also value them for their capacity to coerce and to inflict cost. These abstract failings are not recognized by political warfighters because they concentrate instead on the generation of concrete options. The upshot is that political warfighters have options but do not know what to do with them.

Political warfighters are crippled by an undeveloped conception of Soviet intent. They do not devote much thought to the conditions that would motivate Soviet nuclear weapons use and thus whether these conditions could affect the success of a bargaining strategy. Nevertheless, political warfighters are distressed by the pace and the character of Soviet weapon deployments, and given their uncertainty about Soviet objectives, political warfighters are inclined to prepare for the worst. They are open then to a wide range of U.S. force increases and improvements.

Finally, political warfighters are uncertain of the processes by which deterrence is maintained—whether deterrence has primarily rational or nonrational underpinnings. They suggest that deterrence has a rational basis when they worry if a limited Soviet first strike will leave the United States without rational retaliatory options. The concrete "solutions" (e.g., improved command and control, escalation control) that they promote fail to address this basic problem, though, and at best postpones it: as a conflict escalates, one or both participants could face the assured destruction scenario in which weapon use would be suicide. These concrete solutions also fall short as they have not been devised with awareness of the perceptual factors that complicate intrawar bargaining.

Political warfighters are, in fact, torn between the abstract presumption of rationality and nonrationality. They lean toward a nonrational perspective when they argue for concrete policies that would suspend U.S. rationality to enhance deterrence. But even in this, political warfighters invoke the rational when they require Soviet rationality to make this strategy effective, when they seek to enhance U.S. credibility through capability improvements, and when they struggle to determine the appropriate mix between policy resolve and restraint or risk manipulation and outcome control.

H2: Goals are primarily conceived in concrete rather than in abstract terms.

This study of strategic deterrence converges on a central point: The U.S. goal of deterrence is dominated by one of its components—"capability." However, capability is used here in its crudest sense—weapons and weapons technology—not how, when, or for what it will be used. The adequacy of capability is the dominant element—not its utility or application (though each of these considerations is nominally a function of the others).

Assured destruction advocates elevate the adequacy of U.S. retaliatory capability above all other issues. Confident that the United States has such a capability, assured destruction advocates are not greatly distressed by the argument that retaliation lacks a rational justification. Assured destruction advocates toy with means for reinforcing the credibility of the U.S. deterrent (particularly the extended deterrent) but are confident that the magnitude of potential destruction outweighs in the enemy calculus any probability that retaliatory weapons would not be used.

Warfighters are equally beholden to capability. They look to the elusive nuclear balance to resolve the tensions of U.S. nuclear doctrine. They propose a robust U.S. force posture that will allow the United States to respond to Soviet provocation across the capability spectrum— the so-called stability-instability paradox is treated as, in effect, a capability gap. Political warfighters fail to recognize that while capability diversification could attenuate a nuclear conflict, it does not remove the paradox. Pure warfighters similarly manage the paradox with capability and thereby offer a false image of nuclear war dominated by calculation and devoid of politics, misperception, miscalculation, and emotion.

Capability dominates the conception of deterrence in other ways. Warfighters treat the balance of capability as a virtual balance of intent. They have thus appeared even more committed to a pessimistic view of the Soviet Union, as the Soviets have achieved quantitative and qualitative force advantages. Because of their pessimism and/or their poor sense of Soviet objectives, warfighters are inclined to seek solutions in capability (and even fall under the influence of capability). They are quick to advocate U.S. weapon deployments.

H3: Higher-level goals are conceived to resemble lower-level ones.

Capability enjoys centrality in deterrence policy because military capability is, for a variety of reasons, central to the U.S. foreign policy establishment. First, military capability is central because it defines the low-level goals that direct day-to-day government operations. Much of the business of government is about budgeting, promoting, monitoring, assessing, maintaining, operating, researching, developing, deploying, and employing military capability. Crises come and go, issues emerge, change, and recede, governmental priorities shift and leaders change, but in all of this the requirements of the military establishment remain a central concern. Governments cannot afford to be irregularly attentive to capability—weapons must be developed with sufficient lead time, contingencies for weapon use must be anticipated, long-range technological opportunities and vulnerabilities must be recognized, and force readiness must be maintained. Second, military capability is of concern because it is also a domestic issue. Military programs are funded at the expense of domestic ones and often with indirect economic costs, and these same military programs are for many their professional and economic livelihood, and the basis of service prestige, importance, and budgetary share. Third, military capability is emphasized for strictly American reasons. Military technology has been a manipulable source of U.S. global influence because the United States has an economic base that is unparalleled in the capacity to support a large, diverse, and sophisticated arsenal; it is therefore not surprising that the United States has been partial toward military and/or technological solutions to its global problems. Finally, capability is preeminent in policy by default. A crisis at hand, substantive issues, and more mundane operational concerns are far more salient to policymakers than theory and doctrine—policy instruments are given more attention than policy ends. The result is that strategy is swallowed up by targeting considerations, weapon preferences, and tactical and operational concerns.

These policy deficiencies should not be ignored or understated. Regardless of their source, strategies influence policy at the level at which they are understood by policymakers. The theory of deterrence is not the policy of deterrence, and while personnel and resources freely flow between governmental and nongovernmental institutions and theorists expound on matters of policy, theorists do not direct and control the U.S. nuclear arsenal. In the final analysis, nuclear strategy is whatever policymakers believe it to be.

STRATEGY, ARMS REDUCTIONS, AND THE FUTURE

We live in an untidy world. No amount of wishful or simplistic thinking can change that fact. Nonetheless, strategy originates and thrives in a vacuum and is made to withstand only the most contrived tests against reality. Strategists offer target sets that cannot be distinguished in practice, abstract force requirements that can be used to support any number of competing policies, and strategic force assessments that ignore more factors than they consider. In sum, strategy hinges upon ill-founded and simplistic logic, and these deficiencies will flourish until circumstances, potentially of catastrophic proportions, expose them for what they are.

Strategists do look to the physical world, but unfortunately only to reify its properties. In particular, strategists are preoccupied with weapons characteristics and, accordingly, make weapons choices through criteria that exude an appearance of "truth." The "assured destruction" criterion, for instance, is promoted as if it were based in logic rather than in a professional consensus that could dissipate. But nowhere is this reification more glaring than in recent thinking on limited nuclear war— the belief that nations are constrained from escalating conflict beyond levels of advantage or that limited nuclear actions will be apparent as such, and that levels of conflict are "real," or at least obvious, as if escalation is controlled by physical realities rather than by psychological and political forces.

With the predominance of the physical in strategy, technology provides its own justification. This is intolerable. The strategic problems that we now confront are technological problems only in that they have worsened with technological innovation. What we can do has determined what we want to do and, more importantly, what we believe we *must* do. The answer to "how much is enough?" has changed with each new generation of weaponry as technology has been allowed to define policy objectives. Undeniably, force criteria must change; and indeed, the adequacy of U.S. forces is partly determined by changes in Soviet capability. Nevertheless, it must be remembered that the Soviets were unwilling to challenge the U.S. nuclear arsenal when it was only a fraction of its current size and capability.

Ironically, those who are most attentive to weapons characteristics are most likely to feign indifference to the fundamental physical reality of the nuclear age, a reality captured in the assertion that nuclear weapons serve as an "existential deterrent"—that is, the use of nuclear weapons (and even conventional weapons) is inhibited by the distinctively powerful nature of the bomb and also unfortunately that the use of *any* weapon in a superpower confrontation is a potential trigger and an implicit threat of an all-out exchange. International politics were altered irrevocably at Hiroshima and Nagasaki when weapons of a new order of destructive magnitude were thrust into the public awareness—weapons that would serve as a veritable symbol of a new era. Technology and deployment gimmickry have not changed this fact.

Even those who reject the assertion that nuclear weapons are unique implicitly concede this point by their recognition that others believe this to be true and by their very attention to the subject. The definitive evidence of the importance of the bomb is policymaker perceptions. Simply put, if policymakers *believe* these weapons to be "unusable" or "weapons of last resort" then they *are* unusable or ultimate weapons. Policymakers have devised strategies and weapons to make the bomb more usable, but this is actually a sign of the unreal level at which discourse on nuclear weaponry occurs—the historical record does not suggest that policymakers are cavalier about these weapons when it matters most.

The "existential deterrent" is an "absolute" reality—a challenge to the belief that nuclear effects can be precisely calibrated and differ from conventional effects only in degree. The existential deterrent acquires its power from the nonrational world of fear, psychological bias, and uncertainty and not from the rational world of deduction and mathematical precision. For this reason, strategic decisionmakers find it difficult to deal with nuclear war in probabilistic terms: these decisionmakers might estimate the probability of war to be greater than it is and yet might judge the smallest probability of war to be unacceptable; alternatively, they could be led to precipitous action because of a misplaced faith that nuclear weapons have reduced the probability of war to acceptable levels. The nonrational force of the existential deterrent is also apparent when strategic decisionmakers fail to make fine numerical distinctions:

numbers lack meaning at the higher levels of the destruction continuum —the difference between 1 and 5 million fatalities could be judged phenomenal; the difference between 50 and 55 million fatalities could be judged inconsequential. Indeed, the effects of nuclear weapons are so horrendous that they defy logical evaluation.

Sound nuclear strategies can be devised despite the limits to human logic, awareness, and understanding. Decisionmakers are not perfectly rational, but sound strategy is precluded only when human limitations are ignored. Strategists should be more impressed with human frailties than with a human technology-assisted capability to discriminate, communicate, and reason. A sound strategy will build upon the reputation that nuclear weapons possess and which has prevented their use for almost half a century rather than undermine this reputation with a false image of a decisionmaker that can perform in excess of human capability. Strategists can argue about whether this reputation is deserved, but the fact of this reputation—as witnessed in the symbolic power of nuclear weapons—is inescapable. When strategists allow military considerations to triumph over symbolic ones, in weapons acquisition and deployment, the deterrent power of nuclear weaponry is diminished.

The impediments to sound strategy are often claimed to result from the enormous demands that are placed on strategy—demands that have not declined with increases in Soviet nuclear capability. Accordingly, extended deterrence is assumed to be particularly responsible for the disarray of U.S. nuclear thought. Extended deterrence accounts for deficiencies in all areas of strategy as policymakers grasp at various military and political and rational and nonrational solutions to convince the Soviets that the United States will defend "secondary" interests. However, the dilemmas of extended deterrence have intensified, but did not actually create, the more general dilemmas of strategy. Policymakers are certainly most aware of and distressed about strategic deficiencies that call into question the U.S. willingness to meet commitments to Europe; nonetheless, the dilemmas of extended deterrence serve primarily to underscore strategic problems that would exist even in the absence of these commitments. The issue of whether the United States would use nuclear weapons in support of overseas interests is subordinate to the issue of whether the United States would use these weapons under any circumstances; the issue of whether the United States can use nuclear weapons to accomplish theater military objectives is subordinate to the issue of whether nuclear weapons have any military utility.

This does not mean that the dilemmas can disappear—they are a permanent feature of the nuclear-armed world. The tensions in strategy cannot be erased but they must be made explicit and should not be denied. To do otherwise, is to engage in a ceaseless, costly, fruitless, and even dangerous quest for security.

Weapons counts and features and the mathematics of destruction cannot be ignored—particularly since the Soviets might rely upon them. The Soviets appear to be no more precise, or at least no less arbitrary, than the United States in defining force characteristics. In fact, the Soviets, like their American counterparts, could be wedded perceptually to the status quo and might therefore conclude that unilateral U.S. reductions or unanswered Soviet increases will leave the Soviet Union with a usable military or political advantage. This should not cause undue concern. The new status quo could constrain action as much as the status quo ante, particularly when unilateral reductions are made in the name of force efficiency (note for instance U.S. megatonnage reductions) or other strategic criteria or in the name of existing U.S.-Soviet asymmetries in force structure. The Soviets have no reason to doubt the adequacy of U.S. forces at even a fraction of their current levels. Moreover, the Soviets cannot realize a coercive advantage without U.S. cooperation. A coercive advantage is conceded and not taken—it can exist only if *both* the Soviet Union and the United States believe that it exists and act accordingly.

This is an argument for negotiated arms reductions rather than for unilateral disarmament. If we accept the fact that most nuclear "advantages" are illusionary, negotiating options vastly increase in number. Concessions are not as onerous and "inequities" are more tolerable; a larger number of agreements become acceptable and thus possible.

Certainly, both sides must give up something if the reduction process is to continue and strategic stability is to be preserved. There is hope that such reductions can occur through a Soviet-American consensus derived through the bargaining process. This should not be construed as simply meaning that the United States must "educate" the Soviets. The United States and the Soviet Union are actually not as far apart as their doctrinal and deployment differences might suggest: the Soviet deployment of nuclear forces for warfighting by no means suggests a Soviet desire to use them and appears to be intended mainly to limit the effects of a nuclear conflict—what the Soviets might indeed regard to be the worst of all possible scenarios. Moreover, despite the tone of Soviet military doctrine, the Soviet political leadership appears to acknowledge (often implicitly) the devasting effects of nuclear war in word and in action. The harsh reality of nuclear incineration could indeed be the basis of a U.S.-Soviet consensus. Consensus *is* possible. It should not be forgotten that Soviet negotiators accepted provisions in the INF accords (such as those on verification) that these same negotiators deemed non-negotiable shortly before.

Negotiation certainly requires bargaining ploys and hard-nosed tactics, and Soviet negotiators, like U.S. negotiators, are not likely to purchase what they can get for free. At issue here is not the style or tactics of negotiation but the general spirit and purpose of negotiation. Arms reduction negotiations can be approached in two fundamentally different ways: as a means for achieving unilateral advantages or as a means by which the United States and the Soviet Union can realize their common objectives. In either case, negotiators must make "concessions" only with reluctance, but in doing so they should not assume that they are giving up more than they are. The same applies to the matter of arms control treaty noncompliance: The United States cannot allow small Soviet treaty violations slowly to eat away at agreements, but the United States is hardly an innocent victim either. The United States has interpreted treaties so as to safeguard U.S. deployment and limit Soviet options. The United States must look hard at the benefits of its policies against their costs in U.S.-Soviet trust and cooperation.

These observations are not a precise guide to policy—but that is just the point. Only crude guidelines can be offered. Contrary to conventional wisdom, U.S. security is not tied to exact tallies or more exotic military hardware. The problem is that policymakers mistake the tidy world of strategy for the real world. Until this problem is understood, wisdom will remain little more than convention.

NOTES

INTRODUCTION

1. The predominance of the concrete is partly a by-product of the way in which the abstract is distinguished here from the concrete: That which is treated as concrete might appear to be quite abstract, and indeed, the "concrete" encompasses much of contemporary strategic theory. *Concrete* is a relative term—and thus even those "concrete" aspects of strategy are abstract relative to others like those associated with operational policy—for instance, those related to nuclear weapons targeting.

2. This book adopts a citation convention to identify these policymakers. A citation preceded by *see* means that the position of the person cited can be inferred from the text. A citation preceded by *on this, see* means that the actual position of the person cited cannot be inferred from the text, and refers to a work where the exposition of the given argument can be found.

3. Nevertheless, this study is biased somewhat toward the most articulate among policymakers—those who have contributed to the public debate through contributions to scholarly journals, public speeches, and so on, and thus those who are likely to have the most elaborate set of beliefs.

4. However, policymakers might also appear more consistent and coherent than they actually are.

1. THE PSYCHOLOGY OF FOREIGN POLICY GOAL FORMATION

1. For an opposing view, see Converse 1964:208.

2. To understand is to "select" and, by implication, to "limit," to recognize

what *is* important and what *is not* important in any given context. When concepts bring some aspects of experience into focus, they inevitably divert attention from others.

3. Therefore, insight into the structure of goals can be obtained when goals are recognized to be a particular type of concept, the "constructed type." Constructed types (as kinds of constructs) are "constructed out of a 'combination of the values of several variables" (Stinchcombe 1968:43), but exist as wholes that are more than the sum of these simpler component parts. Thus the meaning of a constructed type is determined by its components and the implicit and explicit relationships among them (or, rather, the "configuration" and varied "accentuation" of these parts; McKinney 1966:11).

It is difficult to reduce goals to their components when their meanings appear to stem from the relationships among these parts. But the parts are vital to the meaning of the whole, and to our understanding of it. "Normally every dismemberment of a whole adds more to its understanding than is lost through the concurrent weakening of its comprehensive features, and again each new integration of the particulars adds more to our understanding of them than it damages our understanding by somewhat effacing their identity" (Polanyi 1969:125). "It would be a mistake to think that, in all domains, the epistemological alternatives reduce to just two options: either admit wholes defined in terms of their structural laws, or allow only for atomistic compounding of prior elements" (Piaget 1970:7).

4. By allowing for the manipulation of its parts, the constructed type serves a heuristic purpose: It is a "prototype" rather than a "typical" instance. It contributes to explanation of the external world, even when it does not directly explain, and it enhances an understanding of the world, even if it does not capture it fully. While constructed types vary in explanatory worth, they are by nature "exaggerations"; as such, they must be judged by their analytical properties (e.g., internal consistency) and utility (Berger 1976:126) and not just by their empirical "correctness."

5. *Abstraction* is used in psychology as a verb or noun to mean "isolating" or "discrimination," the "taking away" of elements. But this chapter is based on a meaning associated with concepts and their formation—the neglect of characteristics by withholding those common to a group (Pikas 1965:10, 111–115).

6. Any goal can be implicitly conceived in terms of its "particularistic" properties—conceptions of strategic deterrence, for example, register the unique aspects of the Soviet-American nuclear relationship.

7. Any concept can be made complex to the point that, for all intents and purposes, it is unique (particular) and can be given a proper name (e.g., the complex of characteristics known as a B-52 bomber). On this, see Russell 1948:298,303.)

8. For example, Converse (1964:213,235) notes that in mass beliefs, central ideas tend to be "simple, concrete, or 'close to home'" and that social "groupings" serve as "attitude objects" (e.g., an economic problem may be seen in racial terms—"they're taking our jobs"). While this does not mean that the concrete

and tangible coincide in those who otherwise think in abstract terms (the elite), it does suggest that concrete thinking is associated with tangible concepts or concepts with clear empirical referents.

9. The predictability of these consequences is enhanced when these goals are defined in tangible terms. If a "power balance" is defined as a "weapons balance," movement toward or away from this objective is more apparent.

10. On these characteristics as they pertain to high-level concepts, see Sartori 1970.

11. Definitions of success are culture-bound and require difficult judgments about such things as the ultimate sources of human happiness and fulfillment and about the relative importance of individual as opposed to collective benefits.

12. People might also think in terms of simple dichotomies because they believe that to fail to realize one of these commanding objectives is to have lost.

13. It is in this regard that March and Simon (1958:156–157) distinguish "nonoperational" goals like "promoting the general welfare" that are not useful in policy assessment and "operational goals" that "substitute" and "replace" these broader goals. The relationship between these sets of goals is "postulated but not testable" and does not appear to be purely instrumental.

14. The study of perception had its earliest origins in attempts to reduce perception to fundamental sensations and their physical receptors, and later in Gestalt theory's rejection of these ideas to study the relationship between environmental form and organization and brain physiology (Hochberg 1978). The modern study of perception continues to examine the human environment, as "stimuli" and "cues," but in order to understand "cognition."

15. The terms *perception* and *attention* are often used interchangeably in the literature.

16. Deutsch and Merritt (1965:134) term this the *focus*.

17. Not everyone experiences similar tension from incongruence, and thus people are not similarly motivated to resolve tension—though tension also depends on the importance of the beliefs involved and the extent of incongruence.

18. A person can be cued to a particular "definition of the situation." For instance, a problem can be clarified when information causes him/her to "recognize" goals that are effected by the problem and the means that are appropriate to address it.

19. The former serve as "symbols" in evoking the "meaning" of those symbols (Whitehead 1927:2,8).

20. There is little evidence that attention "to a particular dimension of experience can prevent the perceptual interpretation of other dimensions." The latter are not easily disregarded when believed associated with another or when relevant to the same entity (Kahneman 1973:110–111).

21. See also Rosch (1975) on the role of "referents."

22. Basic level concepts, however, are not the most concrete concepts, suggesting that, beyond a point, concreteness works against concept centrality. In any case, there is no consensus as to why people are cued to these concepts. In this regard, Rosch et al. (1976) emphasize the peculiar characteristics of basic

level concepts—they are distinguished by their relative informativeness (their number of features) because they are the most abstract concepts for which a "single image" can be formed (e.g., a "hammer" rather than a "tool") and have "members that are interacted with in the same ways" but also have the most apparent dissimilarities. On this, see Tversky and Hemenway 1984:170–171. Tversky and Hemenway (1984), in contrast, argue that basic level concepts assume salience through their "parts"—structural characteristics with which these concepts have generally a monopoly. (Here, parts are distinguished from "attributes": A "car" has "wheels" as a part, but "red" as an attribute.)

23. This tendency has all sorts of fascinating implications. See, for instance, Brown et al. (1985) for its effects on the subjective dating of events.

24. A "red apple" might appear "redder" than a mere "apple" (on this, see Murphy 1988:533).

25. Michotte did not detect similar causal conceptions when qualitative rather than mechanical events were involved, when objects changed appearance or shape rather than movement.

26. When these responsibilities are inadequately articulated, past actions help frame future tasks.

27. And, for this reason, social effects, that is, "outputs," are commonly measured by social "inputs." Spending measures are substituted for measures of social consequences (Bell 1976:333).

28. The case for motivated bias can be found, for instance, in Kull 1985, 1988 and for bureaucratic politics in Allison 1971; Halperin 1974.

29. Sometimes policy is a veritable patchwork quilt of compromise, and it is always a result that reflects the relative capabilities of the contending parties.

30. For example, Lindblom's (1959) "successive limited comparisons" model is a normative model, designed partly as a practical alternative to the classical model.

31. Even if with concerted effort, the search for policy alternatives will remain constrained and limited. As Simon (1979:144–174) has observed, even what appears to be "creative thinking," thinking that is "unconventional" and has "novelty" and "value," may indeed involve the substitution of one set of problem-solving techniques for another. A veteran chessplayer appears to the novice to sacrifice "creatively" a major piece for strategic gain, however, such problem solving does not require "looking for a needle in a haystack", but rather "devices that are capable of narrowing search to a very small part of the haystack."

32. Similarly, limited search behavior is found when U.S. policymakers have adopted compensatory arms sales as a primary means to retain influence and contain conflict within regions like the Middle East. Those policymakers assume, in part, that if U.S. allies are supplied the means to increase their military and economic capability, their regional standing will be bolstered and they will be inclined toward policies that are consistent with U.S. interests. Policymakers have not always appreciated the possibility that rapid development and a conspicuous military can promote popular disillusionment with and resentment of a regime (e.g., the Shah's Iran). Furthermore, policymakers have been insensitive

to the region as a "system." Arms supplied to offset threats in one part of the Middle East reverberate through the region and create demands for offsetting technology, fuel local concerns over misplaced national priorities and increased dependency on the United States, and promote the hostility of others who feel threatened by the weapons (Lebovic 1986). Policymakers, overwhelmed by the complexity of policy effects, might acknowledge only those symptoms that support the policies that they advocate (e.g., domino effects), but they also might not recognize these other effects.

33. These symptoms are not likely to be negative effects of existing policy, since the undesirable effects of policy are not easily recognized by policymakers as such (a matter upon which both cognitive psychologists and organizational theorists generally agree).

2. STRATEGIC ASSESSMENT

1. In this regard, it is important to note that there is a difference between concreteness and complexity and that the latter would seem to reduce concept salience.

2. If the administration did not go to great lengths to discount this doctrine, it may have been because "Eisenhower and Dulles both believed that ambiguity in declaratory policy was not in accord with the dictates of sound deterrence strategy" (George and Smoke 1974:287).

3. In fact, some of the major "nuclear confrontations" of the period could more accurately be regarded as an outgrowth of the integration of U.S. nuclear and nuclear-capable with its conventional forces (Halperin 1987:33).

4. This posture also reflected budgetary constraints. The Eisenhower administration was unwilling to accept the higher costs of conventional defense.

5. This same philosophy of abundance led critics to charge that atomic weapons were inherently weapons of "aggression" and "surprise" (Brodie 1946:73). Like other policymakers of the time, they did not fully anticipate the changes that would result from the joint U.S.-Soviet possession of an assured retaliatory capability.

6. However, these missiles did pose a threat to SAC bomber bases.

7. This position is described in Kahn (1961:15). Kahn distinguishes between those who embrace a "minimum" and a "finite" deterrent—with the latter equivalent to assured destruction.

8. Kennan was the former director of the Policy Planning Staff of the Department of State and a key architect of the U.S. containment policy.

9. When they do not succumb to relativist measures of the military balance and a "political warfighting" perspective.

10. In this regard, it should be noted that the United States possesses many times the capability to meet long-established "assured destruction" criteria, and even then, debate centers on issues that have little to do with the overall destructiveness of U.S. forces (e.g., weapon bans and ceilings) and rarely centers on whether the criteria themselves are inflated.

2. STRATEGIC ASSESSMENT

11. For this reason, this ceiling was not also a floor, and contrary to the absolutist position, McNamara did not claim that destruction below these prescribed levels would be insufficient to deter.

12. These authorizations were made prior to the complete debunking within the intelligence establishment of the "missile gap" myth.

13. In peacetime, U.S. forces were well above these requirements that were estimated by McNamara to be four hundred equivalent megatons, a level that was exceeded by each leg of the U.S. strategic triad (U.S. air, land, and sea forces).

14. See, for instance, Betts 1985:63, 71–72.

15. The annual budget statements of the Secretaries of Defense differed in their treatment of equivalence.

16. This failing is all the more glaring because the "winners" often sustain higher casualties than "losers" (e.g., World War I and II, Vietnam).

17. In such things as allocating its warheads to targets.

18. As "static" indicators, however, these measures can be incorporated into both retaliatory and multiple-exchange indicators.

19. Throw-weight is the weight of the last stage of a missile (after the booster has burnt out), and it includes reentry vehicles, and MIRV bus, penetration aids, et cetera.

20. Overpressure is pressure above normal sea-level air pressure of 14.7 pounds per square inch (PSI). Buildings can be destroyed with overpressure of only a few PSI, while ICBM silos are hardened to thousands of PSI.

21. An increase in the number of warheads will increase equivalent megatonnage, all other things being equal.

22. Though uncertainties exist in the estimates of the yield and resulting overpressures of both U.S. and Soviet weapons (Tsipis 1984:412).

23. The lethal radius of prompt radiation for weapons of one megaton or larger is smaller than that for blast, while the opposite is true for smaller weapons. Given the "smaller" size of U.S. nuclear warheads, blast effects will tend to underestimate Soviet fatality levels (Bennett 1980:34).

24. More recent studies have attempted to model the effects of a wide range of factors that could alter environmental effects such as winds, seasons, geography, and rainfall. These studies have tended to downgrade the probability that the most severe environmental effects would occur and negate the existence of a "threshold" for their onset (on this, see Thompson and Schneider 1986).

25. This is certainly true of popular arguments on the subject.

26. Circular error probability is the radius of the circle in which 50 percent of warheads will fall.

27. Blast primarily affects ICBM kills through overpressures that damage the silo cover and, secondarily, through cratering, silo burial, or shock-induced damage of silo and missile equipment (Tsipis 1984:384).

28. It would take an eightfold increase in hardness to offset a twofold increase in accuracy and an eightfold increase in yield to match the effectiveness of a twofold increase in accuracy.

29. A less important problem of almost all pre-attack indicators is that they implicitly assume that aggregate capability can be distributed freely among targets. Megatonnage is not necessarily available in the units required for adequate target coverage. Adjustments for this specific problem can be made by simple warhead counts—a solution that creates even more problems—or by programming to minimize the number of warheads necessary to destroy specified targets. Moreover, a single warhead cannot destroy two geographically separated targets (such as silos), and thus the excess effects on one blast cannot be applied to other targets. Furthermore, and less problematic, there may be limits to the ability of any two warheads or bombs to combine on any single target; warheads from a single MIRV bus cannot be widely dispersed, and bombers are restricted to so-called bomber tracks.

30. Errors occuring at these other stages include misinformation preprogrammed into the guidance systems (e.g., on the "position, velocity and orientation" of the missile, location of the target, gravitational irregularities), nonrandom effects on the missile guidance system (the accelerometers and gyroscopes) in flight (e.g., vibration, acceleration-, range-, and time-dependent effects, and erratic and nonimmediate rocket-thrust termination) (Tsipis 1984:390–401).

31. This occurs because of contact with debris and the unpredictable aerodynamics associated with the uneven burning of the RV's nose cone upon reentry.

32. This limitation is usually set to two warheads for military targets.

33. They appear to be a random influence because tests are conducted under varying conditions, but in an actual war atmospheric factors would have a more consistent effect on warheads.

34. While the warhead reentry angle can be altered to limit some of these problems, this has its costs (Steinbruner and Garwin 1976:176).

35. These measures are termed *outcome* or *effects* measures and include *retaliatory* and *multiple-exchange* indicators. These measures "thus inherently take into account any asymmetries between sides, whether in weapons technology, military doctrines, or the political structures that produce these doctrines" (Baugh 1984:134).

36. Slow-moving missiles on escape may be less vulnerable than attacking warheads to fratricide.

37. Although such an effort could conceivably engage the attacker's land-, air-, and sea-based strategic weapons, the level of coordination, timing, and weaponry required of such an assault renders it, at best, a hypothetical problem.

38. Elsewhere, very sophisticated measures of retaliatory capability have been offered that measure the ability of a smaller U.S. strategic force to cover the *current* target set (see May et al. 1988).

39. Admittedly, McNamara may have used this indicator because it showed the United States to have nuclear superiority.

40. The military has been a traditional bastion of relativist reasoning and has featured pre-attack indicators in its published reports. Within *Soviet Military Power* and the JCS *Military Posture* can be found U.S.-Soviet comparisons in such things as strategic nuclear delivery vehicles, warheads, throw-weight, hard-

target kill capability, equivalent megatonnage, number of new weapon systems, and various weapon characteristics.

41. This does not mean that rigorous studies of assured destruction capability have not been undertaken. See, for instance, Department of Defense FY1969.

42. Moreover, because they believe that redundancy and diversity assure U.S. force survival and require only that U.S. forces be able to retaliate with devasting indiscriminateness against Soviet society, absolutists are also less concerned with specific force survival issues such as warning time and attack timing.

43. See, for instance, Nitze 1976,1976–77.

44. See Department of Defense FY1975 FY1976 FY1982; Schlesinger 1975.

45. Or that these parameters are otherwise constrained. However, given the current inaccuracy of submarine launched ballistic missiles (SLBMs) and the slowness and limited penetrability of bombers, throw-weight may more validly measure the counterforce potential of land-based ballistic missiles. However, if the United States and the Soviet Union should become dependent upon mobile and unhardened land-based missiles, throw-weight alone, because of its relation to explosive yield, may become a useful indicator of counterforce capability.

46. Throw-weight ceilings would have had an even greater qualitative effect had they been adopted. However, other restrictions did restrain qualitative improvements. For instance, neither side was permitted to test or deploy an existing-type single-warhead missile with a reentry vehicle that constituted less than 50 percent of its throw-weight, preventing the MIRVing of these missiles.

47. Similarly, negotiators relied upon a quantitative standard to produce the 1987 U.S.-Soviet Intermediate Nuclear Forces (INF) treaty. The "zero-zero" solution that requires the destruction of all ground-launched intermediate-range missiles essentially ignores the diverse potentials of these missiles through a common ceiling.

48. The counting principle requires "functionally related observable differences" (Talbott 1980:234), which in this case were lacking. This principle is no longer as important now that the United States and Soviet Union have accepted more intrusive verification means such as on-site inspections. Nevertheless, these principles remain particularly relevant when conventional weapon systems (e.g., cruise missiles) are indistinguishable from their nuclear counterparts.

49. For instance, the throw-weight of missiles might not accurately measure weapons yield; the relationship between throw-weight and yield becomes more complicated when multiple warheads are involved (each warhead requires additional weight for such things as an independent source of fuel) to the point that increases in the number of warheads could conceivably lower the equivalent megatonnage of an arsenal (Bennett 1980:73–74).

50. More specifically, the percentage of weapons that are "groundburst"; see Nitze 1976–77:200,205.

51. Furthermore, counter-military potential is generally reported without accounting for variable weapons reliability or the effect of one country's counter-military potential upon another's.

52. Nevertheless, U.S. strategic forces are not inevitably vulnerable to "de-

capitation." Decapitation is a worst-case assessment that should only be offered with qualification. "It is easy to accumulate an intimidating list of what 'might' go wrong with the command system, but it is usually impossible to arrive at single probabilities of connectivity that do not have variances so large as to make them meaningless" (Carter 1981a:559). Assessment of command and control survivability is, in fact, a more difficult task than strategic weapons assessment.

53. Only when missiles carried multiple warheads could an ICBM attack on enemy ICBMs result in a net gain.

54. This, again, is a favored technique in annual Department of Defense publications.

55. These statistics are found in popular discourse on the nuclear "arms race."

56. And the instances in which U.S. and Soviet arms control negotiators have lectured on the follies of each other's perspective suggests the opposite.

57. For this reason, for instance, the United States could fear a high Soviet warhead-to-missile ratio because it creates a greater Soviet incentive to preempt, or alternatively, the United States could value this high ratio for the more limited number of Soviet targets that the United States must then cover.

58. That is, whether and how their range should be restricted, whether bombers with cruise missiles should count as MIRVs, whether conventionally armed cruise missiles were to be proscribed, and what number of cruise missiles was to be permitted on bombers.

59. In which a single launcher is housed deceptively in any of a number of silos.

60. e.g., limits on ICBM warheads, restrictions on mobile missiles and sea-launched cruise missiles, counting rules for air-launched cruise missiles.

61. e.g., prohibitions on strategic defense.

62. e.g., the phase in which cruise missiles would be discussed, whether intermediate-range systems should be packaged with intercontinental-range systems.

63. Talbott (1985:86) has observed that "it was one of the puzzlements of the INF story that the two sides, working from what were, or should have been, the same data could come up with such wildly divergent measurements of the nuclear balance in Europe. What Reagan read as a six-to-one imbalance in favor of the USSR Moscow professed to see as almost perfect equality. The disagreement was a classic example of how one can prove anything with numbers."

64. Validity of military expenditure data is at least as great a problem as its reliability (partly because a measure that is unreliable cannot also be valid). Nevertheless, cross-national data on military expenditures suffer from serious reliability problems. These problems include double bookkeeping, budgetary categories of impenetrable generality, extra-budgetary accounts and foreign exchange manipulations (where revenues may be channeled directly into arms purchases without being recorded as security expenditures), and military assistance grants that may not be recorded as an expenditure by donor states and may be part of the expenditure totals of recipients (Ball 1984a, 1984b).

65. Indeed, some U.S. high technology is not available at any price—a fact

that could force a ruble assessment toward infinity—and some Soviet defense systems could be "inherently less costly," costing less than U.S. systems with a similar level of performance (Handel 1982:210).

66. The most well-known of these standards differentiates a "first-strike" from a "second-strike" capability. Yet even these terms have not been defined unambiguously and consistently in practice.

67. On the disutility of a time-urgent capability, see Carnesale and Glaser 1982:78–82.

68. This ICBM dominance has been dubbed the *counterforce syndrome*.

69. Interview with Paul Warnke in Scheer 1983:199.

70. Neglecting, for instance, cruise missiles, which have a significant hard-target capability.

71. e.g., industrial assets, sophisticated technology.

72. e.g., dependence upon vulnerable airfields and ports, fewer manpower reserves.

73. e.g., inducing high fatality rates.

74. They may be complacent about the retaliatory capability of U.S. submarines in part because of the devasting destructive power of even a very small number of submarines (i.e., a single surviving submarine could be enough) and the margin for error allowed by excess capability.

75. Even the nuclear winter thesis has been used to justify strategic defensive deployments and nuclear counterforce options (see, for example, Weinberger 1985).

76. For example, the timing of an attack could decrease the problem of fratricide but could also provide a window of escape for enemy missiles.

77. On the dynamics of the perceived balance, see Kull 1988:114–155.

78. As will be shown in chapter 5, the actual capabilities of the United States and the Soviet Union suggest that the game of "chicken" is in order, but the Soviets could have the advantage of not understanding or accepting those rules.

79. It is also true, though, as will become apparent in chapter 5, that assured destruction advocates look upon the uncertainties in capability assessment as a source of strategic stability.

3. STRATEGIC ACTION

1. Various technical limitations combined to make urban-industrial centers the primary targets, though this only served to confuse the purposes of the strategic offensive.

2. The generally pessimistic conclusions of the *Bombing Survey* were given different readings. Many were impressed by the toll that strategic bombing had taken toward the end of the war on some critical German industries such as liquid fuel and transportation and by the fact that the German electric power grid, which had not been expressly targeted, was more vulnerable than had appeared. The implication was that atomic bombs should be employed so as to maximize the disruptive rather than the destructive effects of bombing (see, for

instance, Brodie 1959:107–127). However, SAC, under the strong hand of General LeMay, followed the priorities set by the incendiary bombing of Japan and emphasized attacks on industrial areas over precision targets with the belief that discriminate bombing was neither possible nor desirable (Kaplan 1983:37, 41–42).

3. This ad hoc committee was established by Secretary of Defense James Forrestal and was chaired by air force lieutenant general H. R. Harmon.

4. Indeed, it can be argued that NSC-68 "was 'not' a defense-oriented, status quo-oriented document" (Trachtenberg 1988:13).

5. Tactical warning was provided by the Distant Early Warning line that was completed in 1956. In consisted of a two-thousand-mile-long ground-based system of radars across Canada and was designed to provide up to several hours of warning of an impending Soviet bomber attack.

6. Though the vulnerability problem was recognized actually quite early (Trachtenberg 1988:35, 38).

7. SAC assumed that U.S. strategic bomber bases were only one among a larger set of targets that would be attacked by the Soviet Union in the event of war and that Soviet attacks on other targets on approach to SAC bases would provide hours of warning (Wohlstetter and Brody 1987:166). The JCS had similarly concluded that technical constraints would seriously limit the effectiveness of a Soviet first strike (Betts 1986–87:7).

8. Despite the attention to vulnerability, defensive concerns often did not appear to be logically based. Ironically, it was the Soviet explosion of an H-bomb that appeared to sell Eisenhower on air defense (Quester 1970:100), a development that could as easily be taken as a sign of the pointlessness of nuclear defense.

9. Given the costs and problems of passive defense of these IRBMs and the severity of the Soviet warhead threat.

10. Wohlstetter (1958) addressed the problems created by the overseas deployment of U.S. missiles in a public commentary.

11. The Killian Committee (or the Technological Capabilities Panel) was composed of the Science Advisory Committee of the Office of Defense Mobilization and chaired by James Killian, Jr., of M.I.T. The Gaither Committee (or the Security Resources Panel) was established by the Office of Defense Mobilization at the request of the National Security Council and chaired by H. Rowen Gaither of RAND and formerly of the Ford Foundation.

12. As the work of "outsiders," it rose above bureaucratic compromise (each of the services took exception to at least some of its conclusions or their budgetary implications) and offered sweeping conclusions. For this very reason its political impact was muted.

13. Nevertheless, the report did argue that "the prevention of war would best protect our urban population."

14. This is not meant to imply that there was no interest in civil defense. To the contrary, the air defense of urban-industrial areas had an active constituency within the scientific community throughout the fifties (though many of its sup-

porters were to embrace the antithetical assured destruction position in the sixties), and the Army became an enthusiastic supporter of large-scale ABM deployment for civil defense in the late fifties.

15. To quote Read (1962), "by punishment we mean loss of life, injury, suffering, privation, social upheaval, and destruction of property—in short, all those things that contribute to human anguish on the part of either combatants or noncombatants."

16. This is the sense in which Schelling (1966:192) uses the term.

17. Though it is unclear whether a nation's gains can include the infliction of cost upon an adversary.

18. Some would argue that *warfighting* is a misnomer, for even a nuclear war that was ostensibly limited to "military" targets would assuredly destroy the participants.

19. "It is *not* a new strategic doctrine; it is *not* a radical departure from U.S. strategic policy over the past decade or so" (Department of Defense FY1982).

20. Pure warfighters value coercion partly because the United States lacks a first-strike capability.

21. Counterforce and countervalue attacks do not require a counterforce or countervalue posture, respectively, and refer instead only to the nature of the targets to be struck.

22. Enthusiastic, if not zealous, support of all facets of defense can be found in Kahn 1961.

23. McNamara publically revealed this strategy in 1962 in his famous commencement address in Ann Arbor.

24. The classified five-year Defense guidance of Secretary of Defense Weinberger as cited in Getler (1982).

25. However, a nation with a disarming second-strike counterforce capability could conceivably lack such a first-strike capability. This would depend on the invulnerability of a nation's strategic forces and how its opponent employs its weapons.

26. However, a first-strike option was actively considered within the Department of Defense (Betts 1987:101–102).

27. U.S. officials will sometimes maintain that they adhere to pure warfighter precepts only because the Soviets do. When pressed publicly, officials deny that nuclear war can be won. In public commentary, Secretary of Defense Weinberger, for instance, softened significantly the stance explicit in his Defense guidance that called for the United States to "prevail" in nuclear combat.

28. While it is theoretically possible both to deny another victory and to avoid defeat and yet to not achieve victory, the satisfaction of the former two conditions is tantamount to victory if the United States has as its wartime objective a return to the *status quo ante* (and not some more "permanent solution" to the Soviet problem). This would be true even if the United States were armed only with an impenetrable defense.

29. On this, see Sagan 1989:88–89; see also Gray 1986a.

30. See Slocombe 1981:22–23; Department of Defense FY1982; Brown 1983:75.

31. These theorists sought ways to induce an adversary "to accept limitations of geography, weapons, and possibly time" (see Kaufmann 1956:113).

32. Brodie (1954) placed even less emphasis on force, and he was not optimistic that limits could be maintained once strategic nuclear weapons were employed.

33. These conceptions are elsewhere referred to as a "unilateral" and a "cooperative" approach to damage limitation (Snyder 1977). An early discussion of the difference between these conceptions can be found in Knorr (1962) and a later one in Osgood (1988).

34. Although this chapter focuses on the simple distinction between force and value targets, it must be noted that some limited option advocates rely on a multitude of target distinctions as well as other criteria for limiting conflict. The distinction employed here still usefully highlights the dilemmas and inconsistencies of the strategy.

35. From this perspective, assaults on cities are a confession of weakness.

36. In emphasizing military effectiveness, these warfighters might opt for what Kahn (1968:173) terms an *avoidance* attack over a *constrained* attack—the former requires attempts to limit collateral damage only when this does not entail military costs, and the latter requires unqualified attempts to limit such damage. An avoidance attack is thus more a damage limitation than a city avoidance strategy.

37. This hard-target bias and its attending conceptual problems are recorded, for example, in the claim that the United States should maintain an ICBM force to threaten the "reliable prompt use of small numbers of nuclear weapons against virtually any *meaningful* military targets . . ." (see Allison et al. 1985:226; emphasis added).

38. Given that the countervailing strategy does not challenge explicitly the notion of deterrence based upon mutual vulnerability.

39. The point is not that the Soviets expect victory but that they believe the circumstances to leave them without alternatives. (On Soviet doctrine and deterrence, see Garthoff 1985:768–785; 1988.) However, the Soviets (particularly civilians) have shifted doctrine away from the expectation of victory.

40. Though some believe that the problem is that the United States has to catch up with Soviet thinking (see Cordesman 1982:42; Department of Defense FY1982). On this, see Hart 1984.

41. It is for this reason that some (see, for instance, Gray 1986a:277–280) consider what is termed here *political warfighting* a virtual extension of assured destruction.

42. This scenario is offered by both political and pure warfighters and is attributed to Nitze (1976, 1977) and the private Committee on the Present Danger.

43. The early Department of Defense annual reports emphasized city avoidance, while later reports stressed damage limitation and, to an increasing extent, assured destruction.

44. For a viewpoint that offers the most elongated escalation ladder and

recognizes many rungs between the initiation of nuclear force and an all-out nuclear exchange, see Kahn 1968.

45. The link between mutually assured destruction and political warfighting is apparent in what has been termed a *MAD-plus* posture, a posture devised as a "hedge" that "relies mainly on assured destruction but favors buying some limited options or flexibility for added insurance" (see Art 1985:124).

46. This is not meant to imply that the thin defense had primarily a strategic justification. In fact, the next chapter suggests that the thin defense was, above all else, a result of bureaucratic compromise.

47. The Kennedy administration's interest in passive civil defense waned when the administration recognized that programs aimed at damage limitation could not prevent high casualty levels and offered diminishing marginal returns on investment (Greenwood 1975:69).

48. Bombers might be even more likely to be dispersed to civilian airfields in the future because modern bombers (the B-1) have the capability to take off from shorter and narrower runways (Daugherty et al. 1988:34).

49. Prominent political warfighters, however, have been among the most active opponents of urban-industrial defense.

50. Such a political warfighter might agree with Knorr (1962:30) that theirs is a "bad" and "absurd" war and strategy, "but the question remains whether the available alternatives may not be, or may not come to be, more absurd and worse; and the possibility cannot be ruled out that *our* choices, *and* our opponent's choices, may become as absolutely bad as that implies."

51. See, for instance, Allison et al. 1985; Art 1985; Nye 1986.

52. Even then, many aspects of operational planning, like target selections, are classified and outsiders can never know exactly what they are or when they change.

53. In fact, even retardation targets were mainly fixed industrial installations such as petroleum refineries (Rosenberg 1982:10).

54. These are also termed *aimpoints* and are targets that have been grouped by hardness and proximity (Arkin and Fieldhouse 1985:92).

55. Under the revised SIOP, the United States could technically have withheld attack against any of the three basic target sets (Sagan 1987:38).

56. Rowen 1975:227fn, 230, 233; Rosenberg 1986:45.

57. Until 1974, the smallest planned strike involved the delivery of twenty-five hundred warheads against Soviet nuclear targets (Powers 1982:106).

58. This is the guidance of the Secretary of Defense to the JCS for nuclear weapons employment, and it is used by the JCS to create a more detailed guidance (the Joint Strategic Capabilities Plan) for the Joint Strategic Target Planning Staff (JSTPS) in the preparation of the SIOP. The actual SIOP brings together the work of two JSTPS divisions—one responsible for maintaining and updating a target list and the other for assigning existing weapons to these targets based on considerations of optimal weapons use and operational constraints (Latham and Lane 1987:642–643).

59. Signed by President Carter in July 1980; on this, see Sagan 1989:50–54.

60. C³I improvement required, among other things, a survivable warning system, a protected, relocated, and functioning leadership in control of U.S. strategic forces, the capability to assess damage to U.S. targets, sensors to identify, track and assess damage to Soviet targets, and an extensive communication network to bind the system (Richelson 1983).

61. Including the B-1 and Stealth bombers for use against various Soviet military targets (e.g., mobile missiles), command centers, and so forth.

62. In other words, the United States will employ its air, land, and sea forces to assure their destruction.

63. By 1983, about 10,000 U.S. warheads were available for a full-scale preemptive strike against 50,000 purported targets. While planners theoretically possess great latitude in allocating individual weapons to targets, individual allocation decisions are constrained in practice. Weapons often work in tandem to accomplish their missions and must also be programmed so as to avoid mutual interference.

64. If subject to decapitation attacks, the defender might believe that its opponent is out for military victory at all costs and is unwilling to bargain. The defender, then, is not likely to respond with restraint.

65. In actuality, those given the war task can be distinct from those who make important political decisions, for in war a good deal of authority must be delegated to the military because the time permitted for decisions is limited, technical judgments are required, and centralized command and control is potentially fragile.

66. The Reagan administration gave added emphasis to the importance of this issue by authorizing the development of "burrowing warheads" that could threaten Soviet command centers.

67. This was a controversial issue well before the H-bomb.

68. The Scowcroft commission was officially known as the President's Commission on Strategic Forces, and it was chaired by former presidential National Security Adviser Brent Scowcroft.

69. The Hoffman panel or, as it was officially known, the Future Security Strategy team (FSSS) was one of two major extragovernmental study teams that were formed in 1983 by President Reagan to examine the implications of strategic defense, and it was directed by Fred S. Hoffman of Pan Heuristics.

70. The flight of a missile can be divided into four phases: a "boost phase," during which it is propelled under power, "postboost" phase, during which the postboost vehicle (the "bus") dispenses its warheads, decoys, et cetera, on separate trajectories, a "midcourse" phase, during which the warheads and decoys continue their travel through space, and a "terminal" phase, which commences when the warheads enter the atmosphere.

71. Because of the futuristic nature of much of the technology involved, the actual effectiveness of these systems cannot be judged and the high interception rates that defense advocates posit are, at best, levels to which they aspire.

72. See, for example, Holst and Schneider 1969 for representative arguments of the earlier defense proponents and Chayes and Wiesner 1969 for those of the opponents.

73. This is not contradictory if the instability is due to the false perception that defensive systems will work.

74. That is, split-second performance against the array of Soviet ballistic missile forces.

75. Their pessimism over system performance is justified, and accordingly, the Reagan administration's strategic defense proposals were greeted with widespread skepticism in the civilian scientific community. A recent, still-classified two-year study by the Congressional Office of Technology Assessment, for instance, concluded that the technological challenges mean that there is a "significant probability" that the use of these defenses will result in "catastrophic failure" (Smith 1988c).

76. The size, number, and dispersion of U.S. population centers and their location along an extensive coastline.

77. However, it has been noted that defense advocates "prefer to argue the benefits of defense rather than its feasibility, and doubters prefer to find practical flaws rather than problems of principle" (Carter 1984:6).

78. For a full discussion of the effects of defense on crisis stability, see Wilkening et al. 1987.

79. For the different meanings of cost effectiveness, see Cimbala 1988:117.

80. Lasers could be foiled if missiles were protectively coated or spun in flight, decoy warheads could create problems for target discrimination, boost-phase interception with neutral particle beams could be thwarted if missiles were to complete the boost phase in the atmosphere, and space-based systems could be circumvented if SLBMs were fired on "depressed trajectories."

81. Although they therefore recognize the interdependence of offense and defense, they ignore their interconnection when they discount an arms race explanation for Soviet defensive deployments by narrowly focusing on the lack of prior U.S. defensive deployments.

82. This defense could conceivably allow the defender to marshal its resources to defend certain targets without betraying those targets in advance so that an attacker must expend its offensive resources as if every target were preferentially defended in order to assure the required destruction of targets (Hoffman 1986:10–11).

83. Nevertheless, even an effective point-defense system might give the Soviets an advantage since they are more dependent upon land-based missiles (see Sagan 1989: 116) and because, if many warfighters are correct, the Soviets highly value leadership and command centers that could be protected at the terminal phase.

84. Though it can be argued that such defense induces instability only because it may erroneously be presumed effective (see Glaser 1985:51f).

85. But they also recognize ways in which the defense can destabilize directly. Defense systems that must be launched into space when needed could

limit valuable crisis decision time and may send unintended hostile messages to an opponent (particularly when these systems carry nuclear explosives, e.g., the so-called pop-up X-ray laser).

86. A perfect defense will create stability (though the transition to perfect defense is fraught with peril; see, for example, Burrows 1984:844), and a less-than-perfect defense of force or value targets, in and of itself, will have no effect on stability, for in neither case is a prospective attacker given an increased incentive to preempt.

87. However, when assured destruction advocates argue that a nation that preempts out of fear of preemption will attack enemy value targets, the logic of assured destruction is undermined.

88. However, there is precedent for such major shifts in strategic policy preference. The strongest proponents of defense in the fifties were among the strongest advocates of assured destruction in the sixties.

4. STRATEGIC OBJECTIVES AND WEAPON DEPLOYMENTS

1. This assumption is inherent within the assured destruction stance.

2. Kennan (1983:133), for instance, observes that "there remain, of course, the ever-present possibilities of war by inadvertence: by miscalculation, by mis-read signals, by unacceptable challenges to prestige, by exaggerated anxieties and panic."

3. Though Betts (1985:76) argues, however, that the dangers of a Soviet surprise nuclear attack have nonetheless been overestimated. There are numerous political and technical barriers to a nuclear surprise attack.

4. U.S. proponents of the arms race thesis, however, do have a tendency to overemphasize U.S. culpability, if only because they have less control over Soviet behavior.

5. Harold Brown (1983:11–18), despite his other leanings, joins with pure warfighters to emphasize these same sources of Soviet conduct.

6. For instance, they imply that the Soviets would be out to annihilate by suggesting that the Soviets would lash out in desperation if their empire were crumbling.

7. For one thing, this lack of clarity explains pure warfighter ambivalence toward the purpose of city defense.

8. The Soviets might also be willing to bargain if they determined that war had resulted from accident or miscalculation. Pure warfighters tend to downplay the possibility of inadvertent war, however.

9. Even if they also recognize the possibility of accidental or inadvertent war (see Department of Defense FY1975).

10. It is said that the Soviet Union is "opaque" or a "black box" (see Nye 1984:871) and that "there will always be considerable uncertainty about what deters the Soviet Union" (see Allison et al. 1985:218).

11. With the unlimited objectives of "pure conflict" there can be no limits or

bargaining because "there is no element of common interest" (Snyder and Diesing 1977:116).

12. It can also be argued that the Soviets possess negotiating advantages— e.g., their belief that strategic nuclear war cannot be limited.

13. Where a country is "deterred" when it fails to act because of unacceptable costs or limited gains and "compelled" when it concedes assets or gains because of unacceptable costs.

14. The distinction between deterrence and compellence is important because these policies require different tactics. The threat to deny the Soviet Union further gains could do little to make it concede that which it already has or to renounce a position once taken.

15. They perceive intent, more generally, in the gamut of Soviet foreign policy actions—even to the extent that they treat Soviet WW II casualty levels as indicating the Soviet willingness to incur high costs to achieve expansionist objectives.

16. Warfighters often concede this point, though they argue that the stakes are too high to assume anything but the worst.

17. Other explanations for Soviet behavior can be offered (see Meyer 1984). But the two models explored here are most representative of the views of strategic policymakers.

18. On the positive side, military expenditure figures are standardized and therefore allow the analysis of more than just a few, unrepresentative cases.

19. The arms race literature recognizes that reactions do not always conform to reactions: a nation that is militarily preponderant or grossly inferior or has insufficient resources or faces other internal constraints might not respond to the actions of another nation. For this the arms race literature is fundamentally indebted to the early formulations of Richardson (1960).

20. On the other hand, the Soviets might be less sensitive in other respects because they, unlike the United States, enjoy the logistic advantages of a continental power within the European theater.

21. For example, the Soviets might not be willing to invest in submarines because they pose problems of "attenuated" control (Cimbala 1988:148).

22. This because they tend to believe US-Soviet deterrence to be stable.

23. Even if they might not believe that the Soviets should judge U.S. deployment similarly.

24. The history of international politics can be cast in terms of the changing preeminence of defensive and offensive weapons technology.

25. Interesting also is that defense advocates have argued for U.S. defensive deployments by alluding to Soviet defensive deployments.

26. See U.S. Department of Defense and Department of State 1985.

27. They exhibited this tendency in the "window of vulnerability" debate.

28. Meyer poses these questions in offering a "military superiority model."

29. This appreciation can explain the early Soviet concentration of ballistic-missile forces in the European theater (though, admittedly, Soviet missiles lacked the range for intercontinental operations), the Soviet pursuit of a missile reload

capability (Holloway 1986:153–154), and Soviet plans for an offensive that would include both nuclear and conventional forces (Berman and Baker 1982:26).

30. Shorter-term predictions were better, though they were also consistently underestimates (Berkowitz 1985a).

31. The SS-9 was apparently deployed in numbers sufficient for attacks on hardened ICBM launch-control centers (Berman and Baker 1982:53).

32. For instance, because of the expected Soviet investment in ABM and the considerable expense of large-scale SS-9 deployment, the CIA believed that it was unlikely that the Soviets would invest greatly in ICBMs.

33. These critics also believed it unlikely that the Soviets would invest in a defense that was effective only against bombers.

34. The CIA attributed these procurement decreases to a severe downturn in the Soviet economy, related production bottlenecks, and the costs and complexities of military high technology, and believed that these decreases reflected leadership decisions to stretch out procurement to diffuse costs (Kaufman 1985).

35. See U.S. Congress, Subcommittee on Economic Resources, Competitiveness and Security Economics 1986. The DIA maintained that procurement grew at a rate of 3 to 4 percent in 1982–1984. Discrepancies between the CIA and the DIA figures were due to differences in estimates of both weapons costs and production rates and the DIA practice of looking only at major weapons systems (70 percent of the procurement total).

36. See the *Annual Report to the Congress* and *Soviet Military Power* for that time period.

37. The increase in estimates of the military burden was due to the expression of costs in current dollars—defense prices rose faster than those for civilian goods and services.

38. Under the provisions of the SALT II treaty, the United States and the Soviet Union were both entitled to deploy one new type nonheavy missile, which in the Soviet case the administration maintained was the SS-24.

39. Missile modifications of only 5 percent were permitted for modernization, while the throw-weight of the SS-25 was claimed by the administration to be nearly double that of the SS-13. Moreover, reentry vehicles were required to constitute a minimum of 50 percent of the missile throw-weight for single-warhead missiles, while the SS-25 reentry vehicle was claimed to account for slightly less than half.

40. This radar was in technical violation of the ABM treaty because it was located far from the nearest border and was oriented inward rather than outward as required for early-warning systems.

41. See, for instance, U.S. Congress, Subcommittee on Arms Control, International Security and Science 1987; Arms Control Association 1987.

42. U.S. Congress, Subcommitee on Strategic and Theater Nuclear Forces 1986; Gordon 1986.

43. Therefore, decisions are less likely to reflect strategic doctrine than what has been described as a peculiarly American "doctrine of quality" that manifests itself in a penchant for high-performance, multipurpose weapons (Head 1978:550).

44. Each MIRVed missile carries a "bus," which separates at the end of the boost phase and maneuvers to place each of a given number of warheads on independent trajectories.

45. MIRV appears to have been "a technology whose time had come," and "it is therefore not surprising that MIRV was 'invented' almost simultaneously in several places within the technical community" (Greenwood 1975:14–15).

46. It should also be noted that the H-bomb was envisaged at its inception to be solely a countervalue weapon, a way of inexpensively introducing major increases in weapons yield into the U.S. arsenal. Only with time would the revolutionary contribution of fusion technology to the development of light-weight, low-yield weapons be recognized.

47. It is partly for this reason that the United States has designed its recent arms control proposals to require a minimum restructuring or dismantling of U.S. forces and to shift the burden of disarmament and force restructuring onto the Soviets. It is also for this reason that the military services have resisted program cancellations and have sought to preserve programs through "stretch-outs"—elongated procurement periods (Moore 1987c; Congressional Budget Office 1987).

48. Strategy has certainly affected policy. For the role of "assured destruction" in U.S. operational planning, for instance, see Sagan 1989:11–13.

49. This does not mean that political and economic motives cannot foster incremental technological changes. In fact, Kurth (1973) argues that a "follow-on imperative" dictates that, for economic and political reasons, companies will get contracts for systems that are "structurally similar while technically superior to the system being phased out" that they had produced previously.

50. The incremental model may better fit the Soviet than the American case. Soviet doctrine is mindful of Soviet technological disadvantages and conservatively promotes evolutionary changes and the extensive testing of multiple weapons prototypes (Head 1978:555).

51. This strategy has obvious costs. The B-1 bomber, for example, suffered unexpected deficiencies in flight stability and attack capability that have been attributed to what contractors term *concurrency,* the move into production in advance of R and D completion. Production has been delayed, critical components have failed, and design changes have forced other modifications of the aircraft (Moore 1987a, 1987b).

52. For a thorough presentation of the general bureaucratic politics thesis, see Allison 1971.

53. Military organizations might not be wedded to a particular concrete conception. A fluid conception of service roles certainly underlay the Army–Air Force dispute over development and operational control of IRBMs in the fifties. The Army recognized IRBMs to be an extension of artillery, though of greater range (and thus able to hit deeper targets from less exposed rear positions) and firepower, but also redefined the Army mission to accommodate these missiles so as to challenge Air Force preeminence in strategic bombing (Armacost 1969:94–96).

54. This indefiniteness of purpose also served as a cloak behind which the surface navy could hide its desire to deploy an antiship missile (Art and Ockenden 1981).

55. To support the bureaucratic politics thesis it is argued, among other things, that the Trident assumed its physical characteristics in bureaucratic compromise and that, as a result, in comparison to the Polaris/Poseidon, these characteristics render it more vulnerable (e.g., its size) and fail to give it real advantages (e.g., its greater speed is still insufficient for outrunning Soviet attack submarines) and could have been offered in a simpler, cheaper package (e.g., upgraded missiles could have been placed aboard the existing fleet) (Steinbruner and Carter 1975).

56. To the technical and bureaucratic politics theses can be added other explanations that also center on internal inducements to arms acquisition (e.g., the economic requirements of the so-called military-industrial complex; Kurth 1973).

57. Even then, the arms race and strategy cannot fully explain the deployment decision. These factors cannot explain the differences between the Air Force and the Army on the priority to be given IRBMs (the Air Force argued that IRBMs should only be a by-product of ICBM development). (On the development of IRBMs, see Armacost 1969.)

58. This is certainly the case when the massive Soviet conventional and strategic buildup of the sixties is attributed to the Cuban missile crisis.

59. In the aggregate, all of these forces appear to have influenced U.S. deployment—the U.S. and Soviet arsenals have grown simultaneously (in both quantity and quality), technology has steadily become more sophisticated, and weapons have been deployed that reaffirm the essential mission of each of the nuclear services.

60. Similarly, it can be argued that strategy influenced cruise missile acquisition. Decisions affecting cruise missile development and deployment were made at the highest levels of government and reflected the results of arms control negotiations, U.S. concerns for its alliance commitments, extensive study of missile variants, and assessment of the respective merits and deficiencies of alternative launch platforms.

61. See, for example, Rathjens 1969; York 1970:211; Newhouse 1973:64–65, 74.

62. Paradoxically, those who promoted MIRV as a counter to Soviet defense would also promote U.S. ABM as a counter to the Soviet MIRV threat (claimed to be posed by the SS-9).

63. In fact, MIRV was not planned around a Soviet ABM: The Soviet defensive threat did not become a concern until MIRV was already in development. (MIRV probably gained political momentum, though, because of this threat.)

64. Though the Air Force preferred a higher-yield and then more accurate hard-target-capable warhead.

65. At least one analyst (Kurth 1971:385) regards bureaucratic political motives to have been the primary impetus behind MIRV.

66. Evangelista (1984) discusses the factors that influence Soviet weapon deployment, though others believe that strategic goals dominate Soviet weapon acquisition (see, for example, Jones 1984).

5. STRATEGIC PROCESSES: RATIONALITY AND NONRATIONALITY

1. For example, the narrowing of options, the fragmentation of the decision process.

2. Hence the preference for the term *nonrational* over *irrational*.

3. On the relationship between the "rational" and the "irrational," see Schelling (1960:16).

4. Game theory is often regarded to be the embodiment of the assumption of rational utility-maximizing behavior. But game theory is pliable enough to incorporate limits to rationality. The theory presupposes these limits when outcomes are not preordained (in that the players' choices are contingent upon each other's actions) and variable-sum (nonzero-sum) solutions are possible. Under these conditions, choice might reflect the perception (and therefore the misperception) of adversary alternatives and likely responses and hence a limited understanding of the adversary. Perception and only a limited understanding of the adversary are inherent in "tacit" bargaining, decision strategies like "minimax" (which take account of adversary options but not attending payoffs), observed differences in sequential-play games, the difficulty of deriving solutions to n-person games, and matrices constructed around perceived rather than actual payoffs and choices.

5. In response, it can be argued that decisionmakers could be deterred even with a perfect knowledge of their adversary. Perfect rationality could simply render deterrence less explicit.

6. For an opposing view, see Art 1985:125.

7. Supporting the first interpretation, Kahn (1968:290) takes escalation dominance to be "a function of where one is on the escalation ladder. It depends on the new effect of the competing capabilities on the rung being occupied, the estimate by each side of what would happen if the confrontation moved to other rungs, and the means each side has to shift the confrontation to these other rungs."

8. However, pure warfighters can base their strategy on the assumption that the Soviets will strike out of irrationality, thereby justifying a U.S. capability to deny the Soviets their objectives physically (see Ikle 1973). Nevertheless, against an irrational adversary a denial capability could be inadequate if effective only at lower levels of violence.

9. Though escalation dominance can also be treated as a means of escalation control (see Gray 1986a: 159, 174–177). In any case, escalation dominance is generally regarded to require more than capability dominance and to involve, for instance, "the assurance, morale, commitment, resolve, internal discipline, and so on, of both the principals and their allies" (Kahn 1968:23).

10. Tacit bargaining is conducted through deeds rather than words.

11. These thresholds are reinforced by their overlapping nature. The threshold between the use of what are commonly treated as "strategic" and "tactical" weapons coincides with that between a central (that against the homeland) and a limited war. Of course, the opposite then would also be true. The exceeding of one threshold will undermine others.

12. A threshold could exist even if one party deferred to the other's beliefs.

13. Though warfighters are inclined to view nuclear weapons as "just another weapon," they are still willing to define a threshold between conventional and nuclear weapons use, and though they can argue that conventional explosives can exceed the destructive power of the smallest nuclear weapons, the important question is whether combat participants find the conventional/nuclear distinction to be meaningful. In the final analysis, "the distinction is not physical, but is psychic, perceptual, legalistic, or symbolic" (Schelling 1960:257).

14. These terms are given a more specific meaning here than is common to the literature. There is, however, no standard definition for these terms. (For the origin of the *firebreak* term, see Enthoven 1965.)

15. This is certainly true of Kahn (Brown 1989).

16. However, this argument is superfluous when these warfighters also maintain that the Soviets believe that they can prevail in an all-out nuclear war.

17. SAC, Europe, Atlantic, and Pacific.

18. Tankers are as vulnerable to attack as the planes that they refuel and are likely to be in demand for the servicing of the strategic bomber force.

19. For example, ultrahigh-frequency waves can operate more effectively than others within a nuclear environment but as they are only good for line-of-sight communication, must be propagated through vulnerable relays and are also incapable of reaching submerged submarines. Low-frequency waves have an "over-the-horizon" capability and a partial immunity to electromagnetic disruption (atmospheric ionization), but a ground-based low-frequency relay system could be disabled with the destruction of vulnerable antennae (though these waves are also propagated by aircraft). Extremely low-frequency waves can penetrate to deeply submerged submarines but can communicate only at an extremely low rate of transmission and require antennae of tremendous length and fixed position and that are therefore vulnerable to attack.

20. The distinction between the political and military command would of course break down as the system devolves.

21. These "parts" could at that point be controlled by those who have quite limited peacetime authority. Of course, the extent to and circumstances under which lower-level commanders can authorize nuclear weapons use is classified and remains a matter of speculation (on this, see Shuchman 1987).

22. However, Carter (1987:577–578), for one, minimizes the risk of detection and the utility of submarines in limited warfare.

23. A technical predelegation could similarly constrain Soviet options. In wartime, Soviet theater commands assume an increased role, though they possess both regional and intercontinental-range missiles (Berman and Baker 1982:9–10, 19).

24. On this, see Cordesman 1982:36; Ball 1987; Kelleher 1987:460.

25. Political leader ignorance about military operations led to heated high-level confrontations between political and military leaders during the Cuban missile crisis and might, under other circumstances, have led to a loss of control over the crisis outcome (Sagan 1985).

26. At that point a disintegrating military command might not be able to locate and brief, even if it recognized, the new civilian leader (Bracken 1987).

27. For instance, human error caused by boredom, fatigue, or stress could lead to misrouting of messages or even to weapons mistargeting. This problem would become acute if the United States were to adopt a launch-on-warning policy.

28. This level of responsiveness would be necessary if the United States were to deal with the land-based missile vulnerability problem by adopting a launch-on-warning or launch-under-attack posture.

29. Nevertheless, a sizable percentage of submarines are on alert and can receive communications.

30. It can be argued, though, that the biggest threat to *U.S.* command and control is actually the technical and organizational deficiencies and hence the inferiority of *Soviet* command and control—in other words, that the most problematic "uncoupled" element of U.S. command and control is the deficient Soviet command and control system, a system that is highly centralized and sometimes fragily connected (on Soviet command and control, see Ball 1986a).

31. Though these assertions reflect the long-standing tension between the British role as ally (and subordinate nuclear partner) to the United States—as when British attacks on Soviet air defenses would be used to clear the way for U.S. attacks—and as defender of the British homeland (on this, see Freedman 1985).

32. British and French reliance on a minimum deterrent submarine force requires efficient use of available weapons and thus a "city-busting" strategy.

33. As will be argued, the difference in the clarity of these messages is related to the greater ease with which "deterrent" rather than "compellent" threats can be communicated.

34. Therefore, nonverbal signals are not only evocative and widely applicable but also benefit from "plausible deniability."

35. On the symbolic use of the navy and the importance of context, see Cohen 1981:41–48.

36. On this, see Ball 1986.

37. In this regard, it is important to note the conclusions of a recent Pentagon report on the circumstances surrounding the mistaken identification and downing of an Iranian commerical airliner by the USS *Vincennes* during a series of naval confrontations off the Iranian coast. The report found fault not with the ship's radar and computer systems but with Navy crewmen who distorted data "in an unconscious attempt to make available evidence fit a preconceived scenario" (Moore 1988).

38. Many have noted the human tendency to see an adversary as a coherent

actor—which follows from the tendency to interpret evidence simply and to hold to a belief (in this case the prewar view of the opponent).

39. The Washington terminals are in the White House and the Pentagon and could not survive a direct hit.

40. Freedman's (1988:184) description of the position of McGeorge Bundy.

41. Which President Kennedy is said to have estimated as between one chance in two and one in three (Sorensen 1965:705).

42. Similarly, the United States can be claimed to have executed an effective nuclear power play with the next global nuclear alert, called during the 1973 Middle East war. But U.S. conventional maneuvers and success in pressuring Israel to observe a cease-fire might actually have forestalled Soviet military intervention. On nuclear weapons and the Middle East crisis, see Blechman and Hart 1982.

43. The following remarks do not apply to pure warfighters then.

44. Kissinger (1957:170) contradicts himself on the latter point, though, when he also states that "the psychological equation is, paradoxically, constantly shifting 'against' the side which seems to be winning," for its opponent would be increasingly tempted to launch an all-out attack.

45. See also Steinbruner 1974; Jervis 1976; Snyder 1976; Lebow 1981; Jervis et al. 1985.

46. Schelling (1966:82) has observed that "the very act of compliance—of doing what is demanded—is more conspicuously compliant, more recognizable as submission under duress, than when an act is merely withheld in the face of a deterrent threat."

47. In the standard analogy, two cars race at each other: The driver of the first car to swerve to avoid collision is disgraced, and the other driver is glorified; of course both severely suffer if neither swerves.

48. One recent attempt to strike just such a balance is Allison et al. 1985.

49. For the fullest discussion of signaling in the conduct of nuclear war, see Kahn 1968.

50. Little can be done in the world of diplomacy that does not have information content, and thus no matter how many times a signal is sent, it is the one time when it is not or when its content is changed that will be noticed.

51. The term *rationalized* rather than *made rational* is preferred here because the behavior to which the former refers does not stand up to cost/benefit assessment. Nuclear war would remain a losing proposition.

52. Snyder and Diesing (1977:183) suggest the latter three ideas with the notion of "reputational," "intrinsic," and "strategic" interests.

53. This capability is believed to be needed partly because extended deterrence requires that the United States be the one to initiate strategic nuclear weapons use.

54. It should be noted, however, that a "perfect" Soviet defense would undermine a US extended deterrent.

55. This argument is somewhat justified when strategic weapons would be used to hit what are referred to in the SIOP as "other military targets"—targets

whose destruction would impair the Soviet war effort in Europe (on this, see Jervis 1984:70–71).

56. Given that a nation that relies upon this option is probably without effective alternatives.

57. On the vulnerability of intermediate nuclear weapons, see Sigal 1984:31–32.

58. On the Pershing II, see Sigal 1984:53.

59. This argument is echoed by current proponents of strategic defense.

60. The logic of this argument resembles that offered in the fifties on behalf of NATO conventional forces that would create a defense "shield" to hold a Soviet attack until strategic nuclear forces could be employed.

61. Beyond the European sensitivity to decoupling, thresholds and escalation rungs are bound to mean something different to Europeans than they do to Americans, since these thresholds and rungs relate to the territorial locus of combat.

62. For instance, Kissinger is renowned for his "flip-flops" in thinking about the uses of nuclear weapons (on this, see Quester 1986:89–90).

63. It is this very calculus that the French invoked to question the viability of the U.S. guarantee. U.S. moves toward conventional defense were interpreted as signs of an underlying rationality to U.S. policy that would prevent the United States from incurring annihilation on behalf of France. The French believed that U.S. conventional deployment would proscribe escalation rather than trigger it.

64. As Betts (1987:205) has observed:

> In deploying INF in Europe in the 1980s, Washington played a conceptual double game with its allies and adversary. In dealing with the allies, the United States accepted the doctrinal principle that no separate "Euro-strategic" nuclear balance should be recognized, that the new forces were linked inextricably with U.S.-based strategic forces in the "seemless web" of flexible response. In dealing with the Soviets, in contrast, the United States maintained the diplomatic principle that the new forces "not" be deemed strategic and that they should count against Soviet theater forces —SS-20s, SS-4s, and SS-5s.

This chapter suggests, though, that this strategy reflects strategic confusion rather than brilliant diplomatic tactics.

65. Interestingly, Kissinger coupled his proposal with one for an increased U.S. counterforce capability. Moreover, he has since expressed misgivings about the INF accords because they would remove a class of weapons that link U.S. strategic retaliation to Europe (Dewar 1988).

66. Others would find this logic flawed fundamentally: "Militarily, for the GLCM [ground-launched cruise missile] or Pershing II to serve as a counter to the SS-20 presumes either that both sides have comparable strategies and thus require equivalent forces, which they do not, or that the GLCM and Pershing II are capable of surviving an SS-20 attack and of targeting SS-20 sites in return, which they cannot" (Sigal 1984:45).

67. 1967 NATO Military Committee statement (MC 14/3) codifying "flexible response."

68. See, for instance, Reagan 1988:14.

69. Admittedly, these policies were partly a product of various political constraints and compromises.

70. This has led one critic to charge that Bundy et al. (1982) are "'explicitly' abandoning a nuclear threat, while implicitly continuing to rely on it" (Wohlstetter 1983:28).

REFERENCES

Allison, G. T. 1971. *Essence of Decision: Explaining the Cuban Missile Crisis.* Boston: Little, Brown.

—— 1974. Questions about the arms race: Who's racing whom? A bureaucratic perspective. In R. L. Pfaltzgraff, Jr., ed., *Contending Approaches to Arms Control*, pp. 31–72. Lexington: D. C. Heath.

Allison, G. T., A. Carnesale, and J. S. Nye. 1985. *Hawks, Doves, Owls: An Agenda for Avoiding Nuclear War.* New York: Norton.

Allison, G. T. and F. A. Morris. 1975. Armaments and arms control: Explaining the determinants of military weapons. *Daedalus* 104 (3):99–129.

Ansoff, H. I. 1965. *Corporate Strategy: An Analytic Approach to Business Policy for Growth and Expansion.* New York: McGraw Hill.

Arkin, W. M. 1984. Nuclear weapon command, control and communications. *SIPRI Yearbook.* Stockholm: SIPRI.

Arkin, W. M. and R. W. Fieldhouse. 1985. *Nuclear Battlefields: Global Links in the Arms Race.* Cambridge: Ballinger.

Armacost, M. H. 1969. *The Politics of Weapons Innovation: The Thor-Jupiter Controversy.* New York: Columbia University Press.

Arms Control Association. 1987. Analysis of the President's report on Soviet noncompliance with arms control agreements. *Arms Control Today* 17(3):1A–12A.

Art, R. J. 1985. Between assured destruction and nuclear victory: The case for the "MAD-plus" posture. In R. Hardin, J. J. Mearsheimer, G. Dworkin, and R. E. Gordon, eds., *Nuclear Deterrence: Ethics and Strategy*, pp. 121–140. Chicago: University of Chicago Press.

Art, R. J. and S. E. Ockenden. 1981. The domestic politics of cruise missile development, 1970–1980. In R. K. Betts, ed., *Cruise Missiles: Technology, Strategy and Politics*, pp. 1–28. Washington, D.C.: Brookings.

Axelrod, R. 1976. The analysis of cognitive maps. In R. Axelrod, ed., *Structure of Decision: The Cognitive Maps of Political Elites*, pp. 55–73. Princeton: Princeton University Press.

Ball, D. 1974. *Déjà Vu: The Return to Counterforce in the Nixon Administration*. Santa Monica: California Seminar on Arms Control and Foreign Policy.

—— 1980. *Politics and Force Levels: The Strategic Missile Program of the Kennedy Administration*. Berkeley: University of California Press.

—— 1981. Can nuclear war be controlled?. *Adelphi Paper*, no. 169. London: IISS.

—— 1986a. *Soviet Strategic Planning and the Control of Nuclear War*. The Strategic and Defence Studies Centre, Reference Paper 109. Australian National University.

—— 1986b. The development of the SIOP, 1960–1983. In D. Ball and J. Richelson, eds., *Strategic Nuclear Targeting*, pp. 57–83. Ithaca: Cornell University Press.

—— 1987. *Controlling Theater Nuclear War*. The Strategic and Defence Studies Centre, Reference Paper no. 138. Australian National University.

Ball, N. 1984a. *Third World Security Expenditure: A Statistical Compendium*. Stockholm: Swedish National Defense Research Institute.

—— 1984b. Measuring third world security expenditure: A research note. *World Development* 12(2):157–164.

Barton, J. H. and L. D. Weiler. 1976. *International Arms Control: Issues and Agreements*. Stanford: Stanford University Press.

Baugh, W. H. 1984. *The Politics of Nuclear Balance: Ambiguity and Continuity in Strategic Politics*. New York: Longman.

Beard, E. 1976. *Developing the ICBM: A Study in Bureaucratic Politics*. New York: Columbia University Press.

Bell, D. 1976. *The Coming of Post-Industrial Society: A Venture in Social Forecasting*. New York: Basic.

Bennett, B. W. 1980. *Assessing the Capabilities of Strategic Nuclear Forces: The Limit of Current Methods*. RAND.

Berger, T. 1976. *Max Weber's Theory of Concept Formation; History, Laws, and Ideal Types*. Durham: Duke University Press.

Berkowitz, B. D. 1985a. Intelligence in the organizational context: Coordination and error in national estimates. *Orbis* 29(3):571–596.

—— 1985b. Technological progress, strategic weapons, and American nuclear policy. *Orbis* 29(2):241–258.

—— 1987. *Calculated Risks: A Century of Arms Control, Why It Has Failed, and How It Can Be Made to Work*. New York: Simon and Schuster.

—— 1988. An INF treaty discredits arms control and promotes conflict. *Orbis* 32(1): 119–126.

Berman, R. P. and J. C. Baker. 1982. *Soviet Strategic Forces: Requirements and Responses*. Washington, D.C.: Brookings.

Betts, R. K. 1981. Innovation, assessment, and decision. In R. K. Betts, ed.,

Cruise Missiles: Technology, Strategy, and Politics, pp. 1–28. Washington, D.C.: Brookings

—— 1982. Elusive equivalence: The political and military meaning of the nuclear balance. In S. P. Huntington, ed., *The Strategic Imperative,* pp. 101–140. Cambridge: Ballinger.

—— 1985. Surprise attack and preemption. In G. T. Allison, A. Carnesale, and J. S. Nye, eds., *Hawks, Doves and Owls,* pp. 54–79. New York: Norton.

—— 1986–87. A nuclear golden age?: The balance before parity. *International Security* 11(3):3–32.

—— 1987. *Nuclear Blackmail and Nuclear Balance.* Washington, D.C.: Brookings.

Blair, B. G. 1985. *Strategic Command and Control: Redefining the Nuclear Threat.* Washington, D.C.: Brookings.

—— 1987. Delegation of nuclear command authority. In A. B. Carter, J. D. Steinbruner, and C. A. Zraket, eds., *Managing Nuclear Operations,* pp. 352–372. Washington, D.C.: Brookings.

Blechman, B. and D. Hart. 1982. The political utility of nuclear weapons: The 1973 Middle East crisis. *International Security* 7(1):132–156.

Blight, J. G., J. S. Nye, Jr., and D. A. Welch. 1987. The Cuban Missile Crisis revisited. *Foreign Affairs* 66(1):170–188.

Bracken, P. 1983. *The Command and Control of Nuclear Forces.* New Haven: Yale University Press.

Brennan, D. G. 1969. The case for population defense. In J. J. Holst and W. Schneider, eds., *Why ABM? Policy Issues in the Missile Defense Controversy,* pp. 91–117. New York: Pergamon.

Brodie, B. 1946. *The Absolute Weapon: Atomic Power and World Order.* New York: Harcourt, Brace.

—— 1954. Nuclear weapons: Strategic or tactical? *Foreign Affairs* 32(2):217–229.

—— 1959. *Strategy in the Missile Age.* Princeton: Princeton University Press.

—— 1966. *Escalation and the Nuclear Option.* Princeton: Princeton University Press.

—— 1983. The development of nuclear strategy. In B. Brodie, M. D. Intriligator, and R. Kolkowicz, eds., *National Security and International Stability,* pp. 5–22. Cambridge: Oelgeschlager, Gunn and Hain.

Brooks, H. 1975. The military innovation system and the qualitative arms race. *Daedalus* 104(3):75–97.

—— 1986. The strategic defense initiative as science policy. *International Security* 11(2):177–184.

Brown, H. 1983. *Thinking About National Security: Defense and Foreign Policy in a Dangerous World.* Boulder: Westview.

—— 1985. The strategic defense initiative: Defensive systems and the strategic debate. *Survival* 28(2):55–64.

Brown, N. R., L. J. Rips, and S. K. Sheuell. 1985. The subjective dates of natural events in very-long-term memory. *Cognitive Psychology* 17(2):139–177.

Brown, R. 1989. Strategic Theory and Escalation. Paper presented at the annual meeting of the International Studies Association, April 1989, London.

Brown, T. A. 1976. Missile accuracy and strategic lethality. *Survival* 18(2):52–59.

—— 1977. Number mysticism, rationality and the strategic balance. *Orbis* 21(3):479–496.

Bundy, M. 1969a. To cap the volcano. *Foreign Affairs* 48(1):1–20.

—— 1969b. How to wind down the nuclear arms race. *New York Times Magazine*, November 16, pp. 46–47.

Bundy, M., G. F. Kennan, R. S. McNamara and G. Smith. 1982. Nuclear weapons and the Atlantic alliance. *Foreign Affairs* 60(4):753–768.

—— 1984–85. The President's choice: Star wars or arms control. *Foreign Affairs* 63(2):264–278.

Burrows, W. E. 1984. Ballistic missile defense: The illusion of security. *Foreign Affairs* 62(4):843–856.

Burt, R. 1980. Reassessing the strategic balance. *International Security* 5(1):37–52.

Carnesale, A. and C. Glaser. 1982. ICBM vulnerability: The cures are worse than the disease. *International Security* 7(1):70–85.

Carter, A. B. 1984. Introduction to the BMD question. In A. B. Carter and D. N. Schwartz, eds., *Ballistic Missile Defense*, pp. 1–23. Washington, D.C.: Brookings.

—— 1987a. Assessing command system vulnerability. In A. B. Carter, J. D. Steinbruner, and C. A. Zraket, eds., *Managing Nuclear Operations*, pp. 555–610. Washington, D.C.: Brookings.

—— 1987b. Communications technologies and vulnerability. In A. B. Carter, J. D. Steinbruner, and C. A. Zraket, eds., in *Managing Nuclear Operations*, pp. 217–281. Washington, D.C.: Brookings.

Cattell, D. T. and G. H. Quester. 1986. Ethnic targeting: Some bad ideas. In D. Ball and J. Richelson, eds., *Strategic Nuclear Targeting*, pp. 267–284. Ithaca: Cornell University Press.

Chayes, A. and J. B. Wiesner, eds. 1969. *ABM: An Evaluation of the Decision to Deploy an ABM System*. New York: Harper and Row.

Cimbala, S. J. 1988. *Nuclear Strategizing: Deterrence and Reality*. New York: Praeger.

Cockle, P. 1978. Analyzing Soviet defence spending: The debate in perspective. *Survival* 20(5):209–219.

Cohen, R. 1981. *International Politics: The Rules of the Game*. London: Longman.

Congressional Budget Office. 1987. *Effects of Weapons Procurement Stretchouts on Costs and Schedules*. U.S. Congress.

Conover, C. J. 1977. *U.S. Strategic Nuclear Weapons and Deterrence*. RAND.

Converse, P. E. 1964. The nature of belief systems in mass publics. In D. Apter, ed., *Ideology and Discontent*, pp. 129–155. Glencoe: Free Press.

Cordesman, A. H. 1982. Deterrence in the 1980s. Part I. American strategic forces and extended deterrence. *Adelphi Paper* no. 175. London: IISS.

Cyert, R. and J. March. 1963. *A Behavioral Theory of the Firm.* Englewood Cliffs: Prentice-Hall.

Daugherty, W., B. Levi, and F. von Hippel. 1988. The consequence of "limited" nuclear attacks on the United States. *International Security* 10(4):3–45.

Davis, C. E. and W. R. Schilling. 1973. All you ever wanted to know about MIRV and ICBM calculations but were not cleared to ask. *Journal of Conflict Resolution* 17(2):207–242.

Davis, L. E. 1975. Limited nuclear options: Deterrence and the new American doctrine. *Adelphi Paper* no. 121. London: IISS.

De Rivera, J., ed. 1968. *The Psychological Dimension of Foreign Policy.* Columbus: Merrill.

Deutsch, K. W. 1966. *The Nerves of Government: Models of Political Communication and Control.* New York: Free Press.

Deutsch K. W. and R. L. Merritt. 1965. Effects of events on national and international images. In H. C. Kelman, ed., *International Behavior: A Social-Psychological Analysis*, pp. 132–187. New York: Holt, Rinehart, and Winston.

Dewar, H. 1988. Kissinger backs pact, with misgivings: Rejecting INF treaty would "magnify all difficulties," Senate told. Washington Post, February 24, p. A4.

De Young, K. 1988. NATO closer to deciding future of nuclear forces. *Washington Post*, April 29.

Drell, S. D. and F. von Hippel. 1976. Limited nuclear war. *Scientific American* 235(5):27–37.

Ehrlich, P. R., C. Sagan, D. Kennedy, and W. O. Roberts. 1984. *The Cold and the Dark: The World After Nuclear War.* New York: W. W. Norton.

Enthoven, A. C. 1965. American deterrent policy. In H. A. Kissinger, ed., *Problems of National Strategy*, pp. 120–134. New York: Praeger.

Enthoven, A. C. and K. W. Smith. 1979. *How Much Is Enough?: Shaping the Defense Program, 1961–1969.* New York: Harper.

Evangelista, M. A. 1984. Why the Soviets buy the weapons they do. *World Politics* 36(4):597–618.

Festinger, L. 1962. *A Theory of Cognitive Dissonance.* Stanford: Stanford University Press.

Fisher, R. 1969. *International Conflict for Beginners.* New York: Harper and Row.

Freedman, L. 1977. *U.S. Intelligence and the Soviet Strategic Threat.* Boulder: Westview.

—— 1981–82. NATO myths. *Foreign Policy* (Winter) 45:48–68.

—— 1983. *The Evolution of Nuclear Strategy.* New York: St. Martin's.

—— 1985. British nuclear targeting. *Defense Analysis* 1(2):81–99.

—— 1986. British nuclear targeting. In D. Ball and J. Richelson, eds., *Strategic Nuclear Targeting*, pp. 109–126. Ithaca: Cornell University Press.

Freedman, L. 1988. I exist; therefore I deter. *International Security* 13(1):177–195.

Friedberg, A. L. 1980. A history of the U.S. strategic "doctrine"—1945 to 1980. *Journal of Strategic Studies* 3(3):37–71.

Future Security Strategy Study. 1983. *Ballistic Missile Defenses and U.S. National Security: Summary Report.*

Gaddis, J. L. 1982. *Strategies of Containment: A Critical Appraisal of Postwar American National Security Policy.* Oxford: Oxford University Press.

Garthoff, R. L. 1982. Mutual deterrence and strategic arms limitation in Soviet policy. *Strategic Review* 10(4):36–51.

—— 1985. *Detente and Confrontation: American-Soviet Relations from Nixon to Reagan.* Washington, D.C.: Brookings.

—— 1987. *Reflections on the Cuban Missile Crisis.* Washington, D.C.: Brookings.

——. 1988. New thinking in Soviet military doctrine. *Washington Quarterly* 11(3):131–158.

Gelber, H. G. 1974. Technical innovation and arms control. *World Politics* 26(4):509–541.

George, A. L. 1969. The "operational code": A neglected approach to the study of political leaders and decision-making. *International Studies Quarterly* (June) 13(2):190–222.

—— 1979. The causal nexus between cognitive beliefs and decision-making behavior: The "operational code" belief system. In L. S. Falkowski ed., *Psychological Models in International Politics*, pp. 95–124. Boulder: Westview.

—— 1980. *Presidential Decisionmaking in Foreign Policy: The Effective Use of Information and Advice.* Boulder: Westview.

George, A. L. and R. Smoke. 1974. *Deterrence in American Foreign Policy: Theory and Practice.* New York: Columbia University Press.

Getler, M. 1982. Administration's nuclear war policy stance murky. *Washington Post*, November 10, p. A24.

Glaser, C. L. 1984. Why even good defenses may be bad. *International Security* 9(2):92–123.

—— 1985. Do we want the missile defense we can build? *International Security* 10(1):25–57.

Goertz, G. and P. F. Diehl. 1986. Measuring military allocations: A comparison of different approaches. *Journal of Conflict Resolution* 30(3):553–581.

Gordon, M. R. 1985. Pentagon reassesses Soviet bomber. *New York Times* October 1, p. A8.

—— 1986. C.I.A., in gauging Soviet threat, distances itself from the Pentagon. *New York Times*, July 16, p. A1.

Gray, C. S. 1976. *The Soviet-American Arms Race.* Hampshire, England: Saxon House.

—— 1979. Nuclear strategy: A case for a theory of victory. *International Security* 4(1):54–87.

—— 1984. War-fighting for deterrence. *Journal of Strategic Studies* 7(1):5–28.

—— 1986a. *Nuclear Strategy and National Style*. Lanham: Hamilton.

—— 1986b. Targeting problems for central war. In D. Ball and J. Richelson, eds., *Strategic Nuclear Targeting*, pp. 171–193. Ithaca: Cornell University Press.

Gray, C. S. and K. Payne. 1980. Victory is possible. *Foreign Policy* (Summer), 39:14–27.

Green, P. 1966. *Deadly Logic: The Theory of Nuclear Deterrence*. Columbus: Ohio State University Press.

Greenwood, T. 1975. *Making the MIRV: A Study of Defense Decision Making*. Cambridge: Ballinger.

Hafner, D. L. 1986. Assessing the President's vision: The Fletcher, Miller, and Hoffman panels. In F. A. Long, D. Hafner, and J. Boutwell, eds., *Weapons in Space*, pp. 91–107. New York: Norton.

Halff, H. M., A. Ortony, and R. C. Anderson. 1976. A context-sensitive representation of word meanings. *Memory and Cognition* 4(4):378–383.

Halperin, M. H. 1961. The Gaither committee and the policy process. *World Politics* 13(3):360–384.

—— 1974. *Bureaucratic Politics and Foreign Policy*. Washington, D.C.: Brookings.

—— 1987. *Nuclear Fallacy: Dispelling the Myth of Nuclear Strategy*. Cambridge: Ballinger.

Handel, M. I. 1982. Numbers do count: The question of quality versus quantity. In S. P. Huntington, ed., *The Strategic Imperative*, pp. 193–228. Cambridge: Ballinger.

Hart, D. M. 1984. The hermeneutics of Soviet military doctrine. *Washington Quarterly* 7(2):77–88.

Head, R. G. 1978. Technology and the military balance. *Foreign Affairs* 56(3):544–563.

Hermann, C. F. 1972. Threat, time and surprise: A simulation of international crisis. In C. F. Hermann, ed., *International Crisis: Insights from Behavioral Research*. New York: Free Press.

Heuer, R. J. Jr. 1981. Strategic disception and counterdisception: A cognitive process approach. *International Studies Quarterly* 25(2):294–327.

Hochberg, J. E. 1978. *Perception*. Englewood Cliffs: Prentice-Hall.

Hoffman, F. S. 1986. The SDI in U.S. national strategy. *International Security* 10(1):13–24.

Holloway, D. 1986. *The Soviet Union and the Arms Race*. New Haven: Yale University Press.

Holst, J. J. and W. Schneider, Jr., eds. 1969. *Why ABM? Policy Issues in the Missile Defense Controversy*. New York: Pergamon.

Holsti, O. 1973. Foreign policy decisionmakers viewed psychologically: 'Cognitive process' approaches. In J. N. Rosenau, ed., *In Search of Global Patterns*, pp. 120–144. New York: Free Press.

Holtzman, F. D. 1980. Are the Soviets really outspending the U.S. on defense? *International Security* 4(4):86–104.

Holtzman, F. D. 1982. Soviet military spending: Assessing the numbers game. *International Security* 6(4):78–101.

Howard, M. E. 1981. On fighting a nuclear war. *International Security* 5(4):3–17.

Huntington, S. P. 1961. *The Common Defense: Strategic Programs in National Politics*. New York: Columbia University Press.

Ikle, F. C. 1973. Can nuclear deterrence last out the century? *Foreign Affairs* 51(2):267–285.

—— 1985. Nuclear strategy: Can there be a happy ending? *Foreign Affairs* 63(4):810–826.

Janis, I. L. and L. Mann. 1977. *Decisionmaking: A Psychological Analysis of Conflict, Choice, and Commitment*. New York: Free Press.

Jervis, R. 1976. *Perception and Misperception in International Politics*. Princeton: Princeton University Press.

—— 1979. Deterrence theory revisited. *World Politics* 31(2):289–324.

—— 1979–80. Why nuclear superiority doesn't matter. *Political Science Quarterly* 94(4):617–633.

—— 1984. *The Illogic of American Nuclear Strategy*. Ithaca: Cornell University Press.

Jervis, R., R. N. Lebow, and J. G. Stein, eds. 1985. *Psychology and Deterrence*. Baltimore: Johns Hopkins University Press.

Jones, E. 1984. Defense R & D policymaking in the USSR. In J. Valenta and W. C. Potter, eds., *Soviet Decision-making for National Security*, pp. 116–135. London: Allen and Unwin.

Jordan, A. J. and W. J. Taylor, Jr. 1984. *American National Security: Policy and Process*. Baltimore: Johns Hopkins University Press.

Kahan, J. H. 1975. *Security in the Nuclear Age: Developing U.S. Strategic Arms Policy*. Washington, D.C.: Brookings.

Kahn, H. 1961. *On Thermonuclear War: Three Lectures and Several Suggestions*. Princeton: Princeton University Press.

—— 1968. *On Escalation: Metaphors and Scenarios*. Baltimore: Penguin.

—— 1969. The case for a thin system. In J. J. Holst and W. Schneider, eds., *Why ABM? Policy Issues in the Missile Defense Controversy*, pp. 63–90. New York: Pergamon.

Kahneman, D. 1973. *Attention and Effort*. Englewood Cliffs: Prentice-Hall.

Kaplan, A. 1964. *The Conduct of Inquiry: Methodology for Behavioral Science*. New York: Chandler.

Kaplan, F. 1983. *The Wizards of Armageddon*. New York: Simon and Schuster.

Kaufman, R. F. 1985. Causes of the slowdown in Soviet defense. *Survival* 27(4):179–192.

Kaufmann, W. W. 1956. Limited warfare. In W. W. Kaufmann ed., *Military Policy and National Security*, pp. 102–136. Princeton: Princeton University Press.

—— 1964. *The McNamara Strategy*. New York: Harper and Row.

—— 1983. Nuclear deterrence in Central Europe. In J. D. Steinbruner and

L. V. Sigal, eds., *Alliance Security: NATO and the No-First-Use Question*, pp. 22–42. Washington, D.C.: Brookings.

Kelleher, C. M. 1987. NATO nuclear operations. In A. B. Carter, J. D. Steinbruner, and C. A. Zraket, eds., *Managing Nuclear Operations*, pp. 445–469. Washington, D.C.: Brookings.

Keller, B. 1985. U.S. study finds a Soviet ICBM is less of a threat to missile silos. *New York Times* (19 July): p. 1.

Kennan, G. F. 1983. *The Nuclear Delusion: Soviet-American Relations in the Atomic Age.* New York: Pantheon.

Killian, J. R., Jr. 1977. *Sputnik, Scientists, and Eisenhower: A Memoir of the First Special Assistant to the President for Science and Technology.* Cambridge: MIT.

Kissinger, H. A. 1957. *Nuclear Weapons and Foreign Policy.* New York: Harper.
—— 1979a. *White House Years.* Boston: Little Brown.
—— 1979b. NATO defence and the Soviet threat. *Survival* 21(6):264–268.
—— 1988. START: A dangerous rush for agreement. *Washington Post* (24 April): p. D7.

Knorr, K. 1956. Passive air defence for the United States. In W. W. Kaufmann, ed., *Military Policy and National Security*, pp. 75–101. Princeton: Princeton University Press.
—— 1962. Limited strategic war. In K. Knorr and T. Read, eds., *Limited Strategic War*, pp. 3–31. New York: Praeger.

Krepon, M. 1987. CIA, DIA at odds over Soviet threat. *Bulletin of the Atomic Scientists* (May):6–7.

Kull, S. 1985. Nuclear nonsence. *Foreign Policy* (Spring), 58:28–52.
—— 1988. *Minds at War: Nuclear Reality and the Inner Conflicts of Defense Policymakers.* New York: Basic.

Kuhn, T. 1970. *The Structure of Scientific Revolutions.* Chicago: University of Chicago Press.

Kurth, J. R. 1971. A widening gyre: The logic of America weapons procurement. *Public Policy* 19(3):373–404.
—— 1973. Aerospace production lines and American defense spending. In S. Rosen ed., *Testing the Theory of the Military-Industrial Complex*, pp. 135–156. Toronto: Lexington.

Lambeth, B. S. 1983. Economic targeting in nuclear war: U.S. and Soviet approaches. *Orbis* 27(1):127–149.
—— 1984. On thresholds in Soviet military thought. *Washington Quarterly* 7(2):69–76.

Lambeth, B. S. and K. N. Lewis. 1988. The Kremlin and SDI. *Foreign Affairs* 66(4):755–770.

Lapp, R. E. 1970. *Arms Beyond Debt: The Tyranny of Weapons Technology.* New York: Cowles.

Latham, D. C. and J. J. Lane. 1987. Management issues: Planning, acquisition, and oversight. In A. B. Carter, J. D. Steinbruner, and C. A. Zraket, eds., *Managing Nuclear Operations*, pp. 640–660. Washington, D.C.: Brookings.

Lebovic, J. H. 1986. The Middle East: The region as a system. *International Interactions* 12(3):267–289.

Lebow, R. N. 1981. *Between Peace and War: The Nature of International Crisis.* Baltimore: Johns Hopkins University Press.

—— 1982. Misconceptions in American strategic assessment. *Political Science Quarterly* 97(2):187–206.

—— 1985. Conclusions. In R. Jervis, R. N. Lebow, and J. G. Stein, eds., *Psychology and Deterrence,* pp. 203–232. Baltimore: Johns Hopkins University Press.

—— 1987. *Nuclear Crisis Management: A Dangerous Illusion.* Ithaca: Cornell University Press.

Lee, W. T. 1977. *The Estimation of Soviet Defense Expenditures, 1955–75: An Unconventional Approach.* New York: Praeger.

Lehman, C. M. and P. C. Hughes. 1977. "Equivalence" and SALT II. *Orbis* 20(4):1045–1054.

Lindblom, C. E. 1959. The science of muddling through. *Public Administration Review* 19 (Spring):79–88.

Luttwak, E. 1981. The problems of extending deterrence. In C. Bertram, ed., *The Future of Strategic Deterrence,* pp. 31–37. Hamden: Archon.

March, J. G. and H. A. Simon. 1958. *Organizations.* New York: Wiley.

Mariska, M. D. 1972. The SIOP. *Military Review* 52(3):32–39.

May, M., G. F. Bing, and J. D. Steinbruner. 1988. Strategic arsenals after START: The implications of deep cuts. *International Security* 13(1):90–133.

McKinney, J. C. 1966. *Constructive Typology and Social Theory.* New York: Appleton-Century-Crofts.

McNamara, R. S. 1983. The military role of nuclear weapons: Perception and misperception. *Foreign Affairs* 62(1):59–80.

—— 1986. *Blundering Into Disaster.* New York: Pantheon.

Mearsheimer, J. J. 1986. A strategic misstep: The Maritime Strategy and deterrence in Europe. *International Security* 11(2):3–57.

Meyer, S. M. 1984. Soviet national security decisionmaking: What do we know and what do we understand? In J. Valenta and W. C. Potter, eds., *Soviet Decisionmaking for National Security,* pp. 255–297. London: Allen and Unwin.

—— 1985a. Soviet perspectives on the paths to nuclear war. In G. T. Allison, A. Carnesale, and J. S. Nye, Jr., eds., *Hawks, Doves, and Owls: An Agenda for Avoiding Nuclear War,* pp. 167–205. New York: Norton.

—— 1985b. Civilian and military influence in managing the arms race in the U.S.S.R. In R. J. Art, V. Davis, and S. P. Huntington, eds., *Reorganizing America's Defense,* pp. 37–61. Washington, D.C.: Pergamon-Brassey's.

Michotte, A. 1963. *The Perception of Causality.* New York: Basic Books.

Moore, M. 1987a. B1 bomber repair fund requested: New weapon suffers from major defects. *Washington Post,* January 7, p. A1.

—— 1987b. Travails of the centerpiece weapon: Air Force unsure when B1 problems can be fixed. *Washington Post,* August 10, p. A1.

—— 1987c. Arms stretchouts: Frugal or wasteful? Pentagon increasingly purchases in one of least economical ways. *Washington Post*, December 14, p. A13.

—— 1988. Vincennes report admits errors but urges no disciplinary action. *Washington Post*, August 20, p. A1.

Morgan, P. M. 1977. *Deterrence: A Conceptual Analysis*. Beverly Hills: Sage.

—— 1985. Saving face for the sake of deterrence. In R. Jervis, R. N. Lebow, and J. G. Stein, eds., *Psychology and Deterrence*, pp. 125–152. Baltimore: Johns Hopkins University Press.

Murphy, F. 1988. Comprehending complex concepts. *Cognitive Science* 12(4):529–562.

Murphy, G. L. 1984. Establishing and accessing references in discourse. *Memory and Cognition* 12(5):489–497.

Newhouse, J. 1973. *Cold Dawn: The Story of SALT*. New York: Holt, Rinehart, and Winston.

Nisbett, R. E., E. Borgida, R. Crandall, and H. Reed. 1982. Popular induction: Information is not necessarily informative. In D. Kahneman, P. Slovic, and A. Tversky, eds., *Judgement Under Uncertainty: Heuristics and Biases*, pp. 101–116. Cambridge: Cambridge University Press.

Nitze, P. H. 1956. Atoms, strategy and policy. *Foreign Affairs* 34(2):187–198.

—— 1976. Assessing strategic stability in an era of detente. *Foreign Affairs* 54(2):207–232.

—— 1976–77. Deterring our deterrent. *Foreign Policy* 25(Winter):195–210.

—— 1984–85. Living with the Soviets. *Foreign Affairs* 63(2):360–374.

Nixon, R. M. 1980. *The Real War*. New York: Warner.

Nye, J. S., Jr. 1984. Can America manage its Soviet policy? *Foreign Affairs* 62(4):857–878.

—— 1986. Farewell to arms control. *Foreign Affairs* 65(1):1–20.

Office of Technology Assessment. 1979. *The Effects of Nuclear War*. U.S. Congress.

Osgood, R. E. 1957. *Limited War: The Challenge to American Strategy*. Chicago: University of Chicago Press.

—— 1988. *The Nuclear Dilemma in American Strategic Thought*. Boulder; Westview.

Payne, F. 1977. The strategic nuclear balance: A new measure. *Survival* 20(3):107–110.

Payne, K. B. and C. S. Gray. 1984. Nuclear policy and the defensive transition. *Foreign Affairs* 62(4):820–842.

Piaget, J. 1970. *Structuralism*. New York: Harper and Row.

Pikas, A. 1965. *Abstraction and Concept Formation*. Stockholm: University of Uppsala Press.

Pincus, W. 1987. U.S. may have miscounted some Soviet missiles: Number of SS23s underestimated, cruise weapons overlooked, INF data indicates. *Washington Post*, December 16, p. A6.

Pipes, R. 1977. Why the Soviet Union thinks it could fight and win a nuclear war. *Commentary* 64(1):21–34.

—— 1980. Soviet global strategy. *Commentary* 69(4):31–39.

—— 1982. Soviet strategic doctrine: Another view. *Strategic Review* 10(4):52–58.

—— 1984. How to cope with the Soviet threat: A long-term strategy for the West. *Commentary* 78(2):13–30.

Polanyi, M. 1969. *Knowing and Being*. Chicago: University of Chicago Press.

Powers, T. 1982. Choosing a strategy for World War III. *Atlantic Monthly* (November), pp. 82–110.

Prados, J. 1982. *The Soviet Estimate: U.S. Intelligence Analysis and Russian Military Strength*. New York: Dial.

Prados, J., J. S. Wit, and M. J. Zagurek, Jr. 1986. The strategic nuclear forces of Britain and France. *Scientific American* (August), 255:33–41.

Pringle, P. and W. Arkin. 1983. *SIOP: The Secret U.S. Plan for Nuclear War*. New York: Norton.

Quester, G. H. 1970. *Nuclear Diplomacy: The First Twenty-five Years*. New York: Dunellen.

—— 1986. *The Future of Nuclear Deterrence*. Lexington: Lexington.

—— 1987. Through the nuclear strategic looking glass, or reflections off the window of vulnerability. *Journal of Conflict Resolution* 31(4):725–737.

Rathjens, G. W. 1969. The dynamics of the arms race. *Scientific American* 220(4):15–25.

Rathjens, G. and J. Ruina. 1986. BMD and strategic instability. In F. A. Long, D. Hafner, and J. Boutwell, eds., *Weapons in Space*, pp. 239–255. New York: Norton.

Read, T. 1962. Limited strategic war and tactical nuclear war. In K. Knorr and T. Read, eds., *Limited Strategic War*, pp. 67–116.

Reagan, R. 1988. *National Security Strategy of the United States*. Washington, D.C.: White House.

Richardson, L. F. 1960. *Arms and Insecurity: A Mathematical Study of the Causes and Origins of War*. Pittsburgh: Boxwood.

Richelson, J. T. 1980. Evaluating the strategic balance. *American Journal of Political Science* 24(4):779–803.

—— 1982. Static indicators and the ranking of strategic forces. *Journal of Conflict Resolution* 26(20):265–282.

—— 1983. PD-59, NSDD-13, and the Reagan strategic modernization program. *Journal of Strategic Studies* 6(2):125–146.

—— 1985. Population targeting and U.S. strategic doctrine. *Journal of Strategic Studies* 8(1):5–21.

—— 1986. The dilemmas of counterpower targeting. In D. Ball and J. Richelson, eds., *Strategic Nuclear Targeting*, pp. 159–170. Ithaca: Cornell University Press.

Rosch, E. 1975. Cognitive reference points. *Cognitive Psychology* 7(4):532–547.

Rosch, E., C. B. Mervis, W. D. Gray, D. M. Johnson, and P. Boyes-Braem. 1976. Basic objects in natural categories. *Cognitive Psychology* 8(3):382–439.

Rosenberg, D. A. 1979. American atomic strategy and the hydrogen bomb decision. *Journal of American History* 66(1):62–87.

—— 1982. A smoking radiating ruin at the end of two hours: Documents on American war plans for nuclear war with the Soviet Union, 1954–55. *International Security* 6(3):3–38.

—— 1983. The origins of overkill: Nuclear weapons and American strategy, 1945–1960. *International Security* 7(4):3–71.

—— 1986. Reality and responsibility: Power and process in the making of United States nuclear strategy, 1945–68. *Journal Strategic Studies* 9(1):35–52.

Rowen, H. S. 1975. Formulating strategic doctrine. *Commission on the Organization of the Government for the Conduct of Foreign Policy.* Washington, D.C.: GPO. Appendix K(4):219–234.

—— 1979. The evolution of strategic nuclear doctrine. In L. Martin, ed., *Strategic Thought in the Nuclear Age,* pp. 131–156. Baltimore: Johns Hopkins University Press.

Russell, B. 1948. *Human Knowledge: Its Scope and Limits.* New York: Simon and Schuster.

Russett, B. 1983. *The Prisoners of Insecurity: Nuclear Deterrence, the Arms Race, and Arms Control.* San Francisco: W. H. Freeman.

Sagan, S. D. 1985. Nuclear alerts and crisis management. *International Security* 9(4):99–139.

—— 1987. SIOP-62: The nuclear war plan briefing to President Kennedy. *International Security* 12(1):22–51.

—— 1989. *Moving Targets: Nuclear Strategy and National Security.* Princeton: Princeton University Press.

Salman, M. A., S. Van Evera, and K. J. Sullivan. 1985. Analysis or propaganda? Measuring American strategic nuclear capability, 1969–1984. Manuscript.

Sartori, G. 1970. Concept misformation in comparative politics. *American Political Science Review* 44(4):1033–1053.

——, ed. 1984. *Social Science Concepts: A Systematic Analysis.* Beverly Hills: Sage.

Scheer, R. 1983. *With Enough Shovels: Reagan, Bush and Nuclear War.* New York: Vintage.

Schelling, T. C. 1960. *The Strategy of Conflict.* London: Oxford University Press.

—— 1966. *Arms and Influence.* New Haven: Yale University Press.

—— 1985–86. What went wrong with arms control. *Foreign Affairs* 64(2):219–233.

Schilling, W. R. 1961. The H-bomb decision: How to decide without actually choosing. *Political Science Quarterly* (March), 76:24–46.

—— 1981. U.S. strategic nuclear concepts in the 1970s: The search for sufficiently equivalent countervailing parity. *International Security* 6(2):48–79.

REFERENCES

Schlesinger, J. R. 1975. *Briefing on Counterforce Attacks.* Hearing before U.S. Senate Subcommittee on Arms Control, International Law and Organization of the Committee on Foreign Relations. Washington, D.C.: GPO.

—— 1985. Rhetoric and realities in the Star Wars debate. *International Security* 10(1):3–12.

Schwartz, D. N. 1983. *NATO's Nuclear Dilemmas.* Washington, D.C.: Brookings.

Scoville, H., Jr. 1975. Flexible madness? *Foreign Policy* (Spring), 14:164–177.

Shapley, D. 1978a. ICBM problem a sleeper. *Science* (September), 201(22):1102–1105.

—— 1978b. A world of absolute accuracy. *Science* (September), 201(29):1192–1196.

—— 1978c. Two future arms control problems. *Science* (October), 202(20):289–292.

Shuchman, D. 1987. Nuclear strategy and the problems of command and control. *Survival* 29(4):336–359.

Sigal, L. V. 1984. *Nuclear Forces in Europe: Enduring Dilemmas, Present Prospects.* Washington, D.C.: Brookings.

Simon, H. A. 1957. *Models of Man.* New York: Wiley.

—— 1979. *Models of Thought.* New Haven: Yale University Press.

Simon, H. A. and J. R. Hayes. 1976. The understanding process: Problem isomorphs. *Cognitive Psychology* 8(2):165–190.

Sjoblom, G. 1982. Some problems of the operational code approach. In C. Jonsson, ed., *Cognitive Dynamics and International Politics.* New York: St. Martin's Press.

Slocombe, W. 1981. The countervailing strategy. *International Security* 5(4):18–27.

Sloss, L. and M. D. Millot. 1984. U.S. nuclear strategy in evolution. *Strategic Review* 12(1):19–28.

Smith, B. L. R. 1964. Strategic expertise and national security policy: A case study. *Public Policy* 13(1):69–108.

Smith, E. E. and D. C. Medin. 1981. *Categories and Concepts.* Cambridge: Harvard University Press.

Smith, R. J. 1987. SDI plan draws military critics: Defense board to hear Weinberger bid for limited system. *Washington Post,* June 28, p. A4.

—— 1988a. Pentagon scales back SDI goals: New aim is to shield military installations rather than cities. *Washington Post,* March 27, p. A1.

—— 1988b. Scaled-back SDI scheme considered: Carlucci is advised to initially deploy ground-based system. *Washington Post,* April 25, p. A1.

—— 1988c. SDI seen unlikely to give U.S. edge over Soviets: Hill agency challenges Reagan vision. *Washington Post,* June 8, p. A1.

Smoke, R. 1977. *War: Controlling Escalation.* Cambridge: Harvard University Press.

Snow, D. M. 1979. Current nuclear deterrence thinking. *International Studies Quarterly* 23(3):445–486.

Snyder, G. H. 1961. *Deterrence and Defense: Toward a Theory of National Security.* Princeton: Princeton University Press.

—— 1976. Conflict and crisis in the international system. In J. N. Rosenau, K. W. Thompson and G. Boyd, eds., *World Politics: An Introduction,* pp. 682–720. New York: Free Press.

Snyder, G. H. and P. Diesing. 1977. *Conflict among Nations: Bargaining, Decision Making, and System Structure in International Crises.* Princeton: Princeton University Press.

Snyder, J. L. 1977. *The Soviet Strategic Culture: Implications for Limited Nuclear Operations.* RAND.

Sorensen, T. 1965. *Kennedy.* New York: Harper and Row.

Spinney, F. C. 1985. *Defense Facts of Life: The Plans/Reality Mismatch.* Boulder, Colo.: Westview.

Stanford Research Institute. 1971. *Limited Nuclear Operations.* Declassified portions.

Stein, J. B. 1984. *From H-Bomb to Star Wars: The Politics of Strategic Decision Making.* Lexington: D. C. Heath.

Steinbruner, J. D. 1974. *The Cybernetic Theory of Decision: New Dimensions of Political Analysis.* Princeton: Princeton University Press.

—— 1976. Beyond rational deterrence: The struggle for new conceptions. *World Politics* 28(2)'223–245.

—— 1978. National security and the concept of strategic stability. *Journal of Conflict Resolution* 22(3):411–428.

—— 1981–82. Nuclear decapitation. *Foreign Policy* 45 (Winter):16–28.

Steinbruner, J. D. and B. Carter. 1975. Organizational and political dimensions of the strategic posture: The problems of reform. *Daedalus* 104(3):131–154.

Steinbruner, J. D. and T. M. Garwin. 1976. Strategic vulnerability: The balance between prudence and paranoia. *International Security* 1(1):138–181.

Stinchcombe, A. L. 1968. *Constructing Social Theories.* New York: Harcourt-Brace.

Sullivan, D. S. 1980. Evaluating US intelligence estimates. In R. Godson, ed., *Intelligence Requirements for the 1980's: Analysis and Estimates,* 47–73. Washington, D.C.: National Security Information Center.

Talbott, S. 1980. *Endgame: The Inside Story of SALT II.* New York: Harper and Row.

—— 1985. *Deadly Gambits: The Reagan Administration and the Stalemate in Nuclear Arms Control.* New York: Vintage.

Tammen, R. L. 1973. *MIRV and the Arms Race: An Interpretation of Defense Strategy.* New York: Praeger.

Thompson, S. L. and S. H. Schneider. 1986. Nuclear winter reappraised. *Foreign Affairs* 64(5):981–1005.

Trachtenberg, M. 1985. The influence of nuclear weapons in the Cuban missile crisis. *International Security* 10(1):137–163.

—— 1988–89. A "wasting asset": American strategy and the shifting nuclear balance, 1949–1954. *International Security* 13(3):5–49.

Tsipis, K. 1974. The calculus of nuclear counterforce. *Technology Review* 77(1):34–47.

—— 1975. Physics and calculus of countercity and counterforce attacks. *Science* 187 (February): 393–397.

—— 1984. The operational characteristics of ballistic missiles. *SIPRI Yearbook.* Stockholm: SIPRI.

Tucker, R. W. 1984. The nuclear debate. *Foreign Affairs* 63(1):1–32.

Turco, R. P., O. B. Toon, T. P. Ackerman, J. B. Pollack, and C. Sagan. 1983. Nuclear winter: Global consequences of multiple nuclear explosions. *Science* 222(4630):1283–1292.

Tversky, A. 1977. Features of similarity. *Psychological Review* 84(4):327–352.

Tversky, A. and D. Kahneman. 1982. Causal schemes in judgments under uncertainty. In D. Kahneman, P. Slovic, and A. Tversky, eds., *Judgment Under Uncertainty: Heuristics and Biases*, pp. 117–128. Cambridge: Cambridge University Press.

Tversky, B. and K. Hemenway. 1984. Objects, parts, and categories. *Journal of Experimental Psychology:* General 113(2):169–193.

Ullman, R. H. 1989. The covert French connection. *Foreign Policy* 75 (Spring):3–33.

U.S. Congress. Joint Committee on Defense Production. 1976. *Deterrence and Survival in the Nuclear Age (The Gaither Report of 1957).* Washington, D.C.: GPO.

—— Subcommittee on Arms Control, International Security and Science, Committee on Foreign Affairs. 1987. *Soviet Compliance with Arms Control Agreements.* Washington, D.C.: GPO.

—— Subcommittee on Economic Resources, Competitiveness, and Security Economics of the Joint Economic Committee. 1986. *Allocation of Resources in the Soviet Union and China—1985.* Washington, D.C.:GPO.

U.S. Department of Defense. FY 1961– , *Annual Report to the Congress.* Washington, D.C.: GPO.

—— 1984– , *Soviet Military Power.* Washington, D.C.: GPO.

—— 1985b. *The President's Strategic Defense Initiative.* Washington, D.C.:GPO.

U.S. Department of Defense and Department of State. 1985. *Soviet Strategic Defense Programs.*

U.S. Department of State. 1987. *Soviet Noncompliance with Arms Control Agreements.* Special Report no. 175.

U.S. Joint Chiefs of Staff. 1987. *Military Posture Statement.* Washington, D.C.:GPO.

U.S. Senate Subcommittee on Strategic and Theater Nuclear Forces of the Committee on Armed Services and the Subcommittee on Defense of the Committee on Appropriations. 1986. *Soviet Strategic Force Developments.* Washington, D.C.:GPO.

Walker, R. L. 1983. *Strategic Target Planning: Bridging the Gap between Theory and Practice.* Washington, D.C.: National Defense University Press.

Warnke, P. C. 1984. The illusion of NATO's nuclear defense. In A. J. Pierre, ed., *Nuclear Weapons in Europe,* pp. 75–97. New York: Council on Foreign Relations.

Weida, W. J. and F. L. Gertcher. 1987. *The Political Economy of National Defense.* Boulder, Colo.: Westview.

Weinberger, C. W. 1985. *The Potential Effects of Nuclear War on the Climate: A Report to the United States Congress.* U.S. Department of Defense.

Wells, S. F. 1981. The origins of massive retaliation. *Political Science Quarterly* 96(1):31–52.

Whitehead, A. N. 1927. *Symbolism, Its Meaning and Effect.* New York: Macmillan.

Wilkening, D., K. Watman, M. Kennedy, and R. Darilek. 1987. Strategic defense and first-strike stability. *Survival* 29(2):137–165.

Wilson, G. L. 1988. INF ignites drive for "smart" weapons. *Washington Post,* January 28, p. A4.

Wohlstetter, A. 1958. The delicate balance of terror. *Foreign Affairs* 37(2):211–234.

—— 1964. Strategy and the natural scientists. In R. Gilpin and C. Wright, eds., *Scientists and National Policy-making,* pp. 174–239. New York: Columbia University Press.

—— 1974a. Is there a strategic arms race? *Foreign Policy* 15(Summer):3–20.

—— 1974b. Rivals, but no "race." *Foreign Policy* 16(Fall):48–92.

—— 1983. Bishops, statesmen, and other strategists on the bombing of innocents. *Commentary* 75(6):15–35.

—— 1985. Between an unfree world and none: Increasing our choices. *Foreign Affairs* 63(5):962–994.

Wohlstetter, A. and R. Brody. 1987. Continuing control as a requirement for deterring. In A. B. Carter, J. D. Steinbruner, and C. A. Zraket, eds., *Managing Nuclear Operations,* pp. 142–196. Washington, D.C.: Brookings.

York, H. F. 1970. *Race to Oblivion: A Participant's View of the Arms Race.* New York: Simon and Schuster.

Yost, D. S. 1982. Ballistic missile defense and the Atlantic alliance. *International Security* 7(2):143–174.

—— 1986. French nuclear targeting. In D. Ball and J. Richelson, eds., *Strategic Nuclear Targeting,* pp. 127–156. Ithaca: Cornell University Press.

NAME INDEX

SUBJECT INDEX

ABM treaty, 103, 129-30, 132

Air Force, U.S., 32, 34-35, 70, 74, 92, 97, 100, 125, 126, 127, 137, 138, 140, 216n53, 217n57, 217n64

Alert (rates, nuclear), 34, 49, 58, 63, 156, 157, 159, 168, 175, 184; *see also* Warning

Anti-ballistic missiles (ABM): Soviet, 101, 106, 121, 126, 127, 140; U.S., 91, 103, 138, 142, 207n14, 217n62

Arms control/reduction, 1, 2, 15, 16, 54, 56-57, 59-60, 61, 65, 82, 107, 130, 138, 139, 159, 195-96, 216n47, 217n60; treaty noncompliance, 27, 54, 57, 107, 129-30, 131-32, 140, 196

Arms race, 9, 34, 36, 37, 40, 62, 75, 106-7, 113, 116, 118, 119-22, 123, 139, 140, 141, 142, 187, 205n55

Army, U.S., 96, 127, 138, 207n14, 216n53, 217n57

Attention vs. perception, 17-18

Bargaining, 5, 63, 66, 76, 84-86, 89-91, 94, 107, 114, 115, 116-18, 149-50, 161-63, 165, 189, 190

Bomber gap, 72, 73

Bombers, 50, 59, 120, 122, 123, 203n29, 204n45, 205n58; Soviet, 60, 73, 102, 121, 130, 131; U.S., 34, 58, 63, 64, 66, 67, 72, 73-74, 91, 96, 97, 102, 121, 126, 137, 138, 153, 154, 157, 210n48, 211n61, 215n33

Bombing, strategic, 32, 71, 206n2

British forces and targeting, 60, 159-60, 162-63

Bureaucratic politics, 6, 22, 23-25, 35, 36, 74, 103, 132-33, 135, 136-38, 139, 140-41, 151, 207n12, 210n46

Capability, nuclear, 2, 3, 8, 9, 14, 21, 28, 30-68, 78, 86, 93, 118-24, 147, 150, 165-70, 186, 187, 190-91, 193, 195; assured destruction, 20, 35-36, 37, 39, 192, 201n10, 204n41; asymmetry, 37, 41, 57, 59, 62, 112-13, 121-22, 132, 195; balance, 2, 14, 20, 22, 28, 31, 37, 38, 39, 55, 64, 66-68, 72, 82, 86, 103, 114, 117, 139, 146, 147, 176-78, 182, 183, 189, 190, 191, 205n63, 222n64; city avoidance, 209n36; damage limitation, 14, 59, 72, 76, 107-8, 121, 209n33, 209n36, 210n47; equality/ equivalence, 37, 39, 41, 205n63; inferiority, 37, 41; limited nuclear option, 14; matching, 20, 27, 40-41, 62, 116; parity, 60, 111, 126, 146, 175; prevail-